ABORTION POLITICS

PUBLIC POLICY IN
CROSS-CULTURAL PERSPECTIVE

EDITED by
MARIANNE GITHENS
and DOROTHY McBRIDE STETSON

Routledge   New York and London

Published in 1996 by
Routledge
29 West 35th Street
New York, NY 10001

Published in Great Britain by
Routledge
11 New Fetter Lane
London EC4P 4EE

Library of Congress Cataloguing-in-Publication Data
    Abortion: Public Policy in Cross Cultural Perspective/
    edited by Marianne Githens and Dorothy McBride Stetson.
        p. cm.
    ISBN 0-415-91224-5 (cl.) — ISBN 0-415-91225-3 (pb)
    1. Abortion—Government policy—Cross-Cultural studies.
    I. Githens, Marianne. II. Stetson, Dorothy M.
HQ767, A1858 1996
363. 4 6–dc20

CONTENTS

ABORTION POLITICS

PREFACE

When an issue gets a grip on American politics in the way the abortion issue has, specialists in comparative politics are likely to ask: What is it like in other countries? Is it the same or different and why? In 1986, Lovenduski and Outshoorn assembled a series of case studies of European countries. Their book revealed that in every country, since 1960, long-standing prohibitions on abortion had come up for review and reform. Since 1986 we have seen evidence that abortion law remains a hot issue in many countries, such as Ireland, Germany, Canada, and Poland, as well as in the United States.

We began our search for scholars who have been working on questions of comparative abortion politics and policy by convening a panel at the annual meeting of the American Political Science Association in 1992. Participants in that panel presented results of their original research projects providing information on abortion politics in countries about which little had been previously published. From the discussion begun there, the idea for this book started to take shape.

While political science conferences are places where ideas abound, turning such ideas into books needs the cooperation of many people who are willing to share their work. It also takes time to assemble a set of articles that will provide the necessary range, diversity, and depth of information readers demand. We are grateful to those who participated in the panel—Joyce Gelb, Laura Woliver, Raymond Tatalovich, and Kim Scheppele—for agreeing to allow us to include their excellent papers in this book, and for their patience. We also thank those who joined us later. Joyce Outshoorn, Brian Girvin, Jennifer Merchant, and Don Studlar responded to our requests for original articles, allowing us to complete our goal of providing a comprehensive comparative view of abortion policy.

Edited volumes assemble articles around a theme and are valuable materials for teachers and students. They are, however, often undervalued in academic circles, in comparison with articles in journals. We realize that all contributors had the option of submitting their work to a journal; we also recognize that this book would not have been possible without their support and cooperation.

As editors, we prepared the overall thematic organization of the book and wrote the introductions to each section. We, not the contributors, are responsible for any errors in these summaries or analyses of the various chapters.

Finally, we would like to thank staff and students at Goucher College and Florida Atlantic University for the intellectual as well as clerical support so necessary to the successful completion of an ambitious book project. We would especially like to thank Madeline Kotowski for all her help in preparing the manuscript, Larry Bielawski for his support, and finally Chauna Brocht for her helpful comments and suggestions. And, like countless authors before us, we found the editorial work of Cecelia Cancellaro and the staff at Routledge to be superb.

                    Marianne Githens, Goucher College
                    Dorothy McBride Stetson, Florida Atlantic University

INTRODUCTION

Abortion in the United States is a highly visible and contentious issue whose political ramifications can hardly be overstated. Although in 1973 the Supreme Court ruled in the case *Roe v. Wade* that abortion fell within a woman's zone of privacy and struck down a restrictive Georgia abortion law in the companion case *Doe v. Bolton*, the right to obtain an abortion has continued to be hotly debated and challenged in the public arena. The case for and against abortion is regularly made in homes, in churches, in the media, and in legislatures across the country. Abortion has been an important factor in the appointment of Supreme Court judges and a litmus test of their eligibility. It has played a major role in the Senatorial confirmation hearings on the appointment of a United States Surgeon General. It has influenced the content of political party platforms and the selection of candidates for public office at the national, state, and local levels. Presidents and presidential hopefuls have all carefully weighed their words on this issue, proclaiming positions in the hopes of attracting pro-choice or pro-life support. Abortion has mobilized two powerful social movements: the Women's Movement and the Christian Right. It has also motivated people to stage demonstrations and sometimes to become violent. Abortion clinics and hospitals performing abortions have been picketed and entrances obstructed, and on a number of occasions clinics have been bombed. Doctors who perform abortions have been killed and women seeking to terminate their pregnancies harassed. In this war over abortion, both proponents of choice and pro-life groups have proclaimed their positions to be righteous and truly representative of American values.

Caught up in the shrill claims and counterclaims surrounding the discussion of abortion in this country, we have often come to assume that the same struggle is going on elsewhere. But is it? Is abortion as contentious in other countries? Is the debate always couched in terms of human rights versus God's law? Do religious groups spearhead pro-life movements in other societies? Do women's groups play a vital role in defining the terms of the debate? Is the rhetoric always the same? And if not, what accounts for the differences?

The intensity of the debate in the United States has tended to direct attention primarily to the politics of abortion rather than to the issue of availability. Yet, discussions of rights and morality become somewhat esoteric, if not totally meaningless, when the possibility of obtaining an abortion is very limited or non-existent. After all, the Supreme Court's ruling in the *Roe v. Wade* case signifies little if facilities performing abortions are far away. Similarly, if doctors are unwilling to perform abortions or, as in a recent instance in New York, grossly negligent, then abortion is not a feasible option. Cost is another factor. If abortions are costly and must be paid for by the individual, they are beyond the reach of poor women. In such instances, abortion is only a right for affluent women. State statutes requiring parental consent, prohibitions on the use of federal funds for abortion or abortion related services, and the fact that less than half the states fund abortions in the case of rape and incest also mean that despite what the formal policy says, abortion is not a choice readily available to all women.

To what extent are problems of access and availability peculiar to the United States? With the exception of Spain, Portugal, Monaco, Malta, Ireland, and Germany, Western European countries have liberal abortion policies. The same is true for Canada, and Japan was the first industrialized country to legalize abortion. Prior to the collapse of communism, all the countries of Eastern Europe also had liberal abortion policies, the sole exception being Romania. Have there been similar availability and access problems in these countries?

The frequently held assumption that the struggle over abortion in the United States characterizes the situation everywhere stems in part from the focus of much of the current literature on abortion. There are several recent studies of the politics of abortion and abortion policy that concentrate exclusively on the United States. These include: Craig and O'Brien's *Abortion and American Politics* (1993), which provides an intelligent and thorough examination of the abortion issue in American politics since *Roe v. Wade*; *Understanding the New Politics of Abortion*, edited by Malcolm Goggin (1993), which looks at conflicting values, attitudes, and behavior; and Blank and Merrick's *Human Reproduction, Emerging Technologies, and Conflicting Rights* (1995), which discusses some of the critical policy issues relating to the new technologies and reproductive choice. Over the past decade, research on abortion policy and implementation outside the United States has rarely attempted a comparative analysis, and when it has, its focus has usually been the United States and Britain, or the United States and Canada. For example, Abbott and Wallace's *The Family and the New Right* deals with recent trends in the anti-abortion activities of the Christian Right in Britain and the United States. Country studies of some recent developments in Western Europe and in the former communist nations of Eastern Europe, especially Poland, have also appeared (*Parliamentary Affairs*, Spring 1994; *Feminist Review*, 1991; 1994). However, no literature has dealt with abortion policy in a truly comparative perspective since the publication of Outshoorn and Lovenduski's *The New Politics of Abortion* in 1986. Other than empirical studies of attitudes on abortion in the European Union, there have been virtually no attempts to examine recent events, particularly those in Ireland, Germany, and Eastern Europe, within a comparative framework. Since abortion policy and its implementation is most often analyzed within the narrow context of national politics and policymaking, the effects of different political institutions and the impact of mobilized groups on policy agenda setting elsewhere are lost. As a consequence, the nature of the abortion debate is distorted, and conclusions are then drawn that obscure an evaluation of the pragmatic solutions adopted by some other countries. In the absence of an understanding of how significant prevailing attitudes have been for policy implementation in other countries, the United States's experience is accepted as typical.

The essays in this volume address some of these problems in the current treatment of abortion. Policies in the modern industrialized societies, including the United States, Canada, Western and Eastern Europe, and Japan, are discussed from a comparative perspective and within the framework of public policy analysis. The role of political institutions and groups in defining policy are examined along with their impact on implementation. Emphasis is given to the importance of both the domestic political environment and regional organizations, such as the European Union.

Part I focuses on the rhetoric surrounding the abortion debate. Its bearing on court decisions, constitutional amendments, and legislation is discussed, as well as its effects on the continuing discussion of abortion. Part II examines the complex issue of implementation, and the role political institutions and public opinion play in determining who has access to abortion and how feasible the option actually is. Part III concentrates on the role of the policy environment. The significance of the intersection of domestic priorities and broader, transnational forces, such as the European Union, to attitude formation and policy development is analyzed. Part IV looks at the potential consequences of new reproductive technologies for reproductive choice and assesses the issue of reproductive policies from a feminist perspective.

Several common themes emerge from the various chapters. The first is the role played by political institutions in determining and implementing policy. Since abortion is almost always a divisive issue, governments and parties have traditionally sought to avoid the subject altogether or to depoliticize it. When this strategy fails, and action must be taken, the outcome will be influenced by the particular institution—usually either the legislature or the court—that addresses it. When a legislature sets abortion policy, the results are different than when a court or a small appointed group does. The dynamics of decision-making reflect the extent to which the decision-makers are dependent on the support of the general public. Elected members of a legislature and political parties need to build coalitions if they intend to remain in office. This means that extreme positions must be eschewed. Policy must not be significantly out of step with the attitudes held by the majority. Compromise is necessary. In such circumstances, a liberal abortion policy is likely to emerge. Rigid ideological or theological positions, however, do not encourage the development of broad-based coalitions or electoral support. In seeking to achieve compromise and to balance conflicting pressures exerted by pro-life and pro-choice forces, legislators may opt to pass laws that give the medical profession some real measure of discretion, rather than adopt a feminist reproductive agenda. Doctors, though, often feel uncomfortable about performing abortions when the criteria for deciding their legality is ambiguous. Concerned about legal challenges, they often press for more liberal, term-limit legislation that corresponds more closely to the feminists' demands for reproductive freedom.

In contrast, in countries where legislative decisions can be second-guessed by a court, or when a court or a small appointed group is left to make the decision altogether, there are not the same pressures for compromise. Judges may require political support for their appointment, but afterwards they are usually free to act as they believe appropriate. Without the impetus to compromise generated by the need to be re-elected, courts then may take positions on abortion that are less consistent with prevailing attitudes in the society at large.

It is interesting to note here some variation of this scenario in Poland. Although there is no court in Poland that can make public policy, as there is in the United States, Germany, and Ireland, the development of an abortion policy was left to a small committee selected by Parliament when strong, public opposition to a very restrictive abortion bill sprang up. In delegating the decision on the contents of the bill to this small appointed committee, the members of Parliament were freed, at least in part, from the need to endorse a moderate policy. Efforts by those demanding a liberal abortion policy to involve a larger group in the decision-making process by means of a referendum were subsequently blocked, and a later attempt by a newly elected Parliament whose members understood the importance of broad-based electoral support has been stalled.

A second theme is the critical importance of implementation. Who implements abortion policy, how it is implemented, and the balance struck between the role of the doctor and a woman's right to reproductive choice affects the extent to which abortion is a viable reproductive choice. The role of local authorities and the pressures brought to bear on doctors by local communities and organized pro-life groups impact on both the availability of abortion and the quality of the medical service provided. Similarly, the degree to which abortion is viewed as socially acceptable and the relationship of abortion to family planning have a bearing on implementation. The lack of facilities performing abortions, or a laissez-faire government policy that allows doctors to opt out of performing abortions, may mask an underlying problem with consensus. It may afford a government eager to avoid the consequences of alienating both pro-life and pro-choice groups the means of appearing to satisfy conflicting demands.

Several of the chapters dealing with the implementation strategies pursued by different countries furnish important insights into the importance of the government's commitment to its abortion policy. In countries with a genuine commitment to providing abortion facilities, governments have intervened to make sure that there are qualified doctors available. When abortion is an alternative to birth control, population policies influence implementation. Japan provides a good illustration of this.

The importance of the policy environment is another common theme. In establishing abortion policy, a constitution, legislation, or court decisions define the parameters and often the rhetoric of the debate. Challenges and demands articulated by mobilized groups also contribute to this rhetoric, which frequently assumes highly emotional connotations. Language becomes a means of stigmatizing abortion or placing it in the framework of human rights. Social movements have used this emotional language to create a ground swell to liberalize restrictive policies, to curtail liberal reform, or to jettison it altogether.

Several of the chapters address the issue of the policy environment. They point to the fact that the national policy environment may be modified by policies adopted elsewhere. This is the case in Western Europe, where the European Union has encouraged its citizens to look beyond narrow, national borders and has led to the development of shared values and attitudes.

Last but not least is the issue of feminism. Women's involvement in the reform efforts and their framing of the issue of reproductive rights and freedom have profoundly affected agenda setting, policy formation, and implementation. The extent to which the central role of women will continue in the arena of reproductive choice is partially dependent on the degree to which the new reproductive technologies are defined as exclusively within the purview of the courts and the medical profession.

There are always lessons to be learned from others. This is clearly the case when one looks at abortion policy. The struggle over abortion in the United States is certainly not descriptive of events everywhere. At the same time, it is not wholly unique. In considering where to go from here, the experiences of other modern, industrialized nations suggest both new directions and pitfalls to be avoided.

PART I

RHETORIC AND REFORM:
Struggles over the Law

INTRODUCTION

In Western Europe and North America, debates over abortion policy reform began in the 1960s and 1970s, when policymakers liberalized nearly all laws that had criminalized abortion. For most of these countries, the debate over the basic outlines of that abortion policy has receded from the public agenda. The exceptions—the United States, Canada, Ireland, and West Germany—show how this very contentious issue can travel between legislative and legal arenas. And, along the way, perspectives on the issue seem to become increasingly polarized, resisting resolution. At the same time, dramatic political, economic, social, and ideological changes in the transitional regimes of Eastern Europe since 1989 have brought the Soviet-style legal abortion policies up for review, and this potentially divisive issue has become entangled in society-wide struggles over the place of religion and the organization of the state itself.

The chapters in Part I review the types of abortion debates that characterize these policy conflicts and analyze how they are shaped by different national contexts. Laura Woliver's analysis of *amicus curiae* briefs presented in the *Webster v. Reproductive Services* case counterpoises the rhetorical images of fetus and woman so characteristic of the pro-life/pro-choice contest. The pluralistic nature of interest-group relations with the state in the United States provides what may be a unique situation where the debate is carried out by interest groups in a legal arena: the Supreme Court.

For the most part, the constitutionalizing of the abortion issue constrains debate to a legalist framework, stating it as a contest over rights phrased in absolute terms. Scheppele's description of the efforts of constitutional courts in Canada, Ireland, and Hungary, as well as in the United States, shows how fitting the complex abortion issue into the rules of constitutional discourse distorts the debate, even putting it in a "legal straitjacket." In none of these cases has the constitutionalizing of the abortion issue resulted in a settlement of the conflict.

Following the abortion debates in Eastern European countries, Githens brings out how this issue, which is usually described in pro-life and pro-choice terms, has become currency for major social conflicts over religion, national identity, and the form of the state itself. Although Eastern European feminist activists often employ ideas of reproductive choice, similar to Western feminist demands, they are participating in contests that are unlike any policy controversies in the West. For one thing, the laws under the communist regimes were patterned after the Soviet laws, which permitted abortion while making access to contraceptives difficult. Eastern European women were thus accustomed to using abortion as the primary means of birth control. Yet, at the same time, official ideologies of communism were not supportive of abortion, seeing the need for the procedure as a remnant of class oppression of the poor.

The opening up of these regimes to more democratic processes unleashed institutions, primarily the Catholic Church, as well as nationalist forces who considered access to abortion as one of the oppressive features of the communist regime they hated. The feminists find themselves allying with organizations tied to the old communist parties challenging rhetoric that foresees the idealization of the maternal heroine and the abolition of abortion as the means to "renew the state."

The rhetoric in North America and Europe makes the search for "common ground," as Scheppele points out, difficult and often futile. Readers will note that some of the attempts at compromise yield jerry-rigged policies. The present compromise in the United States continues to guarantee women's right to privacy in making abortion decisions in the first trimester, yet permits the government to erect various barriers to the exercise of her choice. In Germany, the courts ordered that abortion be criminalized, but not punished. Hungary followed the lead of many European countries in drafting laws that permit abortions only in certain conditions of pregnancy and then interpreting conditions, like the social problems of families, very liberally to permit access to abortion. The Irish court has established a hierarchy of rights that prohibits abortions in Ireland but permits women to travel to England to obtain them. The forging of long-term compromises still eludes policymakers in the countries described in this section.

CHAPTER 1

RHETORIC AND SYMBOLS
IN AMERICAN ABORTION POLITICS

LAURA R. WOLIVER

INTRODUCTION

The abortion debate has raged for years in American politics. This controversial issue has drawn in many individuals and interest groups. A distinct pattern of political participation via amicus briefs exists in American abortion politics. Interest groups sometimes submit "friend-of-the-court briefs" in attempts to persuade and educate members of the United States Supreme Court about their position on issues.

The Supreme Court's decision in *Webster v. Reproductive Health Services* in 1989 came after a long campaign by pro-life activists to overturn the ruling in *Roe v. Wade* that had legalized abortion in the United States. The decision expanded the ability of the state and territorial governments to place obstacles in the way of women seeking abortion services. Although the decision was seen as a pro-life victory, legal abortion was retained.

Building on previous research (Woliver, 1991b, 1992a, 1992b), this study looks at the rhetoric and metaphors in the 78 amicus briefs (a record number) filed in *Webster v. Reproductive Health Services*. (Appendix A lists the amicus briefs.) American policies at the time of the preparations for the Webster case were showing steady erosion of many of the principles derived from the landmark *Roe* decision (see Halva-Neubauer, 1990). Many groups on both sides of the abortion debate saw *Webster* as the case that might overrule *Roe* and jeopardize legal abortion. With such high stakes, many groups and professional associations joined in the amicus effort for *Webster*. For this study, these briefs were read with an eye toward the various definitions of fetuses, pregnant women, abortion providers, along with larger issues of women's rights and religious freedom.

Ultimately, more than 300 organizations, using more than 120 lawyers, drafted 31 friend-of-the-court briefs for the pro-choice position in the *Webster* case (Coyle, 1989: 27; see also, Craig and O'Brien, 1993). The pro-choice briefs for *Webster* were coordinated by attorneys at the American Civil Liberties Union (ACLU) Reproductive Rights Project, Planned Parenthood, and the National Abortion Rights Action League (NARAL). The pro-life interests in Webster submitted 46 amici curiae briefs supporting the position of the state of Missouri. In addition, President Reagan's Justice Department offered a Solicitor General's brief. For the first time ever, a United States Solicitor General's brief called for an overturning of *Roe*.

Fascinating coalitions of interests worked together on several of the briefs. There was a unique mobilization of the professional and academic communities to rally around *Roe* and protect legalized abortion. The American Medical Association and other medical groups filed compelling briefs. One-hundred and sixty-seven scientists and physicians signed a brief maintaining that viability for a fetus was still about 24 weeks gestation.

One pro-choice *Webster* brief signed by 281 historians attempted to refute the position of the United States Justice Department and pro-life amici that abortion had been outlawed throughout United States history, therefore making Roe an aberration. Law professors, 885 strong, signed a *Webster* brief. Many of the pro-choice briefs displayed a multi-issue reproductive rights perspective, discussing legal abortion within the context of how women must negotiate their lives in America.

Rhetoric, especially the metaphors, used in the briefs is an important representation of a group's interests. The word choice in the briefs gives clues to the deeper ideological meaning the interest groups and individuals wish to convey. Metaphors are common in rhetorical discourse and are "omnipresent in speech" (Ivie, 198: 167). The metaphors, based on fine distinctions, are not obvious and some terms may not even appear, at first, to be metaphors. For example, pro-life groups frequently label abortion clinics as abortion "industries". Although the differentiation between the two terms, "clinic" and "industry," may appear slight and inconsequential, heavy ideological meanings are embedded in phrases chosen by pro-life groups as well as by pro-choice groups (Woliver and McDonald, 1993).

> *Through words only (not claims), such terms as "property," "religion," "right of privacy," "freedom of speech," "rule of law," and "liberty" are more pregnant than propositions ever could be. They are the basic structural elements, the building blocks of ideology. (McGee, 1980, pp. 6–7)*

Word choice is even more powerful when it is not explained or defended, but accepted as the truth. The danger lies in accepting these terms and words at face value without questioning or analyzing possible hidden meanings. When statements are represented as objective truth, it is important to explore concealed perspectives or ideologies (Mumby, 1989: 30).

Any political speech, then, evokes its most compelling cognitions in a large part of its audience (and in the speaker himself) through the metaphoric views it takes for granted rather than through those it explicitly asserts and calls to people's attention. (Edelman, 1971: 69)

In the amicus briefs filed in Webster, the writers did not shy away from metaphors, and in fact they effectively used these tools of discourse. Their arguments and rhetoric were even more forceful because they often chose to avoid an explanation for word choices, making their phrasing appear to be the correct, proper, or commonly used terminology. In abortion politics, a subject so evocative of emotions and symbols, the language used to frame the debate has heavy implications for policymaking. Whether abortion is defined as murder or a health care option shapes the rest of the policy debate, and very likely the outcome as well.

Throughout this chapter the opposing sides in the abortion debate are referred to as *pro-choice* and *pro-life*. These are the terms that the activists use to describe themselves. Although the accuracy of these terms can be debated, it is preferable to use the self-definition of the activists when describing their political behavior. This follows the decision rule Kristin Luker utilized in *Abortion and the Politics of Motherhood* (1984).

COMPARISON OF RHETORICAL MODES: IMAGES OF FETUSES AND WOMEN

One of the most common metaphors employed by the pro-life interest groups involved substituting the term "fetus" with variations of the term the "unborn." Such consistent use of terms identifying and personalizing the fetus as an individual rests on the premise that a person exists and is alive from the moment of conception. They tend to ignore women altogether or refer to them only in their relation to the fetus.

Striking throughout the over one-thousand pages of these pro-life amicus briefs (single-spaced!) is the careful attention to terms. Fetuses are never called fetuses, they are always "unborn children," "unborn life," "prenatal life," "children in the womb," or "human life before birth." Over forty versions of the term "unborn" were used by pro-life advocates, including "unborn grandchildren," "viable unborn," "minor child," and "unborn human life." Right to Life advocates refer to fetuses as "those who will be citizens if their lives are not ended in the womb" (Brief #10). A couple of pro-life briefs hardly ever use the word "woman" but instead call her the "mother." Discussions abound about "pregnancies," not "pregnant women," glossing over the fact that pregnancies occur within women. The United States Catholic Conference declares that the fetus and the woman are "separate patients" (Brief #20).

The motive for painting this picture is to evoke sympathy for what pro-life groups perceive to be independent human beings. These terms are value laden; they define as true the concept that the fetus is a living being from the moment of conception, a question about which scientists have yet to reach a consensus. Despite this fact, the New England Christian Action Council claims that the "consensus on conception is overwhelming" and there is an "unchallenged positive consensus that human life is fully and legally present 'at every period of gestation'" (Brief #11). Right to Life advocates argue that life beginning at the moment of conception is a "natural and self-evident truism" (Brief #10). Because the pro-life groups assume they are correct and their interpretation of when life begins is the only interpretation, the arguments made are absolute, not allowing the subject to be open for compromise.

Although pro-life briefs make scant mention of what an undesired pregnancy means to women, the briefs do refer to women, mostly in a chastising way. As Baer has noted, "Women are the targets of most moral lectures. On this particular issue [abortion], women get lectured by the religious right, by the male left, by 'feminists for life,' and by politicians who wish the pro-choice movement would disappear" (1990: 578). The dominant voice in the pro-life briefs comes from lawyers, scholars, interest groups, and religious leaders who can never become pregnant and who do not know the thoughts of a woman facing an unwanted pregnancy. "Constitutional law is male, while the decision to have an abortion is female" (Baer, 1990: 560). Missing in the pro-life briefs, for instance, is a central first step recognition of what one scholar has called "the very geography of pregnancy" (Gallagher, 1989: 187).

In several places in the pro-life briefs it is striking how the women actually involved in the debates are invisible. One example, which also shows how pro-life groups use medical advances and fetal medicine in their logic, comes from Brief #15 by The Association for Public Justice et al.:

> Today an embryologist or fetologist can diagnose and treat an unborn child independently of treating the mother, including removing the child from its mother's womb for surgery, and then returning it to the womb to complete gestation. Facing such developments, one can hardly consider the child a mere extension of its mother.

It's as if the fetologist snaps his finger and the fetus separates from the woman, ready for surgery, and is magically returned to "the womb." Masked here is the fact that women undergo major surgery for these procedures, and that the fetus and "the womb" are not independent, they are both within a woman's body. From the moment of fertilization, nevertheless, there are "children who happen to reside within their mothers' wombs" (Brief #19). The desires of these women about what happens to their wombs, though, is not articulated. The heart of the abortion debate for women, the social context of abortion decisions, is either ignored or side-stepped.

Only a couple of pro-life briefs filed in *Webster* address the economic and social causes which help shape women's abortion decisions. The brief submitted by the Lutheran Church–Missouri Synod et al. includes the statement that "as church organizations, we are fully aware, through our own agencies established to counsel and assist pregnant women currently facing the abortion decision, of the burden it places upon them and society in general to decide not to abort their pregnancies" (Brief #1). Private and public funding could be expanded, they continue, "to meet the need for services and facilities for women facing unwanted pregnancies" (Brief #1). Birthright also notes how most women facing an unwanted pregancy "feel abandoned by a family or a society which has no or little patience for a problem unique to women—an unplanned pregnancy"; abortion is a "quick-fix" "cover-up," which "destroys and erodes the very fabric of values in our society," and actually, Birthright argues, harms women (Brief #17). The brief by Covenant House (#32) discusses the social problems of poverty, homelessness, and the abandonment of children and teenagers. Covenant House opposes abortion but does suggest that more care be given to women, children, and families in need. Out of the 47 pro-life *Webster* briefs, these are the only amici that discuss social problems and women's plight. There is scant mention in these briefs, then, of what women actually face when confronted with an unwanted pregnancy.

A clear difference between a pro-life and a pro-choice brief, therefore, is whether the context or rationale for the choice to abort the fetus is presented. While pro-life groups evade the discussion of women's reproductive lives, the social context of what brings women to consider the option of abortion is a key part of the argumentation in the pro-choice amicus briefs.

In court proceedings on abortion, women's rights groups have used a strategy to educate predominantely male judges about what unwanted pregnancy and illegal abortion means to women. Women's rights litigants included the experiences of women with abortion and unwanted pregnancies as equally legitimate "expert testimony" in abortion cases in the early 1970s (Rubin, 1987: 47–48).

Echoes of this same strategy are found in NARAL's *Webster* brief, written with the National Organization of Women (NOW) Legal Defense and Education Fund. In line with their "Silent No More" campaign, which began in

1985, NARAL solicited testimonials from over thirty-five hundred women and their friends who had had illegal abortions before *Roe* or legal abortions after *Roe*. A book-length brief in *Webster* was filed by NOW and NARAL entitled "Brief for the Amici Curiae Women Who Have Had Abortions and Friends of Amici Curia" (Brief #54). NOW and NARAL were able to put together testimony of 2,887 women who had had abortions before and/or after *Roe* (568 of these women signed their real names, while the rest used "Jane Roe") and 627 friends of women who had legal or illegal abortions. The letters listed in the appendix of the brief tell moving stories of frightened, vulnerable, and desperate women who experienced their illegal abortions as nightmares, and other women describing legal ones as respectable choices. Several women describe how their friends died from illegal abortions before Roe.

The women all testify that abortion provided much relief to them and allowed them to get on with their lives, provide better care for their existing loved ones and children, and save their mental and physical health (see also the American Psychological Association's Brief #80; Luker, 1975). They show the diversity of reasons why each decision is individual, a result of the moral, ethical, and philosophical sorting out by each woman. The women and their friends emphasize to the Justices that this highly personal and private decision should be left to the woman to make. In addition, several pro-choice briefs argue that legalized abortion has improved women's health in various ways, especially for poor women who before *Roe* had no safe options. They argue further that restrictions on access to legal abortion in the United States will "disproportionately burden racial minority groups" and poor women (Brief #65).

ISSUE OF RIGHTS

Abortion is not a fundamental right imbedded in the fabric of American history and culture, the pro-life briefs argue. Abortion was criminalized in American law, and the pro-life briefs cite state legal codes and state criminal prosecution cases to bolster this position. According to these pro-life briefs, "the anti-abortion feeling of the period in which the Fourteenth Amendment was proposed and ratified is hard to overstate" (Brief #9). Therefore, the framers of the Constitution, the authors of the Fourteenth Amendment, and numerous state legislatures intended that abortion be criminalized in order to protect the unborn.

"The fact that human life begins at conception is beyond dispute" assert Doctors for Life et al. (Brief #7). "Physicians, biologists and other scientists agree that conception marks the beginning of the life of a human being—of a being that is alive and is a member of the human species. There is overwhelming agreement on this point in countless medical, biological and scientific writings" (Brief #7).

Pro-life advocates are adamant about the citizenship of the fetus at the moment of conception. Their anger and frustration at the Supreme Court majority's position to the contrary is visible throughout their briefs. Some resort to veiled threats—"the civil disobediance in the streets will continue"—while others are moved to sarcasm. Free Speech Advocates (Brief #37) exhorts that the Court's majority should face the clear scientific proof of the humanity of the fetus from fertilization; "at a minimum, the flat earth nonsense of *Roe* must be renounced."

Medical technology has a strong impact on the abortion debate in America (Gallagher, 1989; Oakley, 1987; Rothman, 1986; Woliver, 1989, Woliver, 1991a). Reproductive technologies such as ultrasound construct an image of the fetus that becomes a powerful symbol in abortion politics (Ginsburg, 1989: 104). Images of the fetus used by pro-life activists usually exclude visualization of the woman the fetus is within (Condit: 1990: 79–95; Gallagher, 1989: 187–198; Gorney, 1990: 38; Ginsburg, 1989: 107–109; Petchesky, 1987 and 1984: 353; Woliver, 1989 and 1991a). These carefully constructed fetal images are powerful aspects of the pro-life discourse (Condit, 1990: 80). Technologies, therefore, which allow viewing, studying, and the possibility of medically treating fetuses prenatally, "are likely to elevate the moral status of the fetus" (Blank, 1988: 148; see also Field 1989: 118).

These findings add new elements to the politics of abortion visible in the *Webster* briefs. Many pro-life writers noted the contradictions, from their point of view, in medical technologies that allow and sometimes seem to require doctors to treat fetuses as patients, yet also allow these "patients" to be aborted.

New reproductive technologies have been used to strengthen the pro-life arguments that the fetus is an independent being. These technologies, particularly ultrasound, widen the gap between the mother and fetus and isolate the fetus, making it appear distinct and unconnected to the woman (Ginsburg, 1989: 104–109). An extreme example of this seemingly distant relationship between the mother and fetus is seen in an analogy to the fetus being like "an astronaut" (Brief #6). This framing defines the fetus as a "human being separate and distinct from his mother" (Brief #25).

Neonatal technologies are also altering the perceptions of fetal viability and thus undermining the premise in *Roe* that states may not interfere in abortion decisions before viability, thought in 1973 to be in the third trimester. Neonatal technologies are pushing back the gestational age when fetuses might be viable outside the womb well into the second trimester

(Blank, 1984; Blank, 1988: 64–65). The Knights of Columbus maintain, "More fundamentally, viability is an invalid benchmark for construing the meaning of 'person' in the Fourteenth Amendment because it has nothing to do with attributes of personhood, or a particularized state of being, but only the state of medical technology" (Brief #9; also #40).

The use of new reproductive technologies, combined with pro-life logic, to argue for the separateness of women from their fetuses is displayed in this pro-life brief:

> *In recent years, medical advances have made even more obvious the universally medically known fact that fertilization always means a new individual. In the case of in vitro fertilization, the fertilized ovum can be deposited in the womb of a mother not the donor of the ovum. This makes very obvious the fact that the host mother and the fertilized ovum were separate individuals having absolutely no past contacts when the ovum was in the solution. The coupling of the ovum to the womb does not change the preexisting individuality of each during the pregnancy. In fact a third woman may then adopt and raise the child who would then have three mothers, genetic, nurturing and raising. (Brief #14)*

Viability as used in *Roe* is criticized for implicating dependent people in general as unworthy of life. The Knights of Columbus Brief states, "Indeed, it is doubtful whether there is any such thing as a 'viable' infant at all. Born or unborn, every infant is utterly dependent upon its parents and society. So are many other 'nonviable' persons—the elderly and the handicapped, for example" (Brief #9; see also Brief #19).

Pro-choice groups explore the history of the abortion controversy with a far different outcome. In the brief filed by American Historians (Brief #61), 281 American historians seek to counter the version presented in the pro-life briefs. The pro-choice historians argue that a separate moral value was attached to the fetus only in the late twentieth century, when previous arguments failed (see also Mohr, 1978).

The Historians Brief in *Webster* is also dedicated to disproving the United States Solicitor General's assertion that *Roe* was an aberration, and that the American tradition is to restrict and criminalize abortion. Not only did Roe fit in with a long historic tradition in America, the historians asserted, but also, "Our [the United States's] experience from the 1890s until 1973 amply demonstrates that if women are denied access to legal abortions, many will turn in desperation to self-abortion, folk remedies, or illegal practitioners. Many will die. Others will suffer permanent damage to their reproductive capacity. Still others will bear children for whom they cannot provide adequate care. Apart from these devastating consequences to the lives and health of women, restricting access to abortion will again deny the fundamental legitimacy of women as moral decisionmakers."

Webster Brief #66, filed by 22 international women's health organizations and 22 individuals, similarly attempts to place *Roe* within the long history and tradition in Western democracies of liberalizing abortion laws. This brief also directly argues against the brief by the United States. It warns,

> *Recent history and current events have shown that governments can and will fashion abortion regimes that seek to coerce reproductive choice as official state policy. The nightmarish policies of criminalized abortion in Nazi Germany and the Soviet Union on the one hand and forced abortion in China on the other, are chilling reminders that women must be afforded the ability to make fundamental reproductive decisions free of governmental interference.*

Many other briefs echo this historical and comparative justification for legal abortion (Briefs #65, 84).

The rhetoric of democracy and rights is prominent in pro-choice briefs. They explain why access to safe and legal abortion is necessary for women to fully enjoy their constitutional rights. "Reproductive rights," "liberty of all women," "freedom of choice," "women's privacy and liberty," are commonly used to express the fundamental nature of the rights encircling the abortion debate. Writers also claim that the "right which is naturally a woman's right" has allowed "young women to continue their education and pursue their dreams," "rape victims to begin the healing process," "mothers to sustain their families," and basically allowed women to "maintain control over their bodies, their lives and their futures" (Brief #54).

In fact, Planned Parenthood's brief writers suggest the very nature of "constitutional democracy" is jeopardized by a legal system which does not recognize a woman's "fundamental liberty" of the "right to choose" (Brief #58). Brief writers representing the ideas of NOW hold that the "forced pregnancy" resulting from a lack of facilities where legal abortions are performed would be akin to the involuntary servitude prohibited by the Thirteenth Amendment to the United States Constitution (Brief #59).

Many pro-choice briefs stress the centrality of legal abortion to women's civil rights. "In totalitarian countries," Brief #66 by 22 international women's health centers reminds the Justices, "abortion legislation has routinely been used to force women to bear children or refrain from childbirth according to the dictates of state policy." Examples are provided from the Soviet Union, Nazi Germany, the People's Republic of China, and Romania. "In countries where government is not subject to the processes of Western-style democracy," it continues, "states can use legislative fiat to suppress or to compel abortion and women and their families may be forced to sacrifice their physical integrity to serve the purposes of the state."

The Women's Equality Brief (#56)—signed by 77 organizations including NOW, American Association of University Women, (AAUW), the League of Women Voters, and the National Federation of Business and Professional Women's Clubs—stresses the unequal burden "forced motherhood" would place on women: "If this Court were to uphold abortion restrictions that force pregnant women to bear children, it would render empty the constitutional promise of liberty for women by profoundly structuring their lives. Moreover, it would do so for women alone; men are not required to endure comparable burdens in the service of the state's abstract interest in promoting life." Brief #65, signed by 885 law professors asserts, "For women to achieve the full promise of 'equal protection,' it is necessary for them to control the childbearing decision." The law professors' brief explains, "As long as State laws circumscribe a woman's right to decide whether to continue a pregnancy, her ability to participate fully and equally in American society will be subject to a physical condition that she can avoid only by refraining from sexual relations other than those that are intentionally procreative. If it were possible to fashion a law imposing similar limitations on the ability of men to retain full possession of their lives, the denial of equal citizenship by laws banning abortion would be readily apparent" (Brief #65). Infringement upon women's privacy and bodily integrity by restrictive abortion laws would lead to further erosions of women's autonomy and liberty, the women's equality brief maintains. "Bald assertions of an unabridged state interest in protecting the potentiality of human life, proclaimed to be sufficiently 'compelling' to justify these major invasions of all aspects of women's personal autonomy, must be viewed by this Court with great skepticism. There is no logical stopping point at which such an asserted interest could be cabined." Given the gender-specific nature of abortion restrictions, Brief #75 by the National Coalition Against Domestic Violence argues, in part, that abortion choice should be protected under the Fourteenth Amendment's Equal Protection Clause.

Supporting the women's-rights theme of several of the briefs, Brief #53 (called "The Women of Color Brief") reminds the Court of the poverty, inadequate access to health care, and dangers restrictions on abortion choice pose for women of color in the United States. This brief is a remarkable coalition of interest groups. Fifteen groups are listed on the title page of the brief; an additional 115 groups also signed and are listed in the appendix along with 17 concerned individuals. The coalition includes African American, Hispanic, Latina, American Indian, American Asian, and Puerto Rican women's rights, and women's health groups.

The issue of privacy was addressed by 885 law professors who signed Brief #65. They argue that the woman's right of personal privacy overrides the state's interest in deciding in the legislature how a woman will live her life. The lawyers claim "it is irrational, and incompatible with a decent respect for a pregnant woman's fundamental right of conscientious choice, to suppose that a state legislature's broad prohibition on abortions at any stage of pregnancy can provide a better answer than a responsible and situated woman's own to the questions for multiple human lives, actual and potential, that many pregnancies present" (Brief #65). Much of the rhetoric concerning women's rights and democracy runs parallel to the concept that privacy is a key right and abortion legislation infringes on women's fundamental right to privacy.

FRAMING ABORTION: MURDER OR HEALTH CARE

Abortions are described by pro-life groups as the "mindless dumping of aborted fetuses on to garbage piles" (Brief #8). Personal stories are also included. A woman regretting her abortion describes the process as having her "baby ripped from her body" and the "taking of an innocent life" (Brief #24). Abortion providers are painted by pro-life forces as greedy, money-hungry exploiters of vulnerable or selfish women (Brief #24). One position asks the Court why abortion providers, with a direct economic stake in the outcome, are left to decide when life begins (or when viability exists and an abortion may not proceed). "Such decisions of life and death are simply too important to be left to the technicians," one pro-life group alleges, "especially when the one who makes the actual decision has an economic stake in deciding against life" (Brief #15).

Attacks are directed toward the clinics and facilities where abortions are performed. The medical training of the "technicians" is also questioned. In attempts to undermine the credibility of the establishments, pro-life groups describe the abortion clinics in the worst light. In fact, the abortion clinics are repeatedly referred to as part of the "abortion industry" (Briefs #15, 17, 24). Because these doctors have a "direct financial interest" in abortion, their credibility as physicians is questioned by pro-life groups. What these organizations ignore is the context of the current American health care system, which is based on a fee-for-service situation. The people who perform abortions are referred to as "technicians" and "abortion profiteers" (Brief #24). By referring to these people as technicians, and the clinics as "factories" or "industries," pro-life groups try to make abortion distinct from legitimate health care and birth control; such a word choice is an attempt to undermine and disregard pro-choice arguments and rationale with symbolic images. Because these doctors have a "direct financial interest" in abortion, their credibility as physicians is questioned by pro-life groups.

Important to the image of the abortion "technician" is that this is not a "real" doctor, but a mutant doctor. The pro-life briefs set up two patients that "real" doctors respect and treat with all the procedures available to them. This terminology of the "technician" in the "factory" is important to pro-life image making. Since doctors and medicine are highly legitimate and valued in American culture and politics (Starr, 1982), a separation is attempted between the profession of medicine and these "abortion profiteers."

In contrast, the pro-choice briefs describe the measured way women consider whether to have an abortion or not, the relief women have that such a safe, legal option is available to them since the *Roe* decision, and the important birth control and health care aspects of legal abortion. The image of legal abortion involves terms describing the procedure as safe and not nearly as traumatic as the illegal abortions common before the landmark *Roe* decision (Briefs #54, 58, 59, 62, 64). As Suzanne Staggenborg notes, persuasion has become the strategy of pro-choice activists who previously relied on coercion (Staggenborg, 1991: 30). Arguably, pro-choice brief writers hope to persuade the Court to uphold *Roe* by pointing out the emotional and physical turmoil women experienced in efforts to obtain an illegal abortion when they felt there was no other option.

The harms of illegal abortions are described in efforts to convey the damage done to women when they are denied health care and birth control education. Illegal abortions perpetuate the cycle of poverty by making the tragic situation of unwanted teenage pregnancy worse (Brief #64). The pro-choice stories of the women who have experienced illegal abortions provide emotionally charged testimony of the terrible health crisis created by the "criminalization of abortion" (Brief #54). The horrific stories of back-alley abortions are meant to explain how illegal abortions can become life threatening simply because there are no regulations or professional codes of conduct (Brief #59).

Groups representing the medical profession are also drawn into abortion politics, not solely out of a concern about the rights of women, but also because the outcome of the abortion wars will profoundly affect medicine. Associations of hospitals, doctors, nurses, public health officials, bioethicists, and medical school faculty argued to the Court about the medical nature of abortion, the infringement of government on the doctor-patient relationship, and the ethical obligations of medical professionals in reproductive health. In addition, studies of the United States show that minority and poor women receive less quality health care, are subject to more intrusive medical procedures, and have limited "choice" to use expensive reproductive technologies (Nsiah-Jefferson, 1989; Martin, 1987; Davis, 1990: 53–65; Fisher, 1986). These medical arguments, though, might unnecessarily highlight the science and technology of abortion procedures, with the unintentional result of overshadowing the social context in which women make their abortion decisions, and reifying science as one of the arbiters of abortion jurisprudence.

The power of the medical profession goes beyond its authority and prestige as a rational science and healing enterprise. As Starr writes, "Its authority spills over its clinical boundaries into arenas of moral and political action for which medical judgment is only partially relevant and often incompletely equipped" (1982: 5). Medicine's role in abortion politics will increase in importance as pro-life groups attempt to reframe abortion as a biological issue of human life beginning at conception. This is evident in the *Webster* amici filed by medical associations concerning the patient-doctor relationship and the ability of doctors to practice medicine without government control. Bioethicists for Privacy, in Brief #74, specifically mention the new reproductive technologies and wonder if "it would not be far-fetched to hypothesize a state that would choose to outlaw the use of all prenatal diagnostic techniques by both public and private physicians. . . . What would prohibit states from outlawing new and 'unnatural' means of conceiving a child such as *in vitro* fertilization techniques?" (see also Brief #81). These groups had mostly been silent on abortion politics before, letting the women's rights groups and the ACLU battle this messy fight for them (Woliver, 1992a and 1992b). By the time of the *Webster* brief writing, though, there was much concern in the medical community about the erosion of the doctor-patient relationship concerning proper reproductive health care.

New contraceptives, such as RU 486, and the information derived from new medical research and technologies makes it increasingly difficult to distinguish between abortion and contraception. If there is a future prohibition on abortion, as Richard points out, this "would deprive women of effective contraceptives, increasing the risks of unwanted pregnancy and the health and mental health consequences of illegal abortions or childbirth" (1989: 948). Abortion politics has already had an impact on dissemination of RU 486, the "abortion pill." Pro-life pressure halted for a while the introduction of RU 486 into the United States.

One pro-choice *Webster* brief, from the Association of Reproductive Health Professionals, discusses this problem of the overlap and merging of abortion with some forms of birth control. This brief was the one most often cited by the Court in the *Webster* decision itself. The *Webster* brief for appellees, Planned Parenthood Federation of America as counsel of record, also made these points about birth control (Brief #58).

A compelling aspect of the arguments presented by the pro-choice brief writers is that a generation of young women has grown up enjoying the right to legal abortion and planning their education, lives, and jobs around the idea that this right will always be made available to them. No pro-life advocate adequately responds to the charge that reversing Roe would have devastating consequences on the lives of young women who have never lived with any other legal policies concerning abortion. Indeed, they do not speculate on what policies would be needed to implement an overturning of Roe.

EFFECTS OF ABORTION POLICY

Abortion policymaking "is properly a matter for the legislative, not the judicial, branch of government," pro-life interests assert (Brief #12; see also #15, 27; #51). Returning abortion policymaking to the states, it is argued, will reduce public tension and allow "states to be experimental laboratories in balancing all of the interests involved—maternal, fetal, and societal—to achieve regulations" consistent with public sentiment (Brief #27).

Because a majority of the arguments indicting the Roe decision focus on the logic of the decision itself, pro-life groups tend to argue that the ruling in favor of a decision upholding the previous 1973 abortion case would wreak havoc on the judicial system. Roe's "crazy quilt interpretation of personhood" will lead to such scenarios as "disorder in the streets" (Briefs #10, 6).[2] Pro-life Senators predict "legal instability," "social strife," and "fermented social strife" (Brief #16). Abortion policies "make a mockery of the law. The malleable and uncertain lines separating viability from nonviability, or prematurity from pregnancy, simply cannot support the difference between constitutional rights and crimes . . . such artificiality results in contempt for a legal system full of technicalities that contradict reality" (Brief #19). Several briefs refer to the civil disobedience of "sidewalk counseling" or "rescues" to show the dissention Roe has caused (Briefs #19, 30, 34, for example). This is a compelling example of how establishment interest groups might publicly eschew disruptive or radical acts by other partisans yet find their own disorderly behavior useful for arguments in favor of policy change. Many people are outraged and frustrated by the Court's abortion decisions, notes the Right to Life League of Southern California, "so they are engaged in what is already by far the most widespread civil disobediance in United States history" (Brief #14).

Pro-life groups contend that Roe's logic "reversed reality" and such "violence of abortion" will destroy the moral fabric of society (Briefs #11, 12). On the moral level, Americans United for Life offer the scenario of the "general demoralization" of society due to "widespread popular ignorance of the true character of the crime" of abortion (Brief #12). The "atrocity" and "destruction of human life" that occurs with each legal abortion will inevitably result in a "holocaust" (Brief #6).

The *Dred Scott* (1857) case is a dominant example in this argument. The *Roe* opinion, The National Legal Foundation Brief states, "denies the self evident truth that the unborn child is human and therefore possesses the rights to life and liberty found in the Declaration of Independence. This same rationale was applied in the *Dred Scott* case to arbitrarily deny the self evident humanity of the African-American" (Brief #8, and many others).

"When such protection is denied to the unborn," the National Legal Foundation Brief asserts, "it opens the door for arbitrary withdrawal of such guarantees to all men and women" (Brief #8; see also #21). Many analogies are made between Nazi policies against the "Untermenschen" and United States abortion policies (Briefs #44, 45, 47).

A few pro-life briefs were aimed at proving that *Roe* was harmful to women. Feminists for Life et al. (Brief #24) includes testimonies from the book *Rachel Weeping* by women recounting their bad experiences with legal abortion. Birthright views "abortion on demand not as an act of 'choice', but as an act of despair on the part of a woman" (Brief #17). They continue, "Abortion has become an excuse for not offering real aid to pregnant women . . . abortion is simply a financially cheap way for society to brush troubled women out of the way while claiming to have done them a service. Abortion is indeed a woman's issue, but it is an issue not of women's rights, but of women's oppression."

Abortion has harmed women in many ways, pro-life amici argue, including increased infertility after abortion, post-abortion depression and stress, difficulty in bonding with subsequent children, and increases in divorce (Brief #20; see also #50). Therefore, the argument goes, *Roe's* desire to protect women's health is backfiring. Several pro-choice briefs refute every one of these points.

RELIGION AND POLITICS

The belief that life begins at conception has been painted as a religious position by pro-choice advocates. Important to the pro-life strategy, therefore, is to redefine the religious issue to one of rationality, scientific evidence, and logic, which just happens to coincide with some groups' religious beliefs. Given the very large number of pro-life briefs logged by religious organizations in Webster (15 of the 47 [about 31 percent] pro-life briefs are directly from religious organizations), this is a difficult maneuver to execute. The

Lutheran Church–Missouri Synod et al. Brief offers one example of this position. The position of the religious organizations signing the brief, and statements by the Southern Baptist Convention referenced in the brief, that life begins at conception,

> express profoundly held religious beliefs. However, we do not advocate the imposition of our religious views by law in order to impose upon others our religious beliefs. Rather, those religious beliefs are also deeply seated in the moral and ethical system that forms the basis of much of the civil and criminal law of this nation and, therefore, if the state legislatures so decide, may coincidentally be expressed in legislation.
>
> The fact that a state's law coincides with a deeply held religious belief does not render that law unconstitutional under the first Amendment. (Brief #1)

As the New England Christian Action Council puts it, the courts are defining biology (the humanity of the unborn from conception) as a religious issue: "In other words, they are saying that religious people or groups (the CAC has a Protestant statement of faith) are not allowed to ask public policy questions relative to scientific knowledge. How amazing! . . . And this is an extraordinary affront against the first Amendment's 'free exercise' clause" (Brief #11).

In contrast, pro-choice brief #55, called "The Religious Brief"—and signed by 36 religous groups including the American Jewish Congress, Board of Homeland Ministries–The United Church of Christ, The Presbyterian Church, and the Religious Coalition for Abortion Rights—maintains that overturning Roe would impose a religious belief on the country, in violation of the first Amendment. The brief provides an overview of the diverse perspectives religious people have on abortion politics. It cites the history of religious tolerance for abortion choice and individual freedom. The brief signers are concerned about the possible precedent of the Court siding with one religious opinion (that of pro-life) and violating the religious beliefs of many other Americans. "Given the dramatically contrasting religious views about whether and when abortion is permitted or required," the Religious Brief states, "state statutes drastically curtailing access to abortion unacceptably interfere with constitutionally protected religious and private conscience" (Brief #55). Brief #76 filed by Americans United for Separation of Church and State corroborates these points.

CONCLUSION

Groups have mixed results as amici in federal court cases, not necessarily providing a winning advantage (Epstein and Rowland, 1991; Songer and Sheehan, 1993). Interest groups try to frame the legal reasonings surrounding important Supreme Court cases, and judges respond to this dialogue and "life of the law." Research on recent abortion cases shows the shifting and shaping around abortion jurisprudence based, in part, on important legal doctrines (Epstein and Kobylka, 1992). Both sides also attempt to position themselves as reflective of public opinion, an influence recent scholars have shown plays a role in Supreme Court decisions (Franklin and Kosaki, 1989; Mishler and Sheehan, 1993). Precedents, supportive social movements, and societal socio-economic patterns all shape policy. Courts do not usually cause social reform on their own (Rosenberg, 1991; Rubin, 1987: 3; see also Epstein, 1985; O'Connor, 1980). Effective abortion amicus briefs attempt to highlight these social forces to the judges.

The interest groups' strategy for comparing their own arguments with those of their opponents was to use what Celeste Condit termed "over-weighing." Condit writes, "Since the values of their opposition had, to some significant extent, been accepted, their primary persuasion could no longer be directed toward disallowing the opposition's discourse or toward developing their own values but instead had to show how their values were more important than those of the opposition—over-weighing them" (1990: 159).

In the amicus briefs filed in *Webster*, both pro-life and pro-choice interest groups used the rhetorical tactic of arguing that their position takes precedence over any other. Terms such as "outweighs," "overrides," "balanced against," "on balance," and "counterbalance" are examples of how brief writers attempt to convince readers that the position they support is incomparable.

These groups also rely on value-laden terms and ideas, implying that their arguments and reasoning are morally superior. The careful choice of metaphors in these amicus briefs displays again the power of political language and issue framing (Iyengar, 1991).

The pro-life and pro-choice groups went through their "*repertoires* of collective action" (Tilly as quoted in Rule, 1988: 180) hoping that their lobbying through amicus efforts would sway the Supreme Court to their position. Previous research has established the important role interest groups play in setting the Supreme Court's agenda (O'Connor and Epstein, 1984 and 1983; Caldeira and Wright, 1988). It is unclear, though, what effect these amicus briefs had on the Court. Both sides felt that their amicus brief efforts had been influential in the *Webster* case (Woliver 1992a and 1992b; also Kolbert, 1989a; Grant, 1989). It is clear that the publicity over the *Webster* decision, both before and after it was handed down, helped heighten interest group mobilization around lobbying the Supreme Court.

Both sides, therefore, have continued to lobby the Supreme Court through their amicus briefs, hoping that the number of signatories, the lists of groups who co-sign, the numbers of briefs themselves, the prestige of the brief writers, or perhaps the reasoning within the briefs, will sway justices to their side. If nothing else, the briefs make a public statement, are an organizing tool, and display potential political clout.

The briefs are lengthy and rich in arguments, footnotes, anecdotes, sarcasm, patronizing lectures, heartfelt anger, and dissent. There are differences between the briefs and details in individual brief's arguments that cannot be fully explored here. The briefs offer a fascinating view of pro-life and pro-choice interest group thinking, rhetoric, symbols, and tactics.

NOTES

1   Research for this project was partially funded through a Research and Productive Scholarship Grant, The University of South Carolina—Columbia.

2. This seems almost prophetic given the murders and violence by pro-life activists at abortion clinics recently.

APPENDIX A: AMICUS BRIEFS SUBMITTED IN WEBSTER

NOTE: Pro-life briefs are marked by "**" and are in bold print; the others are pro-choice with the exception of the brief from the American Library Association. The American Library Association brief concerns itself with free speech and the right to have access to information, and takes no position on abortion directly.

#1. **Lutheran Church–Missouri Synod, The Christian Life Commission of the Southern Baptist Convention, and the National Association of Evangelicals.

#3. **The United States [the Solicitor General's Brief; dated November 10, 1988].

#6. **James Joseph Lynch, Jr.

#7. **Doctors for Life, Missouri Doctors for Life, Missouri Citizens for Life, Missouri Nurses for Life, and Lawyers for Life, Inc.

#8. **The National Legal Foundation.

#10. **Right to Life Advocates, Inc.

#11. **The New England Christian Action Council, Inc.

#12. **Certain American State Legislators [more than 200 state senators and representatives signed this brief; counsel for this amici is Americans United for Life, Legal Defense Fund].

#13. **American Collegians for Life, Inc., and The Catholic League for Religious and Civil Rights.

#14. **The Right to Life League of Southern California [Counsel is Robert L. Sassone].

**#15. The Association for Public Justice, and The Value of Life Committee, Inc. [Joseph W. Dellapenna attorney for amici].

**#16. Hon. Christopher H. Smith, Hon. Alan B. Mollohan, Hon. John C. Danforth, and other United States Senators and Members of Congress [9 U.S. Senators and 45 Members of the House signed this brief; counsel for this amici is Americans United for Life, Legal Defense Fund; Counsel of Record is Albert P. Blaustein, Rutgers University School of Law].

**#17. Birthright, Inc.

**#18. The Catholic Health Association of the United States.

**#19. Catholics United for Life, National Organization of Episcopalians for Life, Presbyterians Pro-Life, American Baptist Friends of Life, Baptists for Life, Southern Baptists for Life, Lutherans for Life, Moravians for Life, United Church of Christ Friends for Life, Task Force of United Methodists on Abortion and Sexuality, and the Christian Action Council.

**#20. The United States Catholic Conference.

**#21. The Rutherford Institute and the Rutherford Institutes of Alabama, Arkansas, California, Colorado, Connecticut, Florida, Georgia, Kentucky, Michigan, Minnesota, Montana, Nebraska, Ohio, Pennsylvania, Tennessee, Texas, Virginia, and West Virginia.

**#22. American Life League, Inc.

**#23. Missouri Catholic Conference.

**#24. Feminists for Life of America, Women Exploited by Abortion of Greater Kansas City, The National Association of Pro-Life Nurses, Let Me Live, and Elliot Institute for Social Sciences Research.

**#25. Larry Joyce.

**#26. International Right to Life Federation.

**#27. Certain Members of the General Assembly of the Commonwealth of Pennsylvania [14 Pennsylvania Senators and 56 members of the House signed this brief].

**#28. The American Academy of Medical Ethics [James Bopp, Jr., counsel of record].

**#29. The Catholic Lawyers Guild of the Archdiocese of Boston, Inc.

**#30. The Southern Center for Law and Ethics.

**#31. Alabama Lawyers for Unborn Children, Inc.

**#32. Covenant House and Good Counsel, Inc.

**#33. Bernard N. Nathanson [Robert L. Sassone, counsel].

**#34. National Right to Life Committee, Inc. [James Bopp, Jr., counsel of record].

**#35. The Center for Judicial Studies and Certain Members of Congress [55 members of the U.S. House and Senate signed this brief].

**#36. 127 Members of the Missouri General Assembly [Lynn D. Wardle, Richard G. Wilkins, J. Reuben Clark Law School, Brigham Young University, also listed as attorneys for amici].

**#37. Free Speech Advocates.

**#38. Christian Advocates Serving Evangelism.

**#39. The United States [Acting Solicitor General's brief; dated February 23, 1989].

**#40. The American Association of Pro-Life Obstetricians and Gynecologists and the American Association of Pro-Life Pediatricians [Paige Comstock Cunningham, counsel for amicus; street address listed only; Woliver notes this is also the address for Americans United for Life, Legal Defense Fund and that Comstock Cunningham is a lawyer for AUL].

**#42. Austin Vaughn and Crusade for Life, Inc. [Robert L. Sassone, attorney].

**#43. Human Life International [Robert L. Sassone, attorney].

**#44. Paul Marx [Robert L. Sassone, attorney].

**#45. The Southwest Life and Law Center, Inc.

**#46. Legal Defense for Unborn Children.

**#47. Edward Allen [Robert L. Sassone, attorney].

**#48. The Holy Orthodox Church.

**#50. Focus on the Family, and Family Research Council of America.

**#51. William J. Guste, Jr., Attorney General of Louisiana with Attorneys General joining for the States of Arizona, Idaho, Pennsylvania, and Wisconsin.

**#52. American Family Association, Inc.

#53. The National Council of Negro Women, Inc.; National Urban League, Inc.; The American Indian Health Care Association; The Asian American Legal Defense Fund; Committee For Hispanic Children and Families; The Mexican American Legal Defense and Education Fund; The National Black Women's Health Project; National Institute for Women of Color; National Women's Health Network; Organizacion Nacional de la Salud de la Mujer Latina; Organization of Asian Women; Puerto Rican Legal Defense and Education Fund; Women of Color Partnership Program of the Religious Coalition for Abortion Rights; Women of All Red Nations, North Dakota; YWCA of the U.S.A.; and Other Organizations [more than 100 civil rights, women's, labor and religious organizations and 17 individuals signed this brief; this is called "The Women of Color Brief" by the pro-choice activists].

#54. Women Who Have Had Abortions and Friends of Amici Curiae in Support of Appellees (Names of 2887 Amici Curiae and 627 Friends of Amici Curiae Set Forth in Appendix A) [counsel listed are from NOW Legal Defense and Education Fund and NARAL].

#55. American Jewish Congress, Board of Homeland Ministries–United Church of Christ, National Jewish Community Relations Advisory Council, The Presbyterian Church (U.S.A.) by James E. Andrews as Stated Clerk of General Assembly, The Religious Coalition for Abortion Rights, St. Louis Catholics for Choice, and thirty other religious groups [called the "Religious Brief" by pro-choice activists].

#56. Brief of 77 Organizations Committed to Women's Equality.

#57. 167 Distinguished Scientists and Physicians, including 11 Nobel Laureates [all have separately signed].

#59. National Organization for Women.

**#60. Agudath Israel of America.

#61. 281 American Historians.

#62. The National Family Planning and Reproductive Health Association.

#63. American Public Health Association, et al. [8 other organizations and 5 individuals also signed].

#64. Center for Population Options, The Society For Adolescent Medicine, The Juvenile Law Center, and The Judicial Consent For Minors Referral Panel.

#65. American Law Professors [885 law professors signed this brief].

#66. International Women's Health Organizations [22 international women's health or population organizations and 14 individuals signed this brief].

#67. Attorneys General of the States of California, Colorado, Massachusetts, New York, Texas, Vermont, and West Virginia.

#68. Organizations and Named Women [California National Organization for Women, The San Jose-South Bay Chapter of the National Organization for Women, California Alliance Concerned With School Age Parents, and 6 separately named women].

#69. American Medical Association, American Academy of Child and Adolescent Psychiatry, American Academy of Pediatrics, American College of Obstetricians and Gynecologists, American Fertility Society, American Medical Women's Association, American Psychiatric Association, and American Society of Human Genetics.

#70. The Committees on Civil Rights, Medicine and Law, and Sex and Law of the Association of the Bar of the City of New York and Others [Others are: Arizona Attorneys Action Council, The Beverly Hills Bar Association, Committee on Women's Rights of the New York County Lawyers' Association, Lawyers Club of San Diego, Inc., Women's Bar Association of Illinois, Women's Bar Association of the State of New York].

#71. American Nurses' Association, and The Nurses' Association of the American College of Obstetricians and Gynecologists.

#72. The National Association of Public Hospitals.

#73. Certain Members of the Congress of the United States [25 U.S. senators and 115 members of the House signed this brief].

#74. Bioethicists for Privacy.

#75. The National Coalition Against Domestic Violence.

#76. Americans United for Separation of Church and State.

#77. Catholics for a Free Choice, Chicago Catholic Women, National Coalition of American Nuns, Women in Spirit of Colorado Task Force, et al. [51 individuals also signed].

#78. Americans for Democratic Action, Coalition of Labor Union Women, Committee of Interns and Residents, Federally Employed Women, Public Employee Department, AFL-CIO.

#79. American Library Association, and Freedom to Read Foundation.

#80. American Psychological Association.

#81. The Association of Reproductive Health Professionals, et al. [Et al. includes: 8 associations, 6 medical school deans, 37 chairs of ob/gyn departments, and 64 other doctors and individuals, all separately listed].

#82. Brief on Behalf of 608 State Legislators From 32 States [all separately signed].

#83. Population-Environment Balance, Population Communication, Sierra Club, World Population Society, Worldwatch Institute, Jessie Smith Noyes Foundation, and Zero Population Growth.

#84. Canadian Women's Organizations [listed are The Canadian Abortion Rights Action League, The Ontario Coalition for Abortion Clinics, The National Action Committee on the Status of Women, The National Association of Women and the Law].

#85.   American Civil Liberties Union, The National Education Association, People For the American Way, The Newspaper Guild, The National Writers Union, and The Fresno Free College Foundation.

#86.   National Association of Women Lawyers and National Conference of Women's Bar Associations.

REFERENCES

Baer, Judith A. "What We Know As Women: A New Look At *Roe v. Wade.*" *NWSA Journal* 2, no. 4, Autumn 1990: 558–582.

Blank, Robert H. 1988. *Rationing Medicine.* New York: Columbia University Press.

Blank, Robert H. 1984. "Judicial Decision Making and Biological Fact: Roe v. Wade and the Unresolved Question of Fetal Viability." *Western Political Quarterly:* 584–602.

Caldeira, Gregory A., and John R. Wright. 1988. "Organized Interests and Agenda Setting in the U.S. Supreme Court." *American Political Science Review* 82 (December): 1109–1127.

Condit, Celeste M. 1990. *Decoding Abortion Rhetoric: The Communication Of Social Change.* Urbana: University of Illinois Press.

Coyle, Marcia. 1989. "Pro-Choice Forces Get It Together." *National Law Journal* (May 1): 27.

Coyle, Marcia, and Marianne Lavelle. 1989. "Full Court Press." *National Law Journal* (May 1): 1.

Craig, Barbara Hinkson, and David M. O'Brien. 1993. *Abortion and American Politics.* Chatham, New Jersey: Chatham House.

Davis, Angela Y. 1990. *Women, Culture, and Politics.* New York: Vintage Books.

Edelman, Murray. 1971. *Politics As Symbolic Action: Mass Arousal and Quiescence.* Chicago: Markham Publishing Co.

Epstein, Lee. 1985. *Conservative in Court.* Knoxville: University of Tennessee Press.

Epstein, Lee, and Joseph F. Kobylka. 1992 *The Supreme Court and Legal Change: Abortion and the Death Penalty.* Chapel Hill: University of North Carolina Press.

Epstein, Lee, and C.K. Rowland. 1991. "Debunking the Myth of Interest Group Invincibility in the Courts." *American Political Science Review* 85, no. 1: 205–217.

Field, Martha A. (Summer 1989). "Controlling the Woman to Protect the Fetus." *Law, Medicine and Health Care* 17, no. 2: 114–129.

Gallagher, Janet. 1989. "Fetus as Patient." In Nadine Taub and Sherrill Cohen, eds., *Reproductive Laws For The 1990s.* Clifton, New Jersey: Humana Press, 185–235.

Gallagher, Janet. 1987. "Prenatal Invasions and Interventions: What's Wrong With Fetal Rights." *Harvard Women's Law Journal* 10 (Spring): 9–58.

Ginsburg, Faye D. 1989. *Contested Lives: The Abortion Debate In An American Community.* Berkeley: University of California Press.

Gorney, Cynthia. 1990. "The Dispassion of John C. Willke." *The Washington Post Magazine* (April 22): 21–25, 38–42.

Grant, Edward R. 1989. "Conclusion: The Future of Abortion as a 'Private Choice.'" *American Journal of Law & Medicine* XV, nos. 2 & 3: 233–243.

Halva-Neubauer, Glen. 1990. "Abortion Policy in the Post-Webster Age." *Publius: The Journal of Federalism* 20, no. 3 (Summer): 27–44.

Ivie, Robert L. 1987. "Metaphor and the Rhetorical Invention of Cold War 'Idealists.'" *Communication Monographs* 54: 165–181.

Iyengar, Shanto. 1991. *Is Anyone Responsible? How Television Frames Political Issues.* Chicago: University of Chicago Press.

Luker, Kristin. 1984. *Abortion And The Politics Of Motherhood.* Berkeley: The University of California Press.

Luker, Kristin. 1975. *Taking Chances: Abortion And The Decision Not To Contracept.* Berkeley: University of California Press.

McGee, Michael Calvin. 1980. "The 'Ideograph': A Link Between Rhetoric and Ideology." *The Quarterly Journal of Speech* 66: 1–16.

Martin, E. 1987. *The Woman In The Body: A Cultural Analysis Of Reproduction.* Boston: Beacon Press.

Mishler, William, and Reginald S. Sheehan. March 1993. "The Supreme Court as a Countermajoritarian Institution? The Impact of Public Opinion on Supreme Court Decisions." *American Political Science Review* 87, no. 1: 87–101.

Mohr, J.C. 1978. *Abortion In America: the Origins and Evolution of National Policy.* New York: Oxford University Press.

Mumby, Dennis K. 1989. "Ideology and the Social Construction of Meaning: A Communication Perspective." *Communication Quarterly* 37: 291–304.

Nsiah-Jefferson, Laurie. 1989. "Reproductive Laws, Women of Color, and Low-Income Women." In Nadine Taub and Sherrill Cohen, eds., *Reproductive Laws for the 1990s.* Clifton, New Jersey: Humana Press.

Oakley, Ann. 1987. "From Walking Wombs to Test-Tube Babies." In *Reproductive Technologies: Gender, Motherhood, and Medicine,* ed. Michelle Stanworth. Minneapolis: University of Minnesota Press, 36–56.

O'Connor, Karen. 1980. *Women's Organizations' Use Of The Courts.* Lexington, Massachusetts: Lexington Books.

O'Connor, Karen, and Lee Epstein. 1984. "The Role of Interest Groups in Supreme Court Policy Formation." In *Public Policy Formation,* ed. Robert Eyestone, Greenwich, Connecticut: JAI Press, 63–81.

O'Connor, Karen, and Lee Epstein. 1983. "Court Rules and Workload: A Case Study of Rules Governing Amicus Curiae Participation." *The Justice System Journal* 8, no. 1: 35–45.

Petchesky, Rosalind P. 1987. "Foetal Images: The Power of Visual Culture in the Politics of Reproduction." In Michelle Stanworth, ed. *Reproductive Technologies: Gender, Motherhood, and Medicine.* Minneapolis: University of Minnesota Press, 57–80.

Petchesky, Rosalind Pollack. 1984. *Abortion And Woman's Choice: The State, Sexuality, And Reproductive Freedom.* New York: Longman, 1984. [Also: 1990. Revised edition published by Northeastern University Press.]

Richard, Patricia Bayer. December 1989. "Alternative Abortion Policies: What Are the Health Consequences?" *Social Science Quarterly* 70, no. 4: 941–955.

Rosenberg, Gerald. 1991. *The Hollow Hope: Can Courts Bring About Social Change?* Chicago: University of Chicago Press.

Rothman, Barbara Katz. 1986. *The Tentative Pregnancy: Prenatal Diagnosis And The Future Of Motherhood.* New York: Viking.

Rubin, Alissa. 1991. "Interest Groups and Abortion Politics in the Post-Webster Era." In *Interest Group Politics,* ed. Allan J. Cigler and Burdett A. Loomis, Washington, D.C.: Congressional Quarterly Press, Third Edition, 239–255.

Rubin, Eva R. 1987. *Abortion, Politics, And The Courts: Roe V. Wade and Its Aftermath.* New York: Greenwood Press, Revised Edition.

Rule, James B. 1988. *Theories Of Civil Violence.* Berkeley: University of California Press.

Songer, Donald R., and Reginald S. Sheehan. 1993. "Interest Group Success in the Courts: Amicus Participation in the Supreme Court." *Political Research Quarterly* 46 (June): 339.

Staggenborg, Suzanne. 1991. *The Pro-Choice Movement: Organization And Activism In The Abortion Conflict*. New York: Oxford University Press.

Starr, Paul. 1982. *The Social Transformation Of American Medicine*. New York: Basic Books.

Tribe, Laurence H. 1990. *Abortion: The Clash of Absolutes*. New York: W. W. Norton & Co.

United States Supreme Court. *Webster v. Reproductive Health Services*. 57 L.W. 5023 (June 27, 1989).

Woliver, Laura R. 1992a. "Rhetoric and Symbols in the Pro-Life Amicus Briefs to the *Webster* Case." A paper presented at the 1992 American Political Science Convention, September 3–6, 1992, Chicago, Illinois.

Woliver, Laura R. 1992b. "Symbols and Rhetoric in the Pro-Choice Amicus Briefs to the *Webster* Case." A paper presented at the 1992 Southern Political Science Convention, November 5–7, 1992, Atlanta, Georgia.

Woliver, Laura R. 1991. "The Influence of Technology on the Politics of Motherhood: An Overview of the United States." *Women's Studies International Forum* 14, no. 5: 479–490.

Woliver, Laura R. 1991. "Lobbying the Supreme Court: Coalitions of Abortion Interests and the Webster Decision." A paper presented at the 1991 Southern Political Science Convention, Tampa, Florida.

Woliver, Laura R. 1990. "Reproductive Technologies and Surrogacy: Policy Concerns for Women," *Politics and the Life Sciences*, 8, no. 2: 185–193.

Woliver, Laura R. 1989. "New Reproductive Technologies: Challenges to Women's Control of Gestation and Birth." In *Biomedical Technology and Public Policy*, ed. Robert Blank and Miriam K. Mills. Westport, Connecticut: Greenwood Press, 43–56.

Woliver, Laura R. 1989. "The Deflective Power of Reproductive Technologies: The Impact on Women." *Women And Politics* 9, 3 (November): 17–47.

Woliver, Laura R., and Tracy McDonald. 1993. "Amicus Curia Rhetoric in Abortion Litigation." A paper presented at the 1993 South Carolina Political Science Convention, Presbyterian College, Clinton, South Carolina.

CHAPTER 2

CONSTITUTIONALIZING ABORTION

KIM LANE SCHEPPELE

Few issues in modern politics have been more divisive and apparently less capable of purely political resolution than abortion.[1] Throughout Europe and North America,[2] abortion has emerged as an issue where mutually inconsistent positions are heavily staked out by organized groups and where activists on each side are unlikely to think of compromise as any solution at all.[2] The groups mobilized on each side of this issue have little in common. From the partial information we have, opposing sides generally do not share the same social space, the same picture of the world, or the same sense about what matters or what is to be valued.[3] This lack of a common ground shows up in endless and no-win political fights about abortion, fights from which elected politicians typically want to run, because any answer can only limit the political support politicians get. The intensity of the issue and the tendency of politicians to want to avoid it have caused the interest groups involved to use an appeal to higher law or constitutional principles in the war over abortion. I will argue here that appealing to constitutions changes the ways that the abortion debate may be framed and does not provide final political answers to the question of abortion policy. Constitutions provide discursive spaces that shape claims made in their name into rights claims, which in the abortion case serves primarily to further polarize the debate.

In an earlier article,[4] I showed how the intensity of debate over abortion in Europe and North America often bumped the abortion issue up a notch in abstraction so that constitutionally unusual political procedures (like private members' bills, free votes, unusual invocations of rarely used constitutional procedures, and decisions by constitutional courts) were frequently invoked by all sides when abortion was raised as an issue. I will now focus on one particular strategy within that range: the appeal to textual interpretations of written constitutions to settle questions about abortion. Though having a constitutional decision on abortion is no guarantee that compliant practice will follow, the process of developing constitutional arguments involves seeing abortion within a uniquely *legal* framework, one that comes with its own presumptions, strengths, and limitations. When those involved in the abortion issue turn to the constitution for arguments, they change the nature of the political debate.

This chapter examines constitutional interpretations in the United States, Canada, Ireland, Germany, and Hungary.[5] In each of these countries, abortion has been made explicitly a subject of *substantive* constitutional debate. That is, abortion has been raised as a constitutional issue, and courts examine the text of the constitution to determine whether it allows or prohibits abortion. In Germany, the United States, and Canada, the highest constitutional court has used its power of judicial review to declare duly enacted statutes about abortion invalid because the current laws infringed on constitutionally protected rights. In Hungary, administrative regulations about abortion were declared unconstitutional because constitutional rights were implicated, and this required a statute passed by Parliament and not just a ministerial decree. In Ireland, the Supreme Court interpreted a constitutional provision that explicitly provided guarantees for fetal life and held that the right to life of the unborn was limited by an equal right to life of the mother. Later, the Court ruled that the protections to the fetus could themselves be changed by constitutional amendment.

My analysis concentrates on these constitutional decisions, showing how constitutional discourse tends to frame the issue of abortion in distinctive ways. In brief, my argument is this: The move to take an issue like abortion to a constitutional court for judgment is not just bumping "politics as usual" up to another policy making body. Instead, courts are distinctively *legal* institutions. They operate with a strong, partially autonomous legal ideology that results in issues being framed in particular and unique ways. The law is not just a more technical form of politics or ethics; it is something quite different from either. Making abortion a constitutional question *changes* how abortion can be represented and how competing arguments can be staged. This tends to eliminate gradualist or compromise solutions to contentious problems. Regardless of which side prevails—those who feel abortion should be legal or those who feel abortion should be banned—the very act of invoking constitutional courts means that the issue will be resolved through the lens of constitutional reasoning. Despite substantial national differences in how constitutional reasoning is done, there is a "family resemblance" in constitutional arguments about abortion that makes constitutional solutions to the abortion problem unstable in all countries.

I. CONSTITUTIONAL DECISIONS ABOUT ABORTION
THE UNITED STATES

In the United States, the 1973 decision of the Supreme Court in *Roe v. Wade*[6] burst on the political scene like a bombshell. Credited with shifting the small right-to-life movement into high gear and intensifying public debate on the abortion issue,[7] *Roe* was an extraordinary decision, even by the extraordinary standards of the Supreme Court. The decision struck down the existing laws of 46 states, a highly unusual act. While many of those laws were the ossified product of the nineteenth-century criminalization movement, many other laws represented the recent, reformist successes of the American Law Institute's Model Penal Code. The antique statutes and the modern ones were all similarly judged to be in violation of the Constitution of the United States.

The decision created a controversy in the American legal community, not just for its wide sweep, but also for the method of its reasoning.[8] Justice Blackmun's majority opinion rested on a constitutional right of privacy, which was implied in the Fourteenth Amendment's due process clause but not explicitly mentioned anywhere in the Constitution. He found that this right was "broad enough to encompass a woman's right to choose an abortion." Because of this right to privacy possessed by individuals, the state could not tell a woman, at least in the early stages of a pregnancy, what she and her doctor could decide was best for her. But in the later stages, the interest of the state in "potential life" could be found to be more pressing and government could then regulate abortions to protect a women's health in the second trimester and even prohibit abortions during the third trimester, when the fetus becomes viable. The dissents by Justices Rehnquist and White criticized Justice Blackmun's opinion for its activism, arguing that states were well within their rights to enact legislation on this point and that the federal constitution had nothing whatsoever to say about the subject of abortion. Significantly, however, the justices who opposed the constitutionalization of a right to choose abortion never believed that the Constitution gave independent rights to a fetus. Debate ever since has revolved around whether a women's right to choose abortion is covered by the Constitution and, if so, where.[9]

The intense political conflict that arose after the decision in *Roe* turned confirmation hearings for prospective judges of the federal courts into battles over the nominees' views about abortion. Presidents Ronald Reagan and George Bush, in keeping with the Republican Party's platform statement to overturn *Roe v. Wade*, nominated conservative judges who could be expected to vote to gut *Roe* at the first available opportunity; most senators apparently felt powerless to reject any but the most outrageous nominees. The turmoil caused by *Roe* very nearly engulfed the legitimacy of the Supreme Court itself. It put the politics of the court on open view, inviting speculation that the nominees and even the judging process were more political than judicial.

After two decades of conflict, the opportunity for the Court to overturn *Roe* came in *Planned Parenthood of Southeastern Pennsylvania v. Casey*.[10] Nearly all experts believed that the Court would use the Pennsylvania statute that put in place administrative hurdles—waiting periods, requirements of abortion counseling, parental and spousal consent, and various record-keeping requirements on those involved—as a vehicle for overturning *Roe*. Instead, the Court surprisingly used the case to reiterate that the right to choose abortion is protected by the Constitution, not primarily through the Constitution's implicit privacy provisions but rather through the guarantee of personal liberty in the due process clause of the Fourteenth Amendment.

This ruling came by means of a complicated series of fractured opinions. Four dissenters voted explicitly to overturn *Roe* and the remaining five split 3-2 over the reasons for (and standards to be used in) maintaining a right to choose abortions. While two of the justices voted to leave *Roe* as it was, the three judges in the middle (Justices O'Connor, Souter, and Kennedy—the "troika," as they came to be called), rearranged the constitutional ideas that supported the right.[11] Putting the case on stronger constitutional footing by deemphasizing an implied right of privacy, the troika instead argued that the maintenance of a pregnancy was such an intrusion on a woman's liberty that choices about what to do with a pregnancy could be raised to the status of a fundamental right, involving as it did "a rule of law and a component of liberty that we cannot renounce." To do this, however, the troika jettisoned the earlier trimester framework that had been used in *Roe* and replaced it with another that drew a sharper line at viability of the fetus as a basis of state regulation. Despite the fact that the troika opinion said that "the essential holding of *Roe v. Wade* should be retained and once again reaffirmed," it also went on to overturn two earlier decisions of the Court that had allegedly followed directly from *Roe* and to jettison the concept of trimesters. Most significantly, however, it replaced the absolute ban on state intrusions on pregnancy in the early months with a standard that allows some regulation as long as the regulation does not amount to an "undue burden."[12] The troika opinion said that only an unduly burdensome regulation would create a constitutional violation by significantly infringing the protected liberty of the woman to choose whether or not to have a child. But readers of the troika's opinion might be excused for not understanding how a case could simultaneously say that it was upholding a prior decision while striking down two other cases that had previously relied on it and announcing a new standard to be applied in the future. The troika opinion in *Casey* might have made the current doctrine clearer, but it threw into question the coherence of this new decision with the past decisions of the Court.

The dissenters, this time falling only one vote short of a majority, reiterated their stand that the Constitution could not be used to protect abortion rights and that the issue belonged within the province of the democratic process of the state legislatures.[13] Although there is sharp disagreement both within the Court and among commentators about whether the Court has got it "right"—whether abortion is or is not included as a substantive matter in the Constitution[14]—the case is still generally discussed as if the answer lies within the constitutional text. With the election in 1992 of a pro-choice Democrat, Bill Clinton, as president, focus shifted away from a constitutional strategy, since pro-life supporters know they are unlikely to change the balance of votes on the court to demote a woman's right to choose abortion within the set of protected constitutional guarantees.

CANADA

In Canada, the abortion issue has been raised a number of times as a constitutional question, most spectacularly in the 1988 case of *Morgentaler v. The Queen.*[15] Canada had changed its abortion laws as part of a general revision of its criminal code in 1969, converting abortion from a crime under all circumstances to a crime only under some circumstances. Following the lead of England, which had modernized its abortion laws in 1967, the Canadian Parliament enacted a statute that allowed abortions to preserve the life or health of the mother, but only if an abortion were performed in a hospital and only if a hospital committee of three doctors agreed that the abortion would be necessary on these statutory grounds.

Dr. Henry Morgentaler led a campaign to legalize abortions, opening free-standing clinics that defied the requirements that abortions be done in hospitals with the approval of a three-doctor committee. Morgentaler was arrested—repeatedly.[16] His first arrest came in 1970 in Quebec, the Canadian province that is most overwhelmingly Catholic. After much procedural delay and more arrests for performing abortions, the case finally came to trial in 1973. The jury, despite overwhelming evidence, acquitted him.

In Canadian criminal procedure at that time, the province could appeal from an acquittal, and, in a highly unusual move, the appeals court directed a guilty verdict and ordered Morgentaler sent to jail for eighteen months with three years' probation to follow. Appealing his conviction to the Canadian Supreme Court, Morgentaler was dealt a serious blow. The Court upheld his conviction by a 6-3 vote, though the Court avoided dealing with the abortion issue directly. In his opinion, Justice Dickson noted that the Court had not "been called upon to decide, or even to enter, the loud and continuous public debate on abortion."[17] Instead, the Court looked narrowly at whether the evidence indicated that Morgentaler had violated the criminal law on abortion, and this, they found, he had. Although arguments had been made in favor of his acquittal under the then-existing

Canadian Bill of Rights, the justices noted that the Bill of Rights did not yet rise to the status of constitutional protections in Canada. If people did not like the abortion statute, the Court argued, they would have to go to Parliament to get it changed. The courts would stay out of it.

But as it turned out, the Canadian Supreme Court did not stay out of it for long, nor did Morgentaler. Upon release from prison, Morgentaler continued to perform abortions without making any secret of it. Repeatedly arrested, Morgentaler was repeatedly acquitted by juries until the Quebec Minister of Justice announced that the province would no longer enforce the abortion laws. Morgentaler moved his campaign to other provinces, eventually getting himself arrested in Toronto, Ontario in 1985. Once again, a jury refused to convict, the Ontario Court of Appeals directed a guilty verdict, and the case came up again to the Canadian Supreme Court, just as it had before.

Something important had changed in the meantime, however. The Canadian Charter of Rights had been adopted in 1982, giving Canada its first constitutionally enforceable Bill of Rights. As part of the Charter, the Supreme Court had been explicitly given the power of judicial review (that is, the right to declare statutes invalid if they violated the constitution). With the same case involving the same defendant, the Supreme Court in 1988 changed its ruling. The statute under which Morgentaler was convicted was struck down as unconstitutional by the Supreme Court on a 5-2 vote. This decision showed more than any other what a difference the Charter of Rights made in the Supreme Court's view of its power and in its willingness to confront the constitutionality of statutes.

The provision invoked to declare the abortion statute unconstitutional was Section 7 of the Charter of Rights, which declared that "everyone has the right to life, liberty and security of the person and the right not to be deprived thereof except in accordance with the principles of fundamental justice."[18] In *Morgentaler II*, Chief Justice Dickson, the judge who had previously argued that the Court had no need to get involved in the abortion issue, now argued under the authority of the Charter that the criminal abortion statute violated a woman's right to the security of her person because the statute permitted others to determine what she could do with her body, based on principles that were "unrelated to her own principles and aspirations." He went on to argue that the delays that the statute caused, the effects these delays had on women's health, and the arbitrariness with which definitions of health were applied also infringed the right of a woman to bodily security. This ruling made the existing statute invalid, but did not preclude the enactment of another regulatory statute without these particular offenses.

Four other justices agreed that the abortion statute violated the Charter, but Madam Justice Wilson went even further than the other four justices who wanted to strike down the statute. She wrote an opinion invoking the rights of women to liberty, claiming that *all* abortion regulations in the early stages of pregnancy should be invalidated under the Charter. Only Justices MacIntyre and LaForest, in dissent, maintained that since abortion was nowhere mentioned it was not a constitutional question. All justices agreed that, although the 1969 reform statute was invalid, fetal interests are a valid state concern that would be regulated by at least some constitutionally acceptable means, particularly in the later stages of pregnancy. The Court declined to detail a regime of permissible laws, as the American Supreme Court had in *Roe v. Wade*. Since 1990 the Parliament has not been able to agree on a new law regulating abortion.

IRELAND

In 1983, a majority of Irish voters approved an amendment to the Irish Constitution that said: "The state acknowledges the right to life of the unborn and with due regard to the equal right of the life of the mother, guarantees in its laws to protect, and as far as practicable, by its laws, to defend and vindicate that right." Abortion was already a serious offense in the criminal law at the time of the enactment of the Eighth Amendment to the Irish Constitution. The amendment made it impossible for an ordinary majority of the legislature to repeal the criminal statute. Despite the fact that the language of the amendment nowhere mentions abortion specifically, the context of its ratification made it clear it was designed to prevent any liberalization of the abortion laws.

The strong pro-life forces in Ireland are led by the Catholic Church and supported by all the major political parties, thus securing a nearly two-thirds majority of voters in favor of the constitutional amendment. But the passage of the unborn life amendment was only the first of many constitutional challenges considered by the Supreme Court. In the *Attorney General (at the relation of the Society for the Protection of the Unborn Child) v. Open Door Counselling Ltd. and Dublin Wellwoman Centre Ltd.*,[19] the Irish Supreme Court was called upon to decide whether constitutional protection of the unborn extended to bans of abortion counseling for pregnant women. And in the *Society for the Protection of Unborn Children v. Grogan*,[20] a challenge was raised against university students who published the names and telephone numbers of British abortion clinics in the student manuals. In a pair of decisions that for some raised serious questions under the European law,[21] the

Irish Supreme Court found that the right to life of the unborn could be invoked to limit free speech rights of Irish citizens if they wanted to provide information to women about abortion services in England. In *Society for the Protection of the Unborn Child v. Coogan*,[22] the Court decided that the Eighth Amendment was sufficiently broad to allow any interested party to bring suit to prevent an abortion if the life of an unborn child were at stake. Clearly, the Irish Supreme Court was interpreting the new constitutional amendment broadly to implicate other rights not explicitly limited by the language of the amendment.

By far the biggest and most closely watched constitutional challenge in Ireland was the landmark case of *Attorney General v. X* in 1992.[23] Covered hour by hour by the Western news media, the case involved a fourteen-year-old Irish girl, pregnant as a result of being raped by the father of a friend, who sought to obtain an abortion in England.[24] Believing that preserving the remains of the aborted fetus might provide valuable genetic information to identify the rapist in the upcoming criminal trial, the parents of the girl known only as X contacted the Irish attorney general to find out how they could make this information available for the prosecution, thereby notifying the attorney general that the girl intended to have an abortion. The attorney general decided that going abroad to obtain an abortion arguably violated the right to life of the unborn within Ireland and promptly got a court injunction against the girl and her parents, ordering them not to leave the country and not to get an abortion. After an extraordinary three-day *in camera* hearing at which evidence was presented orally and directly to the justices, the Court issued a stunning judgment: The girl was allowed to go to England for an abortion, but only because carrying the pregnancy to term would threaten her life. The threat involved her repeated statements that if forced to carry the pregnancy to term, she would take her own life. The decision opened up a large exception to the total ban on abortions, because a woman would only have to make a credible threat of suicide to be permitted to have an abortion. A physical threat to the mother's life alone was not required; a psychological threat that might result in suicide was sufficient. All of the five justices who heard the case ruled that the Eighth Amendment protecting the right to life of the unborn implied an equal right to life for the mother, though Justice Hederman thought that the threat to the mother's life in the instant case was not severe enough to allow the injunction to be lifted. The exception to the ban on abortion to save the life of the mother meant that, though a mother's *health* could be subordinated to protect the unborn, her death could not be required, even if the unborn could be saved as a result. None of the justices thought that the exceptions for abortion in Ireland could extend beyond the limited case in which the mother would die without an abortion. The justices differed on how immanent the threat had to be for a threat to a mother's life to allow an abortion, but all agreed that the evidence had to be clear and substantial. In all other cases where a woman might seek an abortion out of the country, she could be prevented from leaving Ireland, since the right to travel of a pregnant woman was clearly less fundamental than the right to life of the unborn child.[25]

The decision caused quite a stir in Ireland, leading to another referendum on the abortion question in the fall of 1992. The referendum essentially asked for popular ratification of the Court's decision in the X case, and the voters supported the decision by a 60 to 40 margin. In addition, other questions that were put on the referendum proposed amendments to liberalize court-imposed restrictions on the rights to travel and to receive information. These referendum questions passed handily as well, thus eliminating the need for a showdown with the European Court of Human Rights on the question.[26] But the outcome led to another challenge before the Irish Supreme Court. The Irish Parliament (the Oireachtas) passed a law in March 1995 that would put into effect the constitutional amendment allowing women access to information about legal abortion facilities abroad but, before signing the law, Irish President Mary Robinson referred the question to the Supreme Court under its special Article 26 jurisdiction for preliminary review of laws.

On May 12, 1995, the Irish Supreme Court ruled that the Fourteenth Amendment to the Constitution (the part of the 1992 referendum that gave the right to women to receive information about legal abortion facilities outside of Ireland) was itself constitutional and that the bill passed by the Parliament to achieve this goal balanced the various rights contained within the Constitution in a fair and reasonable manner.[27] The decision was particularly notable for the way in which it rejected the natural law arguments put forward by the court-appointed counsel for Irish fetuses.[28] While counsel argued that some rights were based in natural law that went beyond the Constitution and therefore could not be altered or amended by the Constitution itself, the Court found that all powers of the government were given by the people, who could legitimately amend the Constitution to which all of the government was then to be subordinated. Moreover, the Court reaffirmed its power as the ultimate interpreter of the Constitution and said that judges must interpret the Constitution "in accordance with their ideas of prudence, justice and charity." Referring to Ireland as a "pluralist society" where different religious traditions had different views of natural law, the Court went on to say that as a result natural law could not be superior to the Constitution. The Fourteenth Amendment and its enacting legislation were constitutional, even if they violated the natural law view represented by the Eighth Amendment. In other words, the criteria for determining the validity of an amendment to the

Constitution would be whether or not it was enacted through appropriate procedures. The court rejected any other substantive standard for the constitutionality of an amendment.

The polarized reaction that followed said that the Supreme Court's decision "recklessly destabilized the whole scaffolding of human rights protection in the constitution,"[29] that it was a "fundamental shift in this State's coming of age,"[30] and that it answered the question "What is Irish democracy?" (pluralistic).[31] But it was clear that the constitutional debate had at least temporarily achieved closure on an important question.

GERMANY

In the early 1970s, as a number of European countries were liberalizing their laws on abortion to allow the procedure under a wider array of circumstances, the German Bundestag considered a series of statutes designed to liberalize abortion in what was then West Germany. The existing law, enacted originally in 1871, provided criminal penalties for any abortion, with the exception of those carried out to save the life or health of the mother. After much deliberation and a confusing set of Parliamentary votes, the Bundestag in 1974 passed the most liberal of several bills under simultaneous consideration. The new law allowed abortion in the first twelve weeks of pregnancy without restriction. After twelve weeks, abortions could be performed up to 22 weeks to save the life or health of the woman, or to abort a fetus suffering from an incurable injury to its health. Right after the passage of the statute, 193 Bundestag members who had voted against it (particularly those from various Christian-based political parties) and the governments of six German *Lander* filed suit in the Constitutional Court to challenge its constitutionality.

The Court's ruling, *The Abortion Decision*, announced on February 25, 1975,[32] struck down the newly passed reform statute for being in violation of the German Basic Law (the Constitution), particularly Article 2, Paragraph 2, Sentence 1, which declares, "Everyone shall have a right to life." This "everyone," according to the Court, includes the fetus from the fourteenth day after conception when "life, in the sense of historical existence of a human individual, exists, according to definite biological-physiological knowledge."[33] The Court found that "the security of human existence against encroachments by the state would be incomplete if it did not also embrace the prior step of 'completed life,' unborn life."[34] This obligation to protect unborn human life exists even against the mother, the Court continued,[35] even though the mother possesses her own right to life and the right to the free development of her personality. But rights, short of a right to life, were not without limits, the Court concluded.

The state must express its condemnation of abortion through its laws, the Court said, and must "reawaken and, if required, to strengthen the maternal duty to protect" the fetus.[36] This does not mean that the pregnant woman can never get an abortion, only that she has to have serious enough reasons to get an abortion so that the infringements on her rights outweigh those to the unborn child in the particular instance. If the pregnant woman's life is at risk, or if her health would be infringed by continuing the pregnancy, then these would be good enough reasons to get an abortion. If the pregnant woman found herself in a desperate situation, then this too would be an acceptable circumstance in which to get an abortion. But the obligation of the state to protect unborn life would require it "to offer counseling and assistance with the goal of reminding pregnant women of the fundamental duty to respect the life of the unborn, to encourage her to continue the pregnancy and—especially in cases of social need—to support her through practical measures of assistance."[37] The liberal abortion law was struck down.

Returning to the drawing board, the Bundestag passed another reform statute, this one criminalizing abortion, except in situations where the pregnant woman's life or health was in danger, where the fetus was substantially deformed, or to "avert the danger of a distress which is so serious that the pregnant woman cannot be required to continue the pregnancy and cannot be averted in any other way she can reasonably be expected to bear."[38] The statute also required mandatory counseling and a three-day waiting period after the counseling before the abortion could be performed. This revised statute was upheld by the European Commission on Human Rights in a challenge brought under the European Convention.[39] But in practice, the decentralized form of the law's practical operation allowed doctors in the Catholic areas of Germany to deny abortions to many women, while doctors in other parts of the country performed something close to abortion on demand.

With one of the most restrictive abortion laws in Europe, West Germany found another challenge to its abortion policy when East and West were united in 1990. In contrast to the relatively restrictive law in the West, East Germany had a liberal law on abortion in force, allowing an abortion in the first twelve weeks of pregnancy without restriction, nearly identical to the law that the Constitutional Court had struck down in 1975. In the hastily drafted unification agreement, which ran to some 900 pages, the two parts of the new Germany were able to agree to common regulations on a vast array of policies—but they could not agree on a uniform law on abortion. At the last minute, negotiators agreed to leave each law intact in its own territory, with an agreement to draft a new abortion law before two years were out. In advance of the deadline, on June 27, 1992, the Bundestag voted by a 357 to 284 margin in favor of a statute that would allow abortion without restriction within the first three months of pregnancy, but only if the woman first underwent counseling and then waited three days before having the procedure.[40] At the time, it looked as if the proponents of the liberal law of the East had prevailed.

Within days of its passage, however, 249 Bundestag members, primarily from the Christian parties, challenged the statute in the Constitutional Court. After several publicly announced delays in the final date of its decision and public challenges to two of the judges who had well-known ties to various pro-life groups, the Court announced *Abortion II* on May 28, 1993. The decision upheld part of the statute while striking down other parts.[41]

The reasoning of the Constitutional Court in the second abortion case is striking, because it opens up a wholly different way of thinking about state responsibility for enforcing rights. At first, the justices appeared to follow the decision of 1975. In fact, the Court substantially modified its earlier ruling while giving lip-service to continuity, just as the American Supreme Court did in the *Casey* decision. While the Federal Constitutional Court had said in 1975 that the German state must use the criminal law to fulfill its obligation to protect unborn life, the 1993 case softened that strong requirement by saying that such criminal law provisions, though still required, did not have to be accompanied by criminal punishment. Thus, the unification law was unconstitutional insofar as it *decriminalized* abortion—but constitutional in saying that the state could substitute "normative counseling" for criminal punishment as a way of fulfilling its obligations to protect fetuses. The 1993 decision required that abortion remain a criminal offense under German law for those cases that still fell outside the Court's 1975 list of acceptable circumstances, but normative counseling that was designed to persuade the woman to have the child could be used instead of criminal sanctions to reduce the number of actual abortions that German women would have. The state did not have to require that women give reasons for getting abortions or to have their personal circumstances subject to scrutiny by third persons, leaving the decision about whether to have an abortion fully in the woman's hands in the first trimester. And the woman could choose to follow the law or not, but the state did not have to inquire or act further.

In practice, then, this meant both that abortion restrictions in the West were greatly eased compared with the previous situation and that women in the East now had to undergo counseling they had not previously had to encounter. But there was a hitch in all this for women seeking abortions. While under both previous laws all approved abortions were paid for by state health insurance, under the new ruling the state must limit funding of abortions. Since some of the abortions that women will get under the new ruling will be illegal (though not punishable) and the government has no way to tell which abortions are legal and which are not, the Court ruled that the state need not pay for *any* of the abortions that women get, unless the woman's life or health is threatened or she is too poor to pay at all.

Finding that both the woman and the fetus had constitutionally protectable rights in its second decision as well as in its first, the Federal Constitutional Court of Germany designed a regime of legal regulation that avoided criminal sanctions while still requiring a state role in providing non-neutral information and advice for women seeking abortions.

HUNGARY

Compared with most of the states under the influence of the former Soviet Union, Hungary had a relatively restrictive abortion law prior to the establishment of a constitutional rule-of-law state in 1989. Women seeking abortions had to go before medical committees that could and did inquire into the personal details of their lives before giving permission for abortions. Only women over age thirty-five or women who had at least two children were exempted from this procedure, which many women found humiliating and intrusive.

Hungary's new Constitution—a heavily amended version of the Stalinist Constitution of 1949—went into effect on October 23, 1989, and on January 1, 1990, the new Hungarian Constitutional Court opened for business. One of the first petitions that the Court received was from a group of Catholic law professors from Miskolc called Pacem in Utero, urging on the Court the view that the fetus had a qualified right to life under the new Hungarian Constitution.

While the Court wrestled with this question, a major public debate over abortion took place in Hungary. Strongly pro-life views were aired for the first time, and small and embattled groups of feminists argued in favor of women's rights of self-determination. The Parliament wanted to avoid the question and managed to do so until a ruling of the Constitutional Court in December 1991.[42]

In its long opinion, the Court held that the existing legal regulations on abortion violated the Hungarian Constitution because they necessarily implicated fundamental human rights. The fetus might have a right to life under the Hungarian Constitution, the Court said; the woman carrying the fetus surely had a constitutional right to self-determination. But rather than reason from these statements directly through to conclusions about what the abortion law should look like concretely, the Court said only that the Parliament had to pass a formal law instead of allowing abortion to be governed by regulations of the welfare ministry (formerly the ministry of health). Within broad parameters that required only that the Parliament take both the rights of the woman and the potential rights of the fetus into account, the Court suggested that it might be possible for the state to meet its constitutional obligations to protect human life and the self-determination rights of women in many ways.

Did the fetus have a right to life protected by the Hungarian Constitution? This question, the Court said, "cannot be resolved by constitutional interpretation."[43] It was instead, according to the Court, a matter of political judgment, to be exercised by the Parliament within broad constitutional parameters. Here, too, the legislature had several options. It could grant the fetus legal personhood, like that given to a corporation, personhood that did not necessarily come with the full complement of rights required by the protection of human dignity. Or, the legislature might provide only general background protection for the survival of human life in general, which would mean that the state would not have to intervene in every individual case to protect a specifically threatened fetus. In this way, the regulation of abortion could be like the laws for the protection of workplace safety or the protection of the environment—generally supportive of healthy conditions without guaranteeing a specific standard to every specific individual. Or the legislature could find that the fetus was a person with full rights to life and dignity. But if the legislature determined that the fetus was a person on an equal par with the woman carrying it, then this would require the logical consequences that the fetus would have stronger claims than the woman, since the right to life was stronger than the right to self-determination. Leaving the decision to the Parliament, the Court hinted that it would revisit the question and consider the balance of rights after the new law was passed.

In 1992, the Hungarian Parliament passed a new abortion law that took effect at the start of 1993. The new law reads like many Western European laws, with abortion formally criminalized, allowing exceptions for a variety of circumstances that include a woman's difficult social conditions. The law stops short of granting the fetus a right to life, but requires informational (not normative) counseling to inform the woman both about state programs designed to assist her with childraising and also about birth control. Since the new law went into effect, about 300 counselors have been trained nationally to do this, and they are finding that they are spending most of their time educating women about birth control.[44] In the first year of the law's operation, the Hungarian abortion rate dropped by nearly 13 percent, but many of those familiar with the law claim that it is the education about birth control, not the apparent restrictiveness of the law per se, that is causing this change. The law may look restrictive, but in practice, abortion is much more widely available with much less restriction than it was under the prior law. This new law has been challenged by new petitions to the Constitutional Court, which has not yet issued a ruling on its constitutionality.

II. THE SPECIAL SPIN OF CONSTITUTIONALISM

Despite the significant differences in the constitutional cultures in the countries under consideration and the substantive content of the five constitutions, certain similarities stand out in the constitutional reasoning of the various courts we have examined. Above all, the justices who have written these decisions think in a lawyerly style that has a recognizable pattern. And though that style differs between the civil law tradition of Germany and Hungary and the common law tradition of the United States, Canada, and Ireland (as well as within the two distinct legal traditions), there is still a remarkable convergence in the moves made by judges in legal reasoning under the constitutions of their respective states. Each of these decisions is recognizable as an instance of a larger genre—the constitutional opinion.

Courts are sites of public discourse that require what is said there to be said in legally recognizable terms. After all, what courts have to offer is the authoritative interpretation of existing laws. Unless arguments brought before courts are framed in terms that give those courts the jurisdiction and the ability to hear those claims as *legal* ones, the claims cannot be heard as valid. When abortion arguments are made to constitutional courts, the issue is *constitutionalized*, in the sense that it is transformed into constitutional arguments using the specialized discourse of law. These "constitutionalized" arguments squash the representation of abortion and what is at stake in abortion debates into predetermined categories that can be understood and elaborated by courts. And though legal cultures vary, there are some strong similarities in the way that these categories are constructed in the different cases examined here.

1. A RIGHTS FRAMEWORK

Most constitutions divide their provisions between those that set out the structure of government and those that spell out the rights citizens can claim against the state. Substantive issues like abortion usually are addressed primarily as questions of rights.[45] Framing an issue as a matter of rights raises the stakes involved in the public debate. The opposition of either "the right to choose" or "the right to the development of personality" against the "right to life" makes the issue even more intense and even less capable of resolution: someone has to lose a right or a claim to a right. And once made in rights terms, such claims are underwritten with the moral force that rights language conveys.

While the deployment of rights language has made important differences in several legal areas (such as civil rights in the United States), rights frameworks are much less effective at resolving deep conflicts where there are strong, irreconcilable personal rights on each side of an opposition. In such cases, courts are pushed into creating hierarchies of rights, as some of the Justices in the Irish Supreme Court did by saying that a right to life clearly was more important than a right to travel. Or courts must "balance" rights, as the German Constitutional Court attempted to do with the right of the woman to the development of her personality and the right of the unborn to life, and as the Hungarian Constitutional Court suggested they would have to do depending on the rights accorded the fetus by the Parliament. Ranking and balancing are activities that lend themselves especially well to charges of bias on the part of judges. Their opinions are least well grounded in the text when they do this because the standards for ranking and balancing are not routinely spelled out explicitly in constitutions but rather are added later by judges.

Moreover, once rights are ranked or balanced, this is usually preliminary to finding that one right is upheld in full and the other right is trumped in full. For example, if a woman has a right to self-determination and the fetus has a right to life, the right to life will generally trump the right to self-determination. This means that the individual woman loses completely because she is the one holding the lesser right. Never mind that there might be some way of valuing all the rights simultaneously by trimming the edges of each. In the abortion case, this might be done by giving the woman the stronger claim in the earlier months and the fetus the stronger claim in the later months of pregnancy. But these sorts of time-dependent solutions, despite their popularity with both courts and legislatures, tend to have weak constitutional pedigrees.[46] Generally, the logic of rights requires some other finding that the fetus is not really a life until the later stages, when it may assert rights of its own. Courts then run into the "bright line" problem (see below).

In addition, for rights claims to be effective, there should be a relatively limited and well-articulated set of rights that can be invoked in the context of law. The right to privacy in the American context came in for attack because it was neither textually grounded nor well-defined. The extension of an existing but limited set of rights to new sorts of cases can also create problems. In the abortion context, the claim of a "right to life" is the ultimate rights claim that, once accepted by a court, very little else can trump. But the "right to life" means something very different when the life in question is a life not yet born than when the life in question is an adult, or at least an already born human being. The German Constitutional Court recognized this by allowing something less than the equal right to life of the pregnant woman to trump the fetus's constitutional right to life, but such gradations of rights that depend on who the rights bearer is are at best controversial. In the Irish case, the woman's "right to life" was held to be threatened by her own threat of suicide, not exactly an elegant reading of this important right.

Rights claims, then, have enormous problems in the area of abortion. They increase the absolutism of claims on both sides; existing rights don't fit the abortion context well; they lead courts to rank and balance according to criteria that are not spelled out in constitutional language. The translation of the abortion debate into rights language squashes the representation of a complicated process into stick-figure language.

2. THE TEXT-BOUND NATURE OF LEGAL INTERPRETATION

Judges, even justices in constitutional courts, are required to do what the law says. However, the law is often not very clear on a particular point, like abortion. Judges, from their training as lawyers, are experts in the interpretation of legal texts. When they are called upon to make constitutional judgments, judges must interpret the specific language of their own constitution.

This requirement is what gave U.S. Justice Blackmun difficulties in *Roe*. He borrowed a right to privacy, not explicit in the Constitution, to ground a right to choose abortions, also not mentioned. The textual thinness of the authority for this argument got the American Supreme Court into trouble on abortion right away, and the "troika" opinion in *Casey* in 1993 eventually tried to completely reground the reasoning. The difficulty is that constitutional language is often more general and therefore less helpful than a specific case requires. In the second *Morgentaler* case in Canada, the language involved was the "right to bodily security"; in Ireland, the language was "with due regard to the equal life of the mother"; in Germany and Hungary, the language was "everyone [not further specified] has a right to life."

The available language sets important limits on the rights that can be claimed and the arguments that can be made for them. That, after all, is the purpose of a constitution: to set out limits in language for legal claims. But in the case of abortion, which has no specific textual peg (except in Ireland, where the text still left important questions unresolved except by interpretive implication), courts are called upon to make judgments from language not well-designed for the purpose. The generality of the rights provisions and the inadequacy of any of them to capture the complex experience of pregnancy and abortion mean that constitutional reasoning will always appear more than a little strained. The American debate, for example, has devolved into a debate over whether the fetus is a person under the Fourteenth Amendment or whether restricting abortions limits women's right to the equal protection of the law. And the German debate tried to squeeze what is at stake for a woman in deciding whether or not to have a child into the "right to the development of personality." The Hungarian court was perhaps the most honest by admitting that they could not work out the problem through constitutional interpretation alone. When they decide the second abortion case, however, they will have to confront the problem directly. The legal concepts in these various constitutions that might be employed to describe the abortion problem are like a straitjacket. They do not describe the problems before the court well; at best they can capture some small bit of what the complex experience at stake is like. Still, for people to argue the merits of particular legal restrictions or permissions for abortion, they must borrow the language from existing legal documents.

3. STATE ACTION

Constitutional law is, first and foremost, *public* law. That is, it pertains to the organization of state institutions, their powers, and the claims an individual can make against them. Passing laws restricting abortion clearly counts as state action (and all of the constitutional abortion cases begin when a law regulating abortion is challenged). But getting rid of laws about abortion does not necessarily mean that abortions are therefore available. Whatever rights they grant are permissive. Doctors may still refuse to perform abortions; many women cannot afford them; facilities that provide them may be distant or hard to find. But these problems cannot generally be raised directly as *constitutional* claims. There may be some basis for the claims to provide particular facilities, services, and resources for residents in constitutional cultures like Ireland, Germany, and Hungary where the government has a broad set of positive duties, but the direct claims individuals can make as against private actors in constitutional systems are almost always less demanding than those that they can make against the state.

Constitutional discourse, then, tends to be limited to specifying the rules of the game between the individual and the state. This does not guarantee that the game is played in such a way that all the players receive what they may legitimately claim as a matter of right unless the state is the actor who might be compelled to perform. Though the legal battles over abortion have all involved state regulation so far, advocates of abortion rights will find the legal system much less helpful in winning access to abortion if suits are brought against private actors to require that abortions actually be available. Constitutions don't help with those sorts of claims.

Constitutional declarations do not typically solve the practical problems for either side when all is said and done. If women have a right to choose abortions, it does not guarantee that abortions will be practically or financially available; similarly, explicit constitutional protection for fetuses doesn't mean that women will not have abortions. In fact, most frequently, the abortion issue is eventually settled in practice through hypocrisy: the state says one thing and does another. Throughout Europe, most abortion statutes generally begin by saying that abortion is illegal, except under certain circumstances, and then go on to provide a list of exceptions, which are in practice interpreted broadly enough to allow abortion under almost all circumstances.[47] In North America, constitutional protection for abortion disguises the unavailability of abortion in practice in many places.[48] The tug and pull of many conflicting demands on politicians and judges has created a system of policymaking where making a formal law on the point is not the end of the matter. In many countries where the law has been "settled," it soon becomes unsettled and the whole question comes up for grabs again, often through the mechanism of a constitutional challenge. As we will see, the abortion issue usually appears not just once, but twice or more at the level of constitutional courts.

4. REASONING BY ANALOGY

What courts typically do when the law pertaining to a case does not provide firm guidance is to figure out what other cases might be reasonably judged as similar to the case at hand. In other words, courts typically solve new problems by finding analogies with old ones. In the case of abortion, however, this turns out to be particularly dangerous for two reasons. First is that there are no perfect or even reasonably good analogies to pregnancy and abortion. These phenomena are not *like* anything else in all the relevant ways. Fetuses are not like born persons, but neither are they like inanimate objects, or tonsils, or animals, though they have something in common with each. Pregnancy is not like an illness or like carrying a package for nine months, though it shares some features of each. But constitutional courts are put in the position of developing analogies whenever a new problem is presented to them to enable them to reason from existing law to new situations.

In *Casey*, for example, the dissent written by Justice Rehnquist emphasized how the analogies between abortion and other rights protected by a right to privacy (the right to teach and learn languages, the right to marry the person of one's choice, the right to attend the school of one's choice) were all inadequate to justify extending privacy protection to abortion. In the German Constitutional Court, aborting a fetus was seen as analogous to the fate of Jews in the Nazi era, when the value of much human life was reduced to nothing. The point of such an analogy was to undermine the legitimacy of public opinion, since in both cases, legalized abortion and Nazi Germany, public opinion found certain forms of life to be beneath protection. But fetuses obviously are not like born persons in crucial ways either, differences the Court chose not to emphasize.

To the American Supreme Court in *Roe*, the relevant analogy was between abortion and other medical procedures, which put the focus on the doctor-patient relationship and worries about infringing upon that relationship.[49] To the Canadian Supreme Court, the relevant analogy was between abortion and other infringements on the body that might produce stress and physical discomfort. In Hungary, the court saw abortion as analogous to the death penalty and euthanasia in that it required a determination of the state role in taking or protecting lives. And to the Irish Supreme Court, the analogy was between abortion and murder, so that the fullest sanctions of the law could be applied to those performing abortions. Each court brought to its analysis some overarching analogical framework within which pregnancy and abortion were to be considered. And the relevant law from the analogized situation was then applied to the abortion case.

Legal arguments invariably get advocates tied up in battles of analogies, which obscure in part the distinctive details of the particular and new situation even while they provide helpful practical guidance. The imperative in legal reasoning to decide "like cases alike" leads to the prominence of analogical reasoning. But any pair of descriptions will have some features in common and other features that distinguish them. Choices of analogy are always choices from a large range of alternatives. Just how that choice is made determines how legal arguments will proceed. But given the very poor fit between the experience of pregnancy and abortion and any other circumstance to which it might be analogized, such a methodology will invariably lead to a lack of recognition of the complexity and distinctiveness of the problem. Moving a problem into a legal arena will always require a battle of analogies, however.

5. BRIGHT LINES

One principle of constitutional jurisprudence common to all the countries under examination is that people should not be punished in criminal law for violations that are unclear or vaguely described. If abortion is to be regulated in the criminal law, as all the countries studied here do, then constitutional courts require something like a "bright line" test. This test would give them a clear point where their judgment would change from favoring one side to favoring the other—for when an offense would become a crime. So, the Irish and German courts were at pains to point out the very specific circumstances that would excuse a woman or a doctor from criminal abortion charges. And the Canadian and American courts were at pains to point out what acts could not be punished by the criminal law. The Hungarian case required a parliamentary debate and judgment, to be followed by a new constitutional review,

but the importance of clarifying just where the line should be was also emphasized in their opinion.

In the case of abortion, drawing bright lines is particularly problematic
because pregnancy is a gradual and developmental process. Bright lines exist
at conception and at birth, and those are the most attractive ones to courts as
a result. Viability seems like another bright line, but it must be determined in
the individual case with expensive tests, and some judges have expressed a
worry that with the advances in medicine, the line will keep shifting.[50] The
gradual and developmental quality of pregnancy has frustrated courts in their
attempts to search for certainty. The German court simply declared that life
begins on the fourteenth day after conception as established by reliable
medical evidence! But courts clearly deal less well with issues where there are
no bright lines than with issues where such lines are easier to draw.

CONCLUSION

In each of the countries examined here, the constitutional (or supreme) court
has used constitutional interpretation to constrain the choices available to
legislators in drafting laws about abortion in the name of rights. If a constitutional decision had not been made, legislators would have been permitted to
balance competing interests and work out compromise solutions.

The discourse of legislative balancing involves dividing up benefits
across different groups, which the rights discourse of courts tends to block. In
addition, the discourse of legislative balancing allows for the possibility that
new problems will be addressed in their own terms and not have to follow
some previous model of reasoning that courts impose by their analogical style
of thinking. If life is protected from conception, for example, then the embryo
has to have rights everywhere—in *in vitro* fertilization as well as in abortion. If
a woman has the right to do whatever she wants with her fetus, then can't she
also deliberately injure its right before it is born? Legislatures might want to
think differently about the two cases in each pair, but such distinctions are
more difficult to make if the usual discourse of rights is invoked.

Constitutional decisions mandate in advance the winners and the losers
in legislative battles. These determinations have come in the name of uncom-
promisable rights, whether of the woman who might seek an abortion or of
the fetus who might therefore be aborted. Court decisions produce winners
and losers, and the losers (or their advocates) go on to fight another day for
issues about which they care passionately. Ironically, then, the constitutional
decisions tend to go through cycles. In the United States, Canada, Ireland,
Germany, and perhaps soon Hungary as well, the high court has been dealing
with the issue repeatedly as the losers from the previous round have come up

with new constitutional arguments to bring back to the courts. Constitutional decisions don't usually settle the question when it has been framed as a choice among rights; these decisions simply provide a pause in the cycle of competing rights claims.

Some of the most recent court decisions seem to make an effort to stop imagining abortion as a contest of individually enforceable rights pinned to the general language of specific constitutions and instead focus on what governments are doing in their formal laws by analogy with other similar cases in the search for bright lines. The second German decision required the legislature to maintain abortion in the criminal code, but said that the legislature did not have to specify punishments for it. So abortion is still criminalized in some cases in Germany, even though there are no negative sanctions. The court's ruling effectively removed criminal law from the abortion issue and turned the regulation of abortion over to counselors instead.[51] Or, even more creatively, the Hungarian Court suggested that the state may be obligated to protect the fetus through measures that ensure that women will want to bring children into the world (and will be able to afford to do so) rather than by zealously protecting individual fetuses through banning abortions.[52] In the German and Hungarian cases, the courts have been trying to find something other than zero-sum answers to reconcile competing demands made through constitutional claims. These decisions may be the beginning of a new rights discourse in which constitutional judgments do not choose between rigidly imagined pre-existing rights, but instead create space for women to exercise their liberties without wiping out the space in which fetuses may also get social support.

NOTES

1. In the fast-changing world of abortion politics, it is always necessary to date one's work. Information in this paper represents to the best of my knowledge the state of affairs up to mid-May 1995. For challenging me to think in different ways, I would like to thank Roger Rouse and Steve Macedo as well as participants in my abortion seminars at the Michigan Law School and the participants in the session at the American Political Science Association in 1992, where these ideas were first presented.

2. There is a good theoretical reason for focusing on Europe and North America, since both regions share a common trajectory for abortion regulation. In particular, many countries in these regions found themselves moving to decriminalize abortion in the 1960s and 1970s at just the moment when their constitutional courts were becoming more aggressive on other issues. This confluence of events may account for some of the patterns described in this chapter.

3. Kristin Luker has shown, among activists in the American context, how little pro-choice and pro-life adherents have in common. In fact, few people have friends whose views on abor-

tion are different from theirs, so different are the social worlds in which pro-choice and pro-life activists reside. Kristin Luker, *Abortion and the Politics of Motherhood* (California, 1984). But Faye Ginsburg's study of abortion activists in Fargo, North Dakota, suggests that in smaller communities, pro-life and pro-choice activists may share a more common world. Faye Ginsburg, *Contested Lives* (California, 1989). Luker: Berkeley: University of California Press. Ginsberg: Berkeley: University of California

4. Kim Lane Scheppele, "Abortion and the Breakdown of Politics as Usual," forthcoming in Katherine LaGuardia and Florence Hazeltine (eds.), *Opportunities in Contraception* (American Association for the Advancement of Science, forthcoming).

5. These are not the only places where the issue could be studied. For instance, in Austria, France, and Italy, the constitutional courts approved in their constitutional decisions what the national parliaments had done. In Poland, the adoption of a new constitution has been blocked by political debate, not incidentally over the issue of abortion. I have not focused on these countries because the use of constitutional trumps has been relatively minor in shaping their national debates. Perhaps this would be an interesting variation to study, but the fact that the constitutional court decisions in France, Italy, and Austria did not have as strong an effect as the decisions in the countries discussed here says something important about constitutional solutions to the abortion debate. That comparison, however, will have to wait until another day.

6. 410 U.S. 113 (1973).

7. Luker, *Abortion and the Politics of Motherhood*. See also Gerald Rosenberg, Gerald *The Hollow Hope*. Chicago: University of Chicago Press, 1991.

8. See the early criticisms of John Hart Ely, "The Wages of Crying Wolf: A Comment on Roe v. Wade," 82 *Yale Law Journal* 920 (1973); Richard Epstein, "Substantive Due Process by Any Other Name: The Abortion Cases," 1973 *Supreme Court Review* 159 (1973); Laurence Tribe, "Foreword: Toward a Model of Rules in the Due Process of Life and Law," 87 *Harvard Law Review* 1 1973), modified by Laurence Tribe, *American Constitutional Law*, 2d ed. (West, 1988). The only immediate academic defenders of the reasoning in *Roe* were Philip Heymann and Douglas Barzelay, "The Forest and the Trees: Roe v. Wade and its Critics," 53 *Boston University Law Review* 765 (1973).

9. For alternative arguments about the constitutional location of the abortion right, see Donald Regan, "Rewriting Roe v. Wade," 77 *Michigan Law Review* 1569 (1979) (equal protection clause); Tribe, *American Constitutional Law*, 2d ed., pp. 1302–1435 (equal protection clause); Catharine MacKinnon, "Reflections on Sex Equality Under Law," 100 *Yale Law Journal* 1281 (1991) (equal protection clause); Cass Sunstein, "Neutrality in Constitutional Law (With Special Reference to Pornography, Abortion and Surrogacy)," 92 *Columbia Law Review* 1–52 (1992) (equal protection clause); Andrew Koppelman, "Forced Labor: A Thirteenth Amendment Defense of Abortion," 84 *Northwestern Law Review* 480 (1990) (13th Amendment).

10. 112 S.Ct. 2791 (1992).

11. One might argue that the troika opinion of Justices O'Connor, Souter, and Kennedy was also implicitly resting its reasoning on an understanding of the equal protection clause as well, since the opinion emphasized the importance of abortion decisions in the lives of women and how her "suffering is too intimate and personal for the State to insist, without more, upon its own vision of woman's role, however dominant that vision has been in the course of history and our culture." Though the plurality opinion does not explicitly ground the abortion right in the equal protection clause, these arguments could have constitutional import only through a further judgment that women were being treated differently from men in ways that denied them the equal protection of the laws.

12. On these controversial deviations from the logic of *Roe*, the troika had only their own votes for the reasoning. The undue burden standard, then, is not official constitutional doctrine

since it has only three votes in its favor. But this standard now forms the practical center of the Court's reasoning, since it provides the lowest common denominator that would allow a regulation to be struck down as unconstitutional. Where the undue burden standard shows a regulation to be acceptable, the troika judges combine forces with the dissenters to uphold the ruling. Where the undue burden standard shows a regulation to go too far, the troika judges side with those who wanted to uphold the strong version of *Roe* to strike down the regulation. In *Casey,* since the dissenters wanted to uphold all the regulations at stake, their four votes combined with the troika's votes were enough to overrule the prior decisions that had struck down almost identical standards. But since the troika disagreed with the four dissenters over the reasons why, none of the reasoning is considered binding on future decisions of the Court. The cases that were overruled were *City of Akron v. Akron Center for Reproductive Health,* 462 U.S. 416 (1983), and *Thornburgh v. American College of Obstetricians and Gynecologists,* 476 U.S. 747 (1986). These cases had previously struck down state regulations on abortion counseling, informed consent, and parental consent, which were upheld in *Casey.* Because the Court composition has changed since *Casey* was decided, just how these standards would play out in votes can only be speculated upon.

13. Chief Justice Rehnquist, in a dissenting opinion joined by Justices White, Scalia, and Thomas, argued that the Court had reached too far in *Roe* in analogizing the abortion decision to the right to teach or learn languages, the right to marry whomever one wanted, and the right to attend a school of one's choosing. A woman may have a "liberty interest" in abortion protected by the Constitution, but not a "fundamental right." Justice Scalia, writing in dissent for another opinion, argued that the Constitution had "absolutely nothing to say" about abortion and that the longstanding traditions of America had permitted abortion to be banned.

14. See, for example, Ronald Dworkin, "The Center Holds!" in *The New York Review of Books,* 13 August 1992, p. 29.

15. [1988] 44 D.L.R. (4th) 385. This case is customarily called *Morgentaler II* because it was the second time Morgentaler's conviction for violating provincial abortion laws was appealed to the Supreme Court. See discussion of *Morgentaler I* below.

16. For a gripping and constitutionally informative history of the abortion fight in Canada, see F. L. Morton, *Pro-Choice vs Pro-Life: Abortion and the Courts in Canada* (University of Oklahoma Press, 1992).

17. *Morgentaler v. The Queen (Morgentaler I),* (1975) 20 C.C.C. (2d) 452.

18. Canadian Charter of Rights, Section 7.

19. [1988] I.R. 593.

20. [1989] I.R. 753.

21. But not for the European Court of Justice, which decided after hearing an appeal in *Society for the Protection of the Unborn Child v. Grogan,* [1991] 3 C.M.L.R. 849, that while abortion counted as a service under the Treaty of Rome, no other European legal issues were raised because the counseling centers involved Irish students distributing information to other Irish students. No citizens of other states were involved, so the ECJ considered this an internal matter of Ireland. It is at least arguable, however, that the European Court of Human Rights would have seen the matter differently, given that the right of free expression was at stake.

22. [1989] I.R. 739, [1990] I.L.R.M. 70.

23. [1992] I.R. 1.

24. This has long been the standard procedure for Irish women. Between 3,000 and 4,000 women a year from the Republic of Ireland go to England to get abortions, and that counts only the women who list Irish addresses when they arrive in England, usually London.

25. Only Justice McCarthy believed that the right to travel should allow a woman to leave the country for an abortion that would not be permitted in Ireland.

26. The European Union has been handling the abortion issue very gingerly. The Maastrict agreement has as a rider a provision that Ireland insisted on, protecting its ability to keep its abortion laws intact. But this agreement does not bind the European Court of Human Rights to interpret the European Convention any differently in Ireland's case.

27. The decision was immediately published in full in the *Irish Times*. "The Supreme Court Judgment on the Abortion Information Bill," *Irish Times*, 13 May 1995, p. 8. Quotations are from that version.

28. The Supreme Court in this case appointed separate counsel to defend the interests of fetuses and of pregnant women under this law. These court-appointed counsel made arguments in addition to those made by the Attorney General, who defended the actions of the Parliament before the Court.

29. William Binchy, "Abortion Ruling One of the Most Significant Legal Decisions Since the Founding of the State," *Irish Times*, 15 May 1995, p. 12.

30. Denis Coghlan, "Supreme Court Closes a Door into the Past," *Irish Times*, 13 May 1995, p. 7.

31. Nuala O'Faolain, "You Could Almost Hear the Creak as We Were Racheted Forward a Notch," *Irish Times*, 13 May 1995, p. 7.

32. 39 BVerfGE 1 [1975]. The German abortion decision was translated into English by Robert E. Jonas and John D. Gorby and appears in 9 *John Marshall Journal of Law and Practice* 605–684 (1976). All textual references are to the English translation.

33. Id. at 638.

34. Id. at 638.

35. Id. at 642.

36. Id. at 644

37. Id. at 649

38. Article 218a of the German Criminal Code, enacted 12 February 1976.

39. In *Bruggemann and Scheuten v. Federal Republic of Germany*, Application number 6959/75, decided 12 July 1977, the European Commission found no violations of human rights, though it did hint strongly that a total ban on abortion might violate the rights of women.

40. Ian Murray, "Women Win Say on Abortion," *The Times of London*, 27 June 1992. See also, "Germany Liberalizes its Abortion Law" from *The Week in Germany*, Lexis, 3 July 1992.

41. The opinion is 183 pages long and has not yet been translated into English. I am very grateful to Gerald Neumann of the Columbia Law School for going step by step with me through a detailed account of the reasoning of the Court right after the decision came out and to Nanette Funk for sharing with me her paper "Reproductive Rights and the Unification of Germany: The 1993 German Constitutional Court Abortion Decision," which translates significant sections of the Court's reasoning.

42. Decision #64/1991 (XII.17), published in English translation in 1 *East European Case Reporter* 3–56 (1994). All citations are to the English translation.

43. Ibid. p. 15

44. This information comes from interviews in April and May 1995 with the directors of the abortion counseling service in Hungary.

45. The leading exception to this generalization is the opinion of the Hungarian Court, which found the existing laws on abortion unconstitutional primarily because they were enacted in an inappropriate way (by the Ministry rather than by the Parliament). But even here, the Hungarian Court based that judgment on the argument that the Parliament needed to get involved in this area because rights were involved.

46. This sort of solution was attacked by the dissenters in *Roe v. Wade* precisely because the Constitution said nothing about the trimester framework that allowed the majority to sort out when different rights could be recognized. And, of course, in *Roe*, the fetus was not held to have rights in itself, but instead the state was held to have interests that could be vindicated when the fetus developed to a certain stage.

47. The importance of hypocrisy is something that Mary Ann Glendon missed in her book *Abortion and Divorce in Western Law* (Harvard, 1987). By reading only the European statutes on abortion and failing to look at the practices that they allowed, Glendon assumed that seemingly restrictive abortion laws in Europe were associated with actually restrictive abortion practices in those countries. But abortion is more widely available in Europe where the laws are more restrictive than in America, where the laws look quite liberal. Glendon: Mary Ann. Cambridge: Harvard University Press, 1987.

48. See Gerald Rosenberg, *The Hollow Hope* (Chicago: University of Chicago Press, 1991) for more evidence on the limited availability of abortion.

49. Such an analogy may have occurred to Justice Blackmun because he had been counsel to the Mayo Clinic before coming to the Supreme Court. *Roe v. Wade* reads more like a doctors' rights opinion than like a privacy case. If one believes *The Brethren* by Scott Armstrong and Bob Woodward, then the privacy language was added on at the last minute when Justice Brennan suggested that the opinion could use a little grounding in some recognizably *constitutional* argument. Scott Armstrong and Bob Woodward. *The Brethren.* New York: Simon and Schuster, 1979.

50. This was the basis of Justice O'Connor's opinion *Akron v. Akron Center for Reproductive Health*, 462 U.S. 416 (1983), where she noted that medical advances were making the trimester system unworkable. In the triply-authored opinion in *Casey*, Justice O'Connor was finally able to throw out the trimester system and replace it with a two-tiered system where pre- and post-viability segments were the only two that mattered for the purposes of regulation. In *Webster v. Reproductive Health Services*, 109 S.Ct. 3040 (1989), the Court upheld a regulation that required viability testing to be used beginning at 22 weeks to ensure a fetus was not yet viable before an abortion could be performed.

51. The danger in the German case is that counselors have instructions to try to talk the women out of having abortions, rather than to provide information and a more neutral setting in which the woman can talk about what she wants. In addition, by cutting funds for abortion as part of this deal, the German Constitutional Court has cut themselves off from the reality that the availability of abortions cannot be ensured simply through abolishing punishments.

52. My preliminary research on this question in Hungary indicates that the less polarizing decision of the Court and the legislation that followed from it have produced generally positive effects—lowering the abortion rate without increasing the birth rate. The system of mandatory non-directive abortion counseling has made birth-control information widely available. In addition, birth-control technology is heavily subsidized in the state health-care system. In late June 1995, the system of pregnancy and infant benefits was saved from the International Monetary Fund knife by a Court judgment that such cuts would be unconstitutional. If these benefits were cut, the Court ruled, women would be deprived of the financial means to have children and might therefore turn to abortion. The state has a positive obligation to financially protect women who want to have children, in the Court's view. Thinking in positive terms rather than punitive ones, the Hungarian Constitutional Court often considers rights as existing through the maintenance of a climate of protection of certain values, rather than being only legal claims that are enforceable in individual cases.

CHAPTER 3

REPRODUCTIVE RIGHTS AND THE STRUGGLE WITH CHANGE IN EASTERN EUROPE

MARIANNE GITHENS

INTRODUCTION

During the past decade the most dramatic change in abortion policy occurred not in Western Europe or North America but in Eastern Europe. There, several of the former Soviet bloc countries, most notably Poland, the Slovak Republic, and Hungary, enacted legislation curtailing a woman's right to terminate her pregnancy. In some respects this was a predictable outcome. Traditional institutions, such as the Roman Catholic Church, sought to fill the political vacuum created by the collapse of Communism. In an effort to increase their power and establish their own agendas during the conversion to a free-market economy, these institutions appealed to sentimental perceptions of a pre-Communist world where home and family were paramount. The economic and political uncertainty occurring during this period coupled with a nostalgia for old values and ideas made women's reproductive freedom an easy target.

Prior to the collapse of Communism, abortion was legal throughout Eastern Europe, with Romania being the sole exception. Legislation permitting abortion had been enacted in all the countries of Eastern Europe, including Romania, during the 1950s, although Romania subsequently prohibited it under Ceausescu. The passage of these laws was not the result of a women's movement or a demand for reproductive freedom. Rather, it was motivated, at least in part, by the state's need to increase women's participation in the labor force. In the absence of adequate family-planning services and contraception, abortion was an important method for limiting family size and freeing women to enter the marketplace. Abortion came to be regarded as an acceptable alternative method of birth control. This chapter will examine the consequences of this legacy of legalized abortion under Communism and the forces currently seeking to criminalize or limit it. It will also address the situation in Romania, where, unlike the rest of Eastern Europe, the current move is to eliminate the constraints imposed under Communism. Since the most protracted and bitter battles over abortion have taken place in Poland, special emphasis will be given to the struggle there.

POLAND

Unquestionably, Poland adopted the most far-reaching restrictions on reproductive rights. Nowhere else in Eastern Europe were the limitations quite as
drastic. Reversing a 1956 law permitting abortion on demand during the first
trimester of pregnancy, the Polish Parliament enacted legislation that criminalized it in most instances. Among the key provisions of this new bill, signed
into law in February 1993 by President Lech Walesa, were the definition of the
right to life as starting with conception and the limitation of abortion to cases
where the mother's life or health was seriously threatened or where there was
evidence of serious and irreversible malformation of the fetus. Although the
law made no provision for jailing women who sought or self-induced an
abortion, doctors who failed to conform to these regulations were liable to a
prison sentence.

The circumstances under which abortion might be performed had been
further restricted by the Medical Ethics Code adopted a year earlier. This code
declared that abortions for fetal deformities could not be justified, since diagnostic tests that could provide confirming evidence, such as amniocentesis,
might injure the unborn and should, therefore, not be performed. It also stated
that abortion was only permissible when three doctors agreed that the
mother's health was seriously endangered or when pregnancy resulted from
rape or incest. Doctors violating these regulations could lose their licenses to
practice medicine.

The harsh restrictions imposed on access to abortion have prompted
some to compare Poland with the Republic of Ireland (Hoff, 1993). While the
two countries have the most restrictive anti-abortion policies in Europe, and
the Roman Catholic Church is a dominant cultural force in each of them, the
two do differ in some important respects. Unlike their Irish counterparts,
Polish women have played a visible role in public affairs for the past forty
years. They participated extensively in the labor market, served both as
elected officials in the government and in Solidarity, and had access to abortion. In 1980 Poland ratified Article 7 of the Convention on the Elimination of
All Forms of Discrimination Against Women, which acknowledged women's
political rights.

The political and economic situation of Polish women was much closer
to that of other Eastern European women. Yet, despite the strength of the
Catholic Church in countries such as Hungary and Slovenia, anti-abortion
policy was much more extreme in Poland. The question one must ask is, why?

The historical context surrounding the issue of abortion, the role that
the Catholic Church played prior to, during and following Communist rule,
and the socialization of women to a traditional, feminine gender role, are cited
as reasons for the emergence of the current Polish policy. Certainly, abortion

has been the subject of controversy for most of this century. Prior to World War I, what is now Poland was under the jurisdiction of three different countries. When its independence was finally recognized in 1918, it had to adopt a single penal code. During the debate over a new code, the Catholic Church pressed to have abortion designated a criminal act regardless of its implications for the mother's health or the conditions causing pregnancy, such as rape or incest. Some voiced opposition to this position, however, and a campaign for limited reproductive rights was initiated in the twenties. Describing the criminalization of abortion as the worst crime in a penal code and citing the health consequences of back-alley abortions, the leader of this movement, Tadeusz Boy-Zelenski, was eventually able to persuade those drafting the new code to allow abortion in cases of rape and incest and for medical reasons. By and large, women remained silent during this debate. Socialized to accept the ideal of the "Polish Mother" who was without sexual desire, they accepted the norm that banned women from discussing sexual matters.

In protesting the effort to liberalize abortion, the Church vilified proponents of reproductive rights and portrayed them as atheists, the enemies of religion and of the nation, Bolsheviks, pimps, and child killers. Although the Church was unable to block the principle of limited abortion advocated by the reproductive rights movement, its opposition persisted. Pro-natal forces, which were highly nationalistic, and the Church continued the campaign to get abortion designated a crime and to use the tactic of characterizing individuals who supported reproductive rights as evil, immoral, and enemies of the nation. Under these conditions it was virtually impossible to create a middle ground where conflicting positions could be discussed dispassionately and some kind of consensus built.

Following the Second World War, the battle against abortion again intensified. Along with the arguments used previously, the anti-abortion forces asserted that the casualties caused by the war necessitated a human as well as material rebuilding of the state. As was the case earlier, those who supported a liberal abortion policy were denounced as evil child killers. Although those opposing abortion were again defeated, it was clear that the society remained deeply divided over the issue. The Pro-Life Lobby, which was mainly Catholic, continued to condemn abortion, as well as contraception, and to denounce all those whose views differed from their own.

In the 1950s Poland, along with several of the other Communist-bloc countries, confronted a series of economic crises. The need to expand the labor market led to the active recruitment of women for employment outside the home. Around this time, legislation making abortion readily available to women was enacted in Soviet-bloc countries, as well as the Soviet Union.

Poland adopted the Abortion Admissibility Law in 1956. In addition to permitting abortion in cases of medical complications and rape, it allowed abortion in cases of hardship, such as poor living conditions or financial burden. For all intents and purposes there was abortion on demand during the first trimester. The Society of Planned Motherhood, subsequently renamed the Society for Family Planning, was established shortly thereafter. Its purpose was to provide information concerning contraception and family planning, and it also reinforced the notion of a woman's right to choose.[1]

Pro-life groups espousing nationalistic rather than religious views, along with the Catholic Church, voiced strenuous objections to these changes. The Church was the major organized force denouncing the new abortion law and was particularly adamant in its condemnation of making contraception readily available.[2] Since the Church had long served as a symbol of Polish national identity, and under Communist rule had became synonymous with resistance to the regime, its stance on abortion took on a distinctly political meaning. Liberal abortion policy became equated with support for the Communist state. Abortion and contraception became symbolic of attitudes toward the government and a barometer for assessing relations between church and state. When interaction between the two improved, the government allocated less money to family planning. When relations were strained, state subsidies increased.

As the Communist regime began to lose power, its policies on family planning shifted. The Society of Family Planning was renamed the Society for Family Development. Larger, more traditional-size families were encouraged, and "natural" methods of family planning—that is, abstinence and rhythm—were encouraged. These incremental changes failed to appease the opponents of government policies on abortion and contraception, however. The Church and pro-life forces demanded fundamental change. This came in the form of the Unborn Child Protection Law, drawn up in 1989 by a group of Church experts. First printed in a Catholic newspaper, it called for a ban on all abortions and provided for prison sentences of up to three years for both doctors performing an abortion and women seeking them.

Shortly after its publication, several members of the Polish Parliament petitioned the chamber for a debate of the bill. Although there was parliamentary support for the bill, media coverage of the debate mobilized public opposition. A number of new women's groups, including the Polish Feminist Association, Pro Femina, and the Democratic Union of Women, emerged and organized resistance to the proposed legislation. Many women responded to the call for action, and there were demonstrations in Warsaw, Pozna, and Bydgoszcz.

To some extent, the negative reaction to the proposed ban on abortion reflected the deficiencies of family planning. The Catholic Church's continuous attacks on contraception dating back to the 1950s and the lack of adequate sex education meant that very few Polish women practiced birth control. With only half or less of them using any reliable method of family planning, abortion was a common method for limiting family size. Various sources claim that somewhere between 60,000 to 300,000 abortions were performed each year (Nowicka, 1994). The elimination of abortion meant that women had virtually no control over their reproductive lives.

Concern with abortion was soon overshadowed, however, by the upcoming parliamentary election. Public protest fizzled out as the election approached. The outcome of the election was an end to Communist control. When the new Senate met, its pro-life majority moved to open debate once again on the proposed Unborn Child Protection Law. The revised draft introduced there removed both criminal grounds, such as rape and incest, and medical reasons for obtaining an abortion. It also provided jail sentences of up to eight years for any individual forcing a woman to have an abortion, and doctors performing abortions were liable for up to three years in prison. In September 1990, by a vote of fifty to seventeen with five abstentions, the Senate adopted a somewhat amended version of the bill that reduced the prison term to two years and made rape and direct threat to mother's life grounds for abortion.

The Senate's passage of the bill has often been cited as evidence of the central role played by the Catholic Church in Polish politics. Indeed, some have claimed that the Church, supported by the Vatican, saw this as an opportunity to mold Poland into the prototype of a Catholic state. This may or may not be true, but nevertheless the Pope praised the Polish Senate's version of the Unborn Child Protection Law. Furthermore, there were grounds to support the contention that the Senate's passage of the bill was a necessary condition for the papal visit to Poland in 1991 (Jankowska, 1991).

Even before the Senate adopted the Unborn Child Protection Law, the Ministry of Health had moved to limit abortion. Under regulations issued in 1990, health insurance no longer covered abortions. With the spiraling inflation that accompanied the move to a free-market economy, this meant that the cost of the procedure was simply out of the reach of many women. Even if a woman could afford the cost of an abortion, there were other obstacles. Women wishing to terminate a pregnancy on social or economic grounds had to make a written application and consult four specialists: two gynecologists, an internist, and a psychologist. Even if the request for an abortion were approved, a doctor had the right to refuse to perform the procedure. This doctor's "conscience clause," the restrictive conditions for approving abortions, and the pressures some doctors claimed were placed on them by pro-life forces led three state hospitals to refuse to perform abortions altogether.

In 1991, these regulations were reinforced and expanded by a "pro-life" Medical Ethics Code, which limited abortion to cases of rape, incest, or serious threat to a woman's health. Prenatal diagnostic tests were condemned on the grounds that they endangered the unborn. Doctors who failed to adhere to the strict limitations on performing abortions were subject to stringent disciplinary action.

Despite the limitations imposed by the Ministry of Health's regulations, the move to pass anti-abortion legislation continued. The Sejm, the lower chamber of Parliament, took up consideration of the Unborn Child Protection Law in 1991. When the initial debate proved to be contentious, the bill was referred to a special commission dominated by pro-life forces. Arguing that there was a need to study public opinion, the commission requested citizens and organizations to forward their views on abortion to them. Although independent opinion polls indicated that 60 percent of the citizens opposed the Senate version of the Unborn Child Protection Law, a mass mobilization effort on the part of the Catholic Church produced a strong show of support for the proposed law, with the commission reporting that 80 percent of the replies it received favored banning abortion.

The anti-abortion bill finally endorsed by the parliamentary commission was even more extreme than the "pro-life" medical code. Abortions were limited to cases where the mother's life was threatened. Prison terms of two years could be imposed on doctors and on women self-inducing an abortion. Asserting that human life began at the moment of conception, the bill also prohibited contraceptives, including birth-control pills and IUDs, defining them as early forms of abortion.

Once again, there was public opposition to the proposed legislation. Many saw the creation of a special parliamentary commission to consider abortion legislation as a means of bypassing the will of the people and viewed it as a threat to the establishment of a truly democratic system. They called for a national referendum on abortion. The movement that emerged from this demand for a referendum generated a petition containing over 1,300,000 signatures. Both the Prime Minister, Hanna Suchocka, and President Walesa rejected the call for a referendum. Justifying her decision, Suchocka stated that "the referendum on abortion will pave the way for social conflict in Poland. It will divide the public" (Engelberg, 1993).

Although the government refused to permit a referendum to be held, it did soften its position on abortion somewhat. The final version of the Unborn Child Protection Act adopted by the Sejm and the Senate in January 1993 did allow abortion in some limited circumstances. A serious threat to the mother's life or health, a serious incurable fetal deformity, or a pregnancy resulting from rape or incest were made grounds for the termination of a pregnancy. These provisions did represent a concession, but the law was still very restrictive. The limitations it imposed became more oppressive still in light of the fact that birth-control pills and IUDs were defined as early abortifacients and could be forbidden. The prohibition on all but "natural methods" of contraception, reinforced by the Church's active campaign against the pill and IUDs on the grounds that they are dangerous to women's health, effectively denied reproductive rights to Polish women.[3]

There were parliamentary elections again in September 1993. This time, the conservative Catholic parties and the centrist Democratic Union lost, and two political parties made up predominantly of former Communists won two-thirds of the seats in the lower chamber. During the campaign, the winning parties had promised to introduce legislation extending the right of abortion for "social conditions" and to be responsive to women's interests. Following the election, the Church once again mounted a drive to oppose any extension of the grounds for abortion. Initially the new government was reticent about challenging the Catholic Church, but in the summer of 1994 an amendment to the 1993 law permitting abortion on social grounds was finally passed by both houses of Parliament and sent to the president for his signature. Walesa, however, steadfastly refused to sign it, claiming that it violated his Catholic beliefs. This meant that the bill had to be sent back to Parliament, where it had to be approved by a two-thirds majority in both houses. To date, efforts to put a more liberal policy in place have been unsuccessful.

There are several observations that might be made about the policymaking process in Poland. The first is that an ongoing, bureaucratized organization, such as the Catholic Church, has a distinct advantage in achieving its policy objectives over ad hoc movements. The Catholic Church has a vast membership and communication networks that allow it to mobilize and maintain support at critical moments. These networks permit it to communicate on an ongoing basis with both its mass and elite membership and to define specific actions for these constituencies. Its material resources, such as newspapers, the pulpit where it could present its views at mass each Sunday, and the reinforcing social community, which the parish structure provided, enabled it to articulate a strategy, galvanize support, and orchestrate the actions necessary to implement its goals. In contrast, nascent democratic organizations, including the newly formed women's groups, which served as the core of opposition to anti-abortion forces, were at a serious disadvantage. They had none of these resources readily available. They lacked organizational structures, which provided an established platform for communicating with mem-

bers. Instead, their membership and network of communication were temporary. Hence, their ability to map out a long-term strategy, to rally support
in the face of setbacks, and to orchestrate their efforts were limited. Under
these circumstances, it is understandable that they had problems in sustaining momentum.

Despite their limited resources, groups opposing the anti-abortion forces
were able to mount impressive campaigns. The attempt to force a national referendum on abortion was a clear example of this, as were the formation of
women's groups and the mobilization of women during the first debate of the
Unborn Child Protection Law. Although some women like Hanna Suchocka
were highly visible in the ranks of the anti-abortion movement, others, despite
their socialization to a traditional, feminine gender role and the pressures of
the Catholic Church, worked actively on behalf of liberalized abortion. Given
the norms governing women's discussion of sexual matters, this was a
remarkable achievement. Nowicka and others reported that public-opinion
polls showed a majority supported access to abortion, with 53 percent approving of it when a woman was in a difficult financial or social situation (1994).
Yet, the attempts to block anti-abortion policies from being adopted failed.
The ad hoc movements were simply no match for the highly developed
organization of the Catholic Church, even though public opinion was opposed
to a highly restrictive abortion law.

Perhaps if the circumstances surrounding the struggle over abortion had
been different, the outcome might have been different. If there had been ad
hoc groups both supporting anti-abortion legislation and opposing it,
neither might have had a distinct advantage over the other. Or if, like
Solidarity, the liberal abortion forces had access to an established institution
like the Catholic Church, which even during the heyday of the Communist
regime was a force to be reckoned with, they might have been successful.
Prior to the 1980s, the Communist party had provided a highly structured organization that could compete with the Catholic Church. Hence, it was possible to pass the Abortion Admissibility Act in 1956. Reorganized remnants of
the old party were able to push through an amendment to the Unborn Child
Protection Law. However, they no longer had access to the same membership
and communications networks as their predecessors. Hence, their amendment
to the 1993 law languished.

The problems posed by the absence of an ongoing organization that
might counter the Church's anti-abortion agenda were compounded by the
fact that abortion had been a highly politicized issue for over seventy years.
Although the abortion laws had been changed twice during this period, no
consensus had ever emerged. Pro-natal, anti-abortion forces never accepted
the principle even of limited abortion, and they continually agitated to

criminalize it. At the same time, a portion of the population accepted the idea of abortion at least under certain circumstances. In the course of the debate, the two positions were posed as irreconcilable. Ideology dominated the discussion. When a liberal abortion policy was associated with support for Communism, discussion became even more emotionally charged. In the absence of a neutral middle ground, the chance of developing any consensus evaporated. Differences of opinion became synonymous with good or evil, with being moral or immoral. Epithets, such as child killer, pimp, Bolshevik, and Communist Jew, were used to describe those who endorsed a liberal abortion policy. There was no possibility for rational debate.

Finally, the rhetoric surrounding the abortion debate made it risky for anyone to take a stand on behalf of a liberal abortion policy. For women who were always marginalized, even under Communist rule, it was particularly difficult to stand up under the barrage of criticism heaped on those who advocated some access to abortion. Catholic pro-life forces have played on notions of maternal devotion and a willingness to sacrifice on behalf of a child. Women have been told that the Catholic ethic demands a maternal heroism even if it is at the cost of their own lives (Heinen and Krasuska, 1995: 30). Arguments for abortion in cases of rape have been countered by assertions that while rapists get a prison sentence, the child receives a death sentence; why should the child be blamed for the crime of its father? A strong, unified organization might have been able to shelter all individuals, especially women, from these onslaughts, but temporary movements provided no such protection. Unable to control the language of the debate, vilified in public, and lacking a permanent supportive community, it was inevitable that the supporters of liberal abortion soon "burned out."

OTHER EASTERN EUROPEAN STATES

As mentioned earlier, laws legalizing abortion were adopted during the 1950s by the other countries of Eastern Europe. In this respect they were similar to Poland. However, the Catholic Church was not as dominant elsewhere, and this may account, at least in part, for the differences in their struggles over abortion policies. In some cases, there have been virtually no policy changes in a women's right to choose in the post-Communist period. In Bulgaria the transition to democracy has had no effect on women's reproductive freedom. Women's social, economic, and political status in Bulgaria is marginal, but then this has always been the case. The absence of a church-state problem has meant that reproductive rights were extraneous to the debates surrounding the social, economic, and political changes that were occurring. There have not been the same pressures to enact anti-abortion legislation there as in Poland.

Although neo-conservative forces have reinforced gender stereotypes and un-employment among women has risen disproportionately, the availability of abortion has remained unchallenged, at least so far.

Similarly, in the Czech Republic, there has been little effort to restrict re-productive rights. The country is predominantly Catholic, but the Church has not played as powerful a role in the public arena as it has in Poland, Hungary, or the Slovak Republic. Some women's groups, along with other conservative forces in the society, have attempted to influence government legislation in a pro-life direction, but so far, there has been no concerted effort to limit abor-tion. To be sure, the position of women has worsened in terms of unemploy-ment and election to public office, and women have felt estranged from the revolutionary reform movement, Civic Forum, but abortion has continued to be available.

In contrast, in the Slovak Republic where the Catholic Church was more prominent in state affairs, a very restrictive anti-abortion law was introduced during the early post-Communist period. There was less resistance to this leg-islation than there was in Poland, although public-opinion poll data indicated that the majority of men as well as women opposed banning abortion (Wolchik, 1994). However, in the subsequent election the government was ousted. Analysis of election returns suggested that some women had voted against the government because of their dissatisfaction with its policies, including abortion, and with the expanded political role that the Catholic Church had come to play.

Interestingly enough, although much of the debate over abortion in the Slovak Republic centered on the sacredness of life, limitations on abortion were also often linked to nationalist sentiments. Curbs on abortion were often linked to the need to revitalize and renew the state. Some of these same ultra-nationalist sentiments were voiced during the crusade against abortion in Poland, but there they were secondary to religious considerations. Perhaps it is the focus on religious belief, rather than on nationalist or secular morality, that accounts for the success of the anti-abortion forces in Poland. It may also be that the advantages afforded by the Catholic Church with its disciplined, structured, chain of command is crucial to the success of an anti-abortion movement and explains the differences between the Polish and Slovak strug-gles over abortion.

In Slovenia, which became an independent republic in 1991, the Catholic Church also exerted considerable influence in public affairs. The preamble to the new Constitution affirmed the sacredness of life as a basic value of society. However, this position was seriously modified by Article 52, which provided women with the option of abortion. During the debate over the new Constitution, pro-life forces and the Catholic Church condemned

Article 52 and demanded its removal. Responding to this threat to reproductive choice, women organized, and pressure groups lobbied Parliament. These efforts helped to persuade members of Parliament to vote for Article 52. As in the Slovak Republic, the struggle over abortion focused on both religious and secular considerations. Forces opposing abortion stressed the sacredness of life as well as the need to renew the state. If different reasons for valuing life could be debated, there was some basis for the arguments presented by the advocates of a liberal abortion policy, and the importance attached to life might be defined in numerous ways.

As elsewhere in Eastern Europe, the transition to democracy in Hungary was accompanied by a decline in women's status and an emphasis on traditional gender roles. Under Communism, Hungarian women enjoyed liberal reproductive rights. Since family planning was not widely available, abortion was often used as a method of contraception. The high rate of abortion led to an extensive debate of the topic in the post-Communist period. As discussed chapter 2, the Catholic Church pressed for strict limitations on abortion. However, parliament passed a bill which allowed abortion for women in a "crisis" situation.

Although Hungary did provide for abortion for "social conditions," it is important to note that during the debate, the rhetoric used to discuss the topic was transformed. Previously, abortion had been discussed from a humanitarian perspective. This was replaced by a dogmatic religious one that emphasized the sacredness of life and described abortion as the killing of unborn children.

In East Germany, women also had the option of abortion. With the collapse of the GDR and the unification of East and West Germany under the Federal Republic, access to abortion was threatened. Limitations placed on abortion in West Germany were not immediately imposed in the East, but eventually there will be a single policy covering all German women. Abortion policy has been the subject of an intense struggle in West Germany. Even if the federal policy is liberalized, East German women will find that their former reproductive rights have been significantly limited.

ROMANIA: THE EXCEPTIONAL CASE

Throughout Eastern Europe, arguments against abortion were often bolstered by the claim that "the nation is dying out." Abortion was denounced because it denied the state the ability to renew itself. Elements of this refrain characterized the abortion debate in the Slovak Republic, Slovenia, and Poland. Perhaps nowhere in Eastern Europe have needs of the state been more central to the adoption of reproduction policy than in Romania. Under Communism, the need to increase the work force produced a two-pronged policy. Women were actively encouraged to enter the work force and, at the same time, they were urged to bear as many children as possible. The fetus was declared the socialist property of the country. A strong pro-natal policy, which banned abortion and made divorce difficult, was first adopted in 1966. Within a year, the birth rate tripled (Fischer and Harsany, 1994). Women's extensive participation in the labor force, coupled with the absence of adequate support services for working mothers, created great hardship for women. By the end of the 1970s, there was considerable resistance to the government policy to have children. The number of illegal abortions grew, despite the fact that a woman would be denied hospital care if she refused to identify the individual who performed the procedure. Increasingly repressive measures to prevent abortion were adopted. Childless couples and the unmarried were heavily taxed. There were monthly examinations of women at their place of work to identify early pregnancies and prevent their illegal termination. Provision was made for a two-year minimum prison term for the woman if it was discovered that she had had an abortion.

The forced reproductive role was particularly onerous to Romanian women. Since abortion had traditionally been an accepted method of contraception, such draconian restrictions meant that women had virtually no control over their reproductive life. No effort was made to reduce the burdens imposed by participation in the work force and responsibility for child care. Faced with the constraints and hardships inflicted on them by the Ceausescu regime, women participated extensively in the 1989 revolution. Following the collapse of his government, anti-abortion laws were abolished, and statutes were enacted that provided for women's maternity leave and child care allowance.

CONCLUSION

Throughout Eastern Europe there have been changes in women's status and reproductive rights since the collapse of Communism. In one instance, Romania, the changes have not only been dramatic but have also restored to women some measure of control over their reproductive lives. In the cases of Bulgaria and the Czech Republic, these changes have been relatively minor. Elsewhere, they have placed varying limitations on reproductive choice, with Poland representing an extreme case. These changes have come about as a result of various pressures imposed by the activities of organized groups, such as the Catholic Church, or those reflecting emerging nationalist sentiments. In the volatile environment of a transitional Eastern Europe, a potent women's movement has not yet emerged. Perhaps if and when such a movement does materialize, abortion policies will shift again.

Until then, with the exception of Romania, easy access to abortion is no longer simply a given.

NOTES

1. The situation in Poland is very similar to that of the USSR. Abortion was legalized there about the same time; like Poland, little attention was given to family planning, with the consequence that abortion was widely considered a form of birth control.

2. The Church's position on birth control, which continues to have a major influence on public policy today, was so intense that little was done to promote family planning. Abortion was the main method for controlling fertility.

3. The grounds for certifying that these conditions have been met are restictive. Furthermore, the pressures applied to physicians make them extremely reluctant to perform an abortion under any circumstance.

REFERENCES

Adamik, Maria. "Hungary: A Loss of Rights?" *Feminist Review* 39 (Autumn 1991): 166–70.

Antic, Milica G. "Democracy Between Tyranny and Liberty: Women in Post-Socialist Slovenia," *Feminist Review* 39 (Autumn 1991): 149–54.

Bystydzienski, Jill M. "Women and Socialism: A Comparative Study of Women in Poland and the USSR." *Signs* 14 (Spring 1989): 668–84.

Castle-Kanerova, Mita. "Czechoslovakia: Interview with Alena Valterova." *Feminist Review* 39 (Winter 1991): 161–65.

Engelberg, Stephen. "Her Year of Living Dangerously." *The New York Times Magazine,* September 12, 1993: 38ff.

Fischer, M. E., and D. P. Harsanyi. "From Tradition and Ideology to Elections and Competition: The Changing Status of Women in Romanian Politics." In *Women in the Politics of Postcommunist Eastern Europe,* ed. Marilyn Rueschemeyer. Armonk, NY: M.E. Sharpe, Inc., 1994.

Fodor, Eva. "The Political Woman? Women in Politics in Hungary." In *Women in the Politics of Postcommunist Eastern Europe,* ed. Marilyn Rueschemeyer. Armonk, NY: M.E. Sharpe, Inc., 1994.

Hadley, Janet. "God's Bullies: Attacks on Abortion." *Feminist Review* 48 (Autumn 1994): 94–113.

Heinen, Jacqueline, and Anna Matuchniak Krasuska. "Abortion in Poland: A Vicious Circle or a Good Use of Rhetoric—A Sociological Study of Political Discourse of Abortion in Poland." *Women's Studies International Forum* 18, no. 1 (1995): 27–34.

Hoff, Joan. "Comparative Analysis of Abortion in Ireland, Poland and the United States." *Women's Studies International Forum* 17, no. 6 (1994): 621–46.

Hoff, Joan, and Christie Farnham. "Editors' Notes and Acknowledgements: The More Things Change the Worse They Become for Women." *Journal of Women's History* 5 (Winter, 1994): 6–9.

Jankowska, Hanna. "Abortion, Church and Politics in Poland." *Feminist Review* 39 (Autumn 1991): 174–181.

Jankowska, Hanna. "The Reproductive Rights Campaign in Poland." *Women's Studies International Forum* 16, no. 3 (1993): 291–96.

Jogan, Maca. "Redomestication of Women in Slovenia?" *Women's Studies International Forum* 17, nos. 2/3 (1994): 307–309.

Kissling, Frances. "The Church's Heavy Hand in Poland." *Planned Parenthood in Europe* 21, no. 2 (May 1992): 18–19.

Kligman, Gail. "The Politics of Reproduction in Ceausescu's Romania: A Case Study in Political Culture." *Eastern European Politics and Society* (Fall 1992): 364–418.

Kostova, Dobrinka. "The Transition to Democracy in Bulgaria: Challenges and Risks for Women." In *Women in the Politics of Postcommunist Eastern Europe*, ed. Marilyn Rueschemeyer. Armonk, NY: M.E. Sharpe, Inc., 1994.

Mezei, Smaranda. "Gendering the Social Body in Postcommunist Romania—From Homogenization to Diversity: New Discourses, Old Practices." *Women's Studies International Forum* 17, nos. 2/3 (1994): 313–14.

Meznaric, Silva, and Mirjana Ule. "Women in Croatia and Slovenia: A Case of Delayed Modernization." In *Women in the Politics of Postcommunist Eastern Europe*, ed. Marilyn Rueschemeyer. Armonk, NY: M.E. Sharpe, Inc., 1994.

Nicolaescu, Madalina. "Post-Communist Transitions: Romanian Women's Responses to Changes in the System of Power." *Journal of Women's History* 5 (Winter 1994): 117–28.

Nowicka, Wanda. "Two Steps Back: Poland's New Abortion Law." *Journal of Women's History* 5 (Winter 1994): 151–55.

Pakszys, Elzbieta, and Dorota Mazurczak. "From Totalitarianism to Democracy in Poland: Women's Issues in the Sociopolitical Transition of 1989–1993." *Journal of Women's History* 5 (Winter 1994): 144–50.

Penn, Shana. "The National Secret." *Journal of Women's History* 5 (Winter 1994): 55–67.

Rueschemeyer, Marilyn, ed. *Women in the Politics of Postcommunist Eastern Europe*. Armonk, NY: M.E. Sharpe, Inc., 1994.

Siemienska, Renata. "Women in the Period of Systematic Changes in Poland." *Journal of Women's History* 5 (Winter 1994): 70–90.

Tarasiewicz, Malgorzata. "Women in Poland: Choices to be Made." *Feminist Review* 39 (Autumn 1991): 182–85.

Titkow, Anna. "Polish Women in Politics: An Introduction to the Status of Women in Poland." In *Women in the Politics of Postcommunist Eastern Europe*, ed. Marilyn Rueschemeyer. Armonk, NY: M.E. Sharpe, Inc., 1994.

Todorova, Maria. "Historical Tradition and Transformation in Bulgaria: Women's Issues or Feminist Issues." *Journal of Women's History* 5 (Winter 1994): 129–43.

Wolchik, Sharon. "International Trends in Central and Eastern Europe: Women in Transition in the Czech and Slovak Republics: The First Three Years." *Journal of Women's History* 5 (Winter 1994): 100–107.

Wolchik, Sharon. "Women and the Politics of Transition in Czech and Slovak Republics." In *Women in the Politics of Postcommunist Eastern Europe*, ed. Marilyn Rueschemeyer. Armonk, NY: M.E. Sharpe, Inc., 1994.

Zielinska, Eleonora, and Jolanta Plakwicz. "Strengthening Human Rights for Women and Men in Matters Relating to Sexual Behavior and Reproduction." *Journal of Women's History* 5 (Winter 1994): 91–99

PART II

THE REALITY FACTOR:
Availability and Access
to Abortion Services

INTRODUCTION

Formal, legal constraints on abortion are, of course, profoundly important in defining reproductive choices. When abortion is outlawed, or limited solely to reasons of maternal health or fetal deformity, women wishing to terminate a pregnancy have almost no options available to them. In such situations, they have often sought the services of "back-alley" abortionists, who are often poorly trained and carry out the procedure under highly unsanitary conditions. The consequences of these illegal abortions for women's health were one of the compelling arguments used to press for liberalizing abortion policy in the 1960s and 1970s.

Legalizing abortion is crucial to extending choice, but so too is implementation. Access and availability are particularly important. If there are barriers imposed by inadequate or non-existent public funding that make abortion an option available only to women who can pay for it, if there are a limited number of facilities performing abortions, if facilities only exist in certain geographic areas, or if the final decision is determined by the medical profession, reproductive choice is illusory. Similarly, if negative attitudes about abortion are widely held in the society at large, abortion is not truly a viable option. Using a comparative perspective, the chapters in Part II examine the extent to which barriers have affected the implementation of abortion policy choices in the United States, Canada, Russia, France, and Japan, and their implications for reproductive choice.

Several common themes influencing implementation are discussed in the three chapters in this section. They are the relationship of societal values and belief systems to the availability of abortion services; the political environment in which implementation decisions are made; the lobbying activities of organized groups; and the participants in the policy-making and policy implementation processes. Each of the chapters shows that the legal provisions sanctioning abortion are not adequate by themselves in guaranteeing reproductive choice. An argument is made that the degree to which reproductive choice exists is dependent on funding, the number of facilities providing abortion services, and the acceptance of abortion either as a backup to failed contraception or as an alternative method of birth control. A case is also made that societal belief systems and the mix of groups involved in the policy process play a significant role in determining policy implementation in all of the countries, regardless of the differences in their political and governmental institutions.

Chapter 4 begins by focusing on the role of political institutions in the implementation of abortion policy in the United States and Canada. Studlar and Tatalovich argue that the existence of federalism has allowed the

American states and the Canadian provinces considerable latitude in implementation. In Canada, the administration of health care at the provincial level, for example, has permitted significant variation from one area to another in terms of public funding. Similarly, in the United States, the Supreme Court's decisions upholding the right of states to place limitations on a women's right to an abortion have also contributed to significant variations. Although the courts have played an important role in defining abortion policy in both countries, some differences in the politics of abortion may be attributed to different political institutions. A parliamentary system and strict party discipline in Canada, the authors contend, may well explain the reason why abortion is a much less contentious issue there than it is in the United States.

Political institutions account for some but not all aspects of the implementation of abortion policy in Canada and the United States, however. In each country there is real variation in implementation from one region to another, and there are some major similarities shared by particular regions in Canada and the United States. In looking at a woman's access to abortion, the authors have found that some states and provinces have adequate hospital or clinic facilities, whereas others provide few or no services. Availability in both countries appears to be affected by factors such as the extent to which the area is urbanized, its geographical location (some states and provinces providing far fewer opportunities for women seeking abortions), and attitudes about abortion dating back to pre-liberal abortion laws. For example, both Canadian and United States prairie and Western mountain areas provide few facilities offering abortion services. Old attitudes about abortion, the authors assert, seem relevant to the implementation of current laws. The United States provides some evidence to support this position; states that had not moved to liberalize abortion policy prior to the Supreme Court's decision in *Roe v. Wade* are much more likely to place restrictions on a woman's right to choose.

Although chapter 5 does not deal specifically with the part played by political institutions in implementing policy, it does explore the differences in policymaking and policy implementation that emerge from the roles played by what Stetson describes as the policy triad of doctors, women, and policymakers. Like Studlar and Tatalovich, she notes the shortage of facilities where abortions might be performed in the United States and attributes this to a laissez faire policy, with the government refusing to assign abortion resources to either doctors or women. As a consequence, the abortion debate in the United States, she contends, has come to be dominated by women and family planners on the one hand and religious fundamentalists on the other. Physicians have increasingly withdrawn from the policy arena, and have come to view abortion as a "dirty" business. In contrast, in Russia the government has supported physicians who determine policies related to implementation. Who receives abortions is a medical decision, with women having little say in the policymaking process. finally in France, the government has shifted its resources for state abortion to women and encouraged reluctant physicians to provide the services.

Although the government, doctors, and women compose the policy triad in all three countries, Stetson claims that the role that each group plays in its country's triad is tied to the political role of physicians and feminists. In Russia, which has the highest abortion rate of the three countries, the government has been a dominant force in all policymaking processes. Whereas feminist activity, which has been at best sporadic, has been unsuccessful in establishing the meaningful participation of women in the policy-making process, physicians have been designated as official public experts and play a dominant role. In the United States, a laissez faire triad has produced a government that has withdrawn from the fray and left the policy debate to feminists and pro-life activists. With fewer and fewer doctors performing abortions, continued availability is threatened. In France, which has a low rate of abortion and safe and available services, the pattern is one of an inactive medical profession and an activist feminist presence.

Japan, which is the focal point of the last chapter in this section, liberalized its abortion law in 1948. Unlike the reasons advanced for legalizing abortion in the other countries dealt with in this section, Japanese abortion policy was predicated on the notion of "enhancing the gene pool." Indeed, abortion policy in Japan has been consistently linked to demographic concerns. Although abortion is legal in Japan and socially available, its rate is only half that of the United States. Gelb suggests several reasons for this. In the first place, societal constraints on discussion of sexual matters, even between husband and wife, have contributed to serious underreporting. Then, the high priority placed on virginity before marriage is also a factor both in underreporting and discouraging sex before marriage. Finally, abortion is not funded through a national health insurance, and although the claim has been made that money is not a constraint on obtaining an abortion, the cost and the fact that women often conceal an abortion from their husbands suggests that it ought to affect access, certainly for poorer women.

The higher tolerance level for abortion in Japan and its general accessibility, Gelb argues, is related to the country's birth-control policies. Condoms and a Japanese form of the rhythm method are the major forms of available contraception. After a brief period in the 1960s and early 1970s, the pill has been unavailable except through a doctor's prescription, and then only for therapeutic reasons. Although the pill may be obtained illegally and is used by some women, there appears to be some reluctance among women to use it. Reported male sterilization rates appear to be very low, and although the popularity of female sterilization appears to be growing, it is still insignificant as a method for controlling fertility. In the absence of effective, modern methods of contraception, abortion has provided a major means of regulating fertility.

CHAPTER 4

ABORTION POLICY IN THE UNITED STATES AND CANADA: DO INSTITUTIONS MATTER?

DONLEY T. STUDLAR AND RAYMOND TATALOVICH

The political institutions of the United States and Canada are different in that the United States has a congressional/presidential separation of powers system, and Canada has a parliamentary/cabinet government inherited from Britain. They are alike, however, in that both have a federal structure. Over the past 30 years Canadian federalism has become progressively decentralized, partly as a result of pressure from Quebec, partly from other regional loyalties. In contrast, federalism in the United States has moved in the opposite direction, at least until the 1990s (Riker, 1964; Gibbins, 1982; Weaver, 1992). Nevertheless, the existence of a federal system has affected abortion policy in both countries, as exemplified by the *Morgentaler* decision in Canada and the 1989 *Webster* decision in the United States. The sub-national level in policy-making is critically important in each country, since state/provincial decision makers, as well as national political elites, participate in determining procedures that affect abortion policy implementation. Moreover, the role of states and provinces, as well as regions, in providing facilities for abortion often determines the extent to which abortion is accessible.

Studies of abortion policy have reflected these institutional characteristics. In the United States they have focused on central governmental institutions, especially the courts (Tatalovich and Daynes, 1981; Craig and O'Brien, 1993), particular states (Segers and Byrnes, 1995), or comparisons among states (Halva-Neubauer, 1990; Meier and McFarlane, 1993; Mooney and Lee, 1995). In the case of Canada, they have explored the role of the courts and central policymakers (Pal, 1991; Brodie, Gavigan, and Jenson, 1992; Morton, 1992).

There have been a number of efforts to compare abortion policy in the two countries. Schwartz (1981) illustrated the dynamics of "politicized moral causes" in a comparative study that found that despite similarities of opinion and controversy in both countries, the Canadian central government, with its disciplined single party majority in a parliamentary system, was better able to control agenda setting and policy formation on abortion than was its counterpart in the United States. McDaniel (1985) focused on abortion policy implementation in Canada and used selective comparisons to the United States. This approach was pursued more systematically by Brodie (1994) and in two public opinion studies (Nevitte, Brandon, and Davis, 1993; Jelen and Chandler, 1994). More recently, Tatalovich and Studlar (1995) found that, prior to the time that the Canadian judiciary entered the policymaking arena on abortion with the *Morgentaler* decision of 1988, there were similar rates of access to abortion in both countries. These findings led them to conclude that the implementation of abortion policy did not depend on the differences between legislative and judicial enactment of policy that Schwartz (1981) had identified.

This chapter will address abortion policy comparatively, in terms of problem definition, policy development, implementation, and the impact of political institutions on the policy process. Following a brief overview of abortion policy in the two countries, in terms of how the issue arose, how it was defined, and what actions were taken in the late 1960s and early 1970s to liberalize previously restrictive policies, it will examine the impact of the *Morgentaler* decision of 1988 and the *Webster* decision of 1989 on policy implementation and the overall formulation of policy in the two countries.

ABORTION POLICY IN THE UNITED STATES

As discussed elsewhere in this volume, by the early twentieth century, abortion was proscribed in the criminal codes of all fifty states of the United States. Abortions to save the mother's life were the sole exception. Only the statutes of Alabama, Oregon, Colorado, Maryland, and New Mexico made any reference to maternal health, bodily injury, or safety (Tatalovich and Daynes, 1981: 24). As medical technology improved and more births occurred in hospitals, physicians became uneasy with informal decision making about terminating pregnancies and desired legal protection for their decisions. In 1959, the American Law Institute (ALI) formulated a model penal code that included a provision legalizing abortions for therapeutic reasons other than saving the mother's life. The demand for reform was widely publicized in 1962 when an Arizona woman, Sherri Finkbine, had to travel to Sweden to obtain an abortion of a fetus deformed by her ingestion of the drug thalidomide during her pregnancy. The pressure for reform continued, and in 1965 the National Association for Humane Abortion was organized. Two years later, the American Medical Association incorporated the ALI recommendations in its policies. During this period reformers used newspaper accounts of personal tragedies to bring the issue before the public as a serious health problem. However, there was little advocacy of abortion as a legal right (Tatalovich and Daynes, 1981: 60).

Beginning in 1964, nineteen states liberalized their anti-abortion laws, and in 1970, Alaska, Hawaii, New York, and Washington removed abortion from their criminal codes, thus legalizing it as an elective procedure (Mooney and Lee, 1995). The leading advocates of abortion reform were physicians and attorneys who, in addition to documenting the evils of the existing policies, made the argument that the criminal law should reflect prevailing medical practices (Brodie, 1994). Women's rights groups, which were just beginning to emerge in the early sixties, were not prime movers in getting abortion on the policy agenda. By the end of that decade, however, they did begin to take a stand, and, along with the Roman Catholic Church, which was concerned about the rights of the fetus, they injected a moral dimension into the debate (Tatalovich and Daynes, 1981; Mooney and Lee, 1995).

Although there were state statutes, there was no national policy on abortion until 1973, when the Supreme Court in *Roe v. Wade* and its companion case *Doe v. Bolton* nullified all state abortion laws and affirmed the right of abortion during the first trimester under the "zones of privacy" doctrine of the Ninth Amendment. However, the *Roe* decision left many unanswered questions about the extent of state regulation of abortion, public funding of the procedure, and the structure of the abortion delivery system. Variations among the fifty states in such procedures as public funding, waiting periods, parental consent (Meier and McFarlane, 1993; Halva-Neubauer, 1993), and the availability of hospital abortion services (Tatalovich and Daynes, 1989) and clinic providers (Henshaw and Van Vort, 1994) remained.

Litigation that came before the Supreme Court subsequently addressed some of these questions, but the issue of access to abortion services was left to the marketplace. *Roe* created choices: a constitutional right for women to choose abortion in the first trimester of pregnancy and a choice for doctors and hospitals to offer these services. Since it did not require that health care professionals perform abortions, it did not provide an implementation strategy. Instead, questions of compliance were left to hospitals and physicians.

The *Roe* decision provoked a backlash throughout the United States (Tatalovich, 1988). Pro-life groups lobbied all levels and branches of government to limit the effects of the ruling. In response, Congress and Republican presidents enacted anti-abortion curbs on federal agencies and programs, the most famous being the Hyde Amendment, which banned Medicaid payments for all abortions except those performed to save the mother's life. This constraint on federal funding, which was upheld as constitutional in *Harris v. McRae* (1980), stipulated that no state could use federal funds to pay for abortions other than to save the mother's life, although state revenues could be used to pay for non-therapeutic abortions.

Republican administrations' sympathy toward pro-life groups was reflected in their appointments to the United States Supreme Court. By 1989, when the case of *Webster v. Reproductive Health Services* reached the court, there were only four reliable pro-choice votes among the nine judges. Indeed, there was considerable apprehension that the court might overturn *Roe v. Wade*. To the consternation of both pro-life and pro-choice forces, the court both opened the door for further regulation by the states and stopped short of reversing its 1973 landmark decision.[1] All aspects of the Missouri law were upheld by a five-to-four vote, but the justices could not agree on a single majority position. The decision did, however, effectively end the idea that women enjoyed an "absolute" constitutional right of abortion, and it signaled the states that they had authority to impose reasonable restrictions on abortion. *Planned Parenthood of Southeastern Pennsylvania v. Casey* (1992) further confirmed the right of the states to place restrictions on abortion.

CANADIAN ABORTION POLICY

Most of Canada's Criminal Code, including its abortion laws, followed British practices closely. Referring Canadian constitutional disputes to the British Privy Council for final adjudication had formally ended in 1949, but British influence on Canadian law was still substantial in the 1960s (Morton, 1992). The British Labour Party, when it came to power in Britain in the mid-1960s, allowed the first liberalized abortion law in Western Europe to pass through the infrequently used procedure of a free vote.[2] It was against this background that the Canadian move to liberalize abortion took place. In 1959 the Canadian women's magazine *Chatelaine* published an article calling for legalized abortions, pointing to the debate about the issue which had just started to come to the fore in Britain and in the United States (de Valk, 1974). By 1966 the Canadian Medical Association (CMA) and the Canadian Bar Association also advocated therapeutic abortion. The Canadian Medical Association was considered the most influential lobby, but, as Morton observes, "their principal motivation appears to have been neither sexual equality or social engineering, but rather professional self-interest: to protect doctors against the legal uncertainties of the current law" (1992: 5). This concern later resurfaced in the wake of the 1988 *Morgentaler* decision. Ultimately the law approved by the Canadian Parliament in 1969 closely resembled the earlier Medical Association proposal (Morton, 1992).

Three Private Member's bills to legalize abortion were introduced in 1966 and 1967. As non-government bills, their chances of passage were slim, but they did bring the issue onto the formal agenda of Parliament. After public hearings, the Standing Committee on Health and Welfare offered an

Interim Report in December 1967, which found the existing abortion law ambiguous and recommended that the criminal code be amended to "allow therapeutic abortion under appropriate medical safeguards where a pregnancy will seriously endanger the life or health of the mother" (de Valk, 1974: 55). Two days after the Interim Report appeared, the Liberal government introduced Bill C-195, an omnibus bill to change the criminal code and which included provisions on abortion, homosexuality, and lotteries. Abortions would be allowed when the pregnancy was likely to endanger the life or health of the mother (de Valk, 1974). In contrast to the United States, this reform was formulated by the government as part of a concerted philosophical effort to remove private morality from the criminal code.

After the Liberals were reelected, the government reintroduced an identical bill in the new Parliament, Omnibus Bill C-150. The abortion provision generated such rancorous debate in the House of Commons that the government finally allowed one free vote, on a motion to strike the abortion provision from the bill. The motion lost by 107 to 38, and five days later C-150 passed its final vote in the House of Commons and went into effect on August 26, 1969. Although restrictive, this new legislation formalized what was already common practice in many Canadian hospitals (Glendon, 1987). A national policy on abortion now existed although considerable authority was retained by the provinces, which were responsible for health administration.

The provisions regarding abortion contained in the new criminal code stipulated that hospitals seeking to provide abortion services had to create a three-doctor Therapeutic Abortion Committee (TAC). These committees, which were to be comprised of not less than three medical practitioners, were to consider individual applications for abortions, although their decisions did not necessarily involve dealing with patients individually. In practice, the composition and practices of these committees varied considerably across the country (McDaniel, 1985).

How stringent the restrictions on abortion were under the new law is a matter of dispute. Some commentators argued that expansive interpretations of "health" allowed women to obtain abortions relatively easily (Glendon, 1989: 573), while others who advocated abortion as a woman's right contended that too much variation occurred in abortion availability across Canada (McDaniel, 1985). Culminating a personal crusade against restrictive abortion practices, Dr. Henry Morgentaler challenged the legality of the code under Section 7 of the 1982 Canadian Charter of Rights and Freedoms, which declared: "Everyone has the right to life, liberty and security of the person and the right not to be deprived thereof except in accordance with the principles of fundamental justice." Voting 5 to 2, the Supreme Court in *R. v. Morgentaler* (1988) removed abortion from the criminal code. Unlike *Roe v. Wade*, this decision was not based on privacy rights and did not preclude legislative restrictions on abortion. Instead, it was based on the "unworkable" nature of the existing abortion law, which posed a threat to the "security" of women. In short, it was a decision about appropriate regulations, not constitutional rights.[3]

While the immediate effect of the 1988 ruling was to make abortion a medical issue between the woman and her doctor, three of the Justices who supported Morgentaler indicated that they would accept some federal restrictions on abortion. The provinces could not make abortion a criminal offense, but they could regulate it as they did any health service. This situation led to further litigation, primarily concerning provincial payments for clinic rather than hospital abortions under Canadian public health-care insurance.

In July 1988, immediately following the *Morgentaler* ruling, the Conservative government introduced a bill that allowed relatively easy access to abortion in the early stages of pregnancy, while making it more difficult later. After two days of debate, the MPs rejected the proposal by 147-to-76 on a free vote. There was no consensus for a compromise on this issue within the 167-person Tory caucus (Pal, 1991).

After much delay, the Conservative government, which was re-elected in November, 1988, made another attempt to regulate abortion by introducing Bill C-43 in 1990. It was hardly restrictive by the standards of the pro-life lobby in the United States Congress. It granted no rights to the fetus, specified no time limit for abortions, and did not apply to drugs that prevented the implantation of a fertilized ovum. C-43 simply eliminated the Therapeutic Abortion Committee requirement of the 1969 law and allowed any *one* medical practitioner to determine whether the mother's health—physical, mental and psychological—or life was likely to be threatened if the pregnancy were carried to term.

When this government-sponsored bill was considered by the House of Commons, Conservative party members were allowed a modified free vote, with government ministers, but not back benchers, required to adhere to the party line. Since anything other than a party-line vote is unusual in the Canadian Parliament (Stewart, 1993), the use of this procedure indicated how deep divisions within the governing party were on the issue. The Liberals, the major opposition party at the time, were also split on abortion. Only the socialist New Democrats supported freedom of choice (Pal, 1991). Following the debate, all amendments, pro-life as well as pro-choice, were rejected, and the 140-to-131 outcome on the final vote was strongly influenced by partisanship (Tatalovich, Overby, and Studlar, 1993).

When the bill came before the upper chamber, the Senate, in February 1991, the members, who unlike their counterparts in the United States are appointed through Prime Ministerial patronage, were also freed from party discipline. Bill C-43 was defeated on a tied vote, 43 to 43. With that, the Conservative government gave up its effort to shape a compromise position, and the subsequent Liberal government, elected in October 1993, has never broached the issue. As of 1995, there is no federal abortion statute, and the *Morgentaler* ruling remains the law of Canada.

The defeat of the abortion bill might be attributed to a variety of reasons. Both pro-choice and anti-abortion Senators were not entirely happy with the bill. In addition, physicians increasingly voiced their concern that the law provided for penalties of up to two years in prison for any doctor who performed an abortion but who could not prove that the woman's "health and life" had been threatened. As in the 1969 legislation, physicians' fears of legal repercussions were an important consideration in the policymaking process.

In the aftermath of *Morgentaler*, there have been efforts by all the provinces except Ontario, Quebec, and Saskatchewan to curb abortions through funding limits and through requiring hospital approval of individual abortions. Almost all of these efforts have been challenged in the courts, and several of them have been overturned (Dunsmuir, 1991: 17–20; Brodie, 1994). Informal pressure, including threats of violence, have reduced the supply of physicians willing to perform abortions, especially in the Maritime provinces.

COMPARING ABORTION IMPLEMENTATION

Abortion in both Canada and the United States was defined as a medical problem, not a personal right, in the early reform period of the 1960s, but by the early 1970s distinctions emerged. In the United States, the *Roe* decision made abortion part of women's right to privacy; in Canada, the parliamentary reform of the criminal code defined abortion in terms of women's right to health care. While pro-choice advocates in Canada, were envious of the constitutional status achieved for abortion rights in the United States, thoughtful feminists were uncomfortable with its grounding in civil rights and individual privacy, which reinforced "the long-standing boundary between the public and private spheres fundamental to patriarchal domination within the family . . . . American women could make a private decision about abortion, but the equally critical issue of access to abortion services was also privatized" (Brodie, 1994: 128). These concerns were confirmed by the abortion funding cases, in which the United States Supreme Court unequivocally asserted that the right to an abortion is not an entitlement mandating the federal or state governments to pay for abortions, even for indigent women. Abortion became an issue in the proposed National Health Care plan in early 1990s, when it appeared that the federal government would compel private insurers to cover the procedure under President Clinton's managed competition proposal. In contrast, without a constitutional right to abortion, the Canadian government could regulate the conditions for abortions, but, as part of the universal health-care system, financed by public insurance, the state paid for the procedure (Brodie, 1994).

However abortion is defined, the critical question is whether these distinctions have an impact on the availability of abortion services. The implementation of abortion policy in both countries went through two phases. In Canada the first phase began with the reform of the criminal code, and in the United States four years later with *Roe v. Wade*. The second phase came during the late 1980s with the *Morgentaler* and *Webster* decisions, which have been widely depicted as imposing more restrictions on abortions in the United States but fewer in Canada. This characterization has been contested by Brodie (1994), who has argued that there is a convergence of policy as well as process in the two countries, because both the *Webster* and *Morgentaler* decisions decentralized policymaking on abortion.

Although statistics for the two countries on rates of abortion and abortion providers show some differences over time, they also indicate that by the 1990s convergence was occurring. The abortion rate has been rising in Canada and declining in the United States in the 1990s, although it is still almost twice as high in the latter. Table 1 indicates that just two years after *Roe* the number of abortions in the United States reached the one million mark. Since 1979 it has stabilized at about one-and-a-half million per year, although recently it has declined somewhat. In Canada, which has a population only one-tenth the size of the United States, the number of abortions each year is one-fifteenth that of its neighbor (see table 1).

Although Canadian law mandated that abortions should be done only in hospitals, Morgentaler operated his clinics openly in Quebec from 1976. Quebec, the second-largest province, began reporting clinic abortions in 1978. For 1988, the United States clinic abortion rate of 27.3 was more than double the Canadian rate of 11.6, but in 1990, following the *Morgentaler* case, there was a substantial jump to 14.6 in the Canadian rate. This increase reflected the opening of other clinics across Canada. The total of 21,443 clinic abortions for 1990 were distributed among six provinces (Statistics Canada, 1991: 28): Newfoundland (63), Nova Scotia (81), Quebec (8,919), Ontario (10,200), Manitoba (1,051), and British Columbia (1,129). Greater access to abortion clinics, particularly in Ontario, has allowed the abortion rate to increase, although some of this may have occurred because Canadian women no longer have to travel to the United States for clinic abortions. In 1990 clinics accounted for 22 percent of total abortions, up from only 9 percent in 1989. By 1992 clinics accounted for nearly 30 percent of abortions. These trends, if

TABLE 1
ABORTIONS AND ABORTION RATES IN THE UNITED STATES AND CANADA

| | CANADA | | | | UNITED STATES | | | |
| | Hospital | Non-Hosp.[a] | | | Hospital | Non-Hosp.[b] | | |
Year	Number	%	%	Rate[c]	Number	%	%	Rate
1970	11,152[d]	100		6.6				
1971	37,232	100		9.9				
1972	45,426	100		10.4				
1973	48,720	100		10.8	744.6	52	48	16.3
1974	52,435	100		10.4	898.6	47	53	19.3
1975	53,705	100		11.2	1,034.2	40	60	21.7
1976	58,712	100		11.4	1,179.3	35	65	24.2
1977	59,864	100		11.8	1,316.7	30	70	26.4
1978	66,710	96	3.9[e]	12.3	1,409.6	25	75	27.7
1979	69,745	95	5.2	12.3	1,497.7	23	77	28.8
1980	72,099	94	6.5	12.2	1,553.9	22	78	29.3
1981	71,911	94	5.9	12.3	1,577.3	19	81	29.3
1982	75,071	94	6.0	11.6	1,573.9	18	82	28.8
1983	69,368	95	5.2	11.4	—			
1984	69,449	95	5.1	11.4	1,577.2	14	88	28.1
1985	69,216	95	5.4	11.3	1,588.6	13	87	28.0
1986	69,572	96.2	3.8	11.2	—			
1987	70,023	94.7	5.3	11.3	1,559.1	11	89	26.8
1988	72,693	93.6	6.4	11.6	1,590.8	10	90	27.3
1989	79,315	91.1	8.9	12.6	—			
1990	92,901	78.2	21.8	14.6	—			
1991	95,059	75.4	24.6	14.7	1,556.5	7	93	26.3
1992	100,497	70.6	29.4	14.9	1,528.9	7	93	25.9

[a] Source: Statistics Canada. *Therapeutic Abortions.* 1992, p. 15, Table 10.

[b] Source: For total number of abortions: Stanley K. Henshaw and Jennifer Van Vort, "Abortion Services in the United States, 1991 and 1992," *Family Planning Perspectives* 26 (May/June 1994), p. 101, Table 1. Distributions between hospitals/non-hospitals: for 1973–82, Maureen Muldoon, *The Abortion Debate in the United States and Canada: A Source Book* (New York: Garland Publishing, 1991), p. 12, Table 4; for 1983–86, Stanley K. Henshaw and Jennifer Van Vort, eds., *Abortion Factbook 1992 Edition* (New York: Alan Guttmacher Institution, 1992), Table 6; for 1991–92, directly from Alan Guttmacher Institute.

[c] The number of abortions per 1,000 females aged 15–44 years.

[d] Based on the total number of abortions, the percentage done in clinics was derived and the remainder was attributed to hospitals, although a number of abortions were done on Canadian residents in the U.S. with no indication how many were clinic or hospital procedures. The number of abortions done on Canadian women in the U.S. was over 6,000 in 1971 but generally fell since then; fewer than 3,000 were reported in 13 of the 22 years.

[e] For 1981–1989 only Quebec reported clinic abortions; later data reflects clinic abortions in Newfoundland, Nova Scotia, Quebec, Ontario, Manitoba, and British Columbia (for 1990) and also Alberta (for 1991 and 1992).

they continue, would mean that the demand for abortions and the supply of abortion services in Canada will more closely approximate patterns in the United States.

Until *Morgentaler*, one substantial difference in abortion services in the two countries was who provided them. In Canada, 90 percent of the abortions were performed in hospitals; in the United States, non-hospital providers had long accounted for the vast majority of abortions, and by 1988 they performed 90 percent of them (Table 1). In 1992, hospitals represented 36 percent of abortion providers but they performed only 7 percent of all abortions (Henshaw and Van Vort, 1994: 106); specialized abortion clinics (19 percent) performed 69 percent; other clinics (19 percent) accounted for 20 percent more; and four percent of all terminated pregnancies took place in physicians' offices (27 percent). With one in six United States hospitals doing abortions in 1992 as compared to nearly one in three in Canada (Table 2), and with a record high of 84 percent of United States counties having *no* abortion provider (Henshaw and Van Vort, 1994: 105), lack of access to abortion services indicates a considerable maldistribution.

Morgentaler argued in the Canadian Supreme Court that the 1969 law failed to provide equitable access to abortion services. This had already been documented a decade earlier by the government-appointed Committee on the Operation of the Abortion Law, which concluded that obtaining a therapeutic abortion was "illusory" for many women. It explained:

> *Coupled with the personal decisions of obstetrician-gynecologists, half of whom (48.9 percent) in eight provinces did not do the abortion procedure in 1974–75, the combined effects of the distribution of eligible hospitals, the location of hospitals with therapeutic abortion committees, the use of residency and patient quota requirements, the provincial distribution of obstetrician-gynecologists, and the fact that the abortion procedure was done primarily by this medical specialty resulted in sharp regional disparities in the accessibility of the abortion procedure. (Committee on the Operation of the Abortion Law, 1977: 140)*

When Doctors for Repeal of the Abortion Law (DRAL) petitioned Parliament in 1975 to remove abortion from the criminal code, they cited a 1971 Canadian Medical Association declaration that the statute was unworkable and that abortion should be a decision made by a woman and her physician. Since there was a dearth of reliable information about abortion practices, the DRAL decided to undertake its own study. Using the 1973 *Canadian Hospital Directory*, it determined how many general hospitals with 10 or more

TABLE 2
PERCENT OF UNITED STATES AND CANADIAN HOSPITALS WITH ABORTION
CAPACITY WHICH PROVIDE ABORTION SERVICES, 1971-1992

| YEAR | UNITED STATES | | | CANADA | | |
| | Abortion Capacity[a] | Abortion Services[b] | | Abortion Capacity[c] | Abortion Services[c] | |
	N	N	%	N	N	%
1971				862	143	16.6
1972				861	247	28.7
1973				867	261	30.1
1974				862	259	30.1
1975	5,875	1,629	27.7	862	274	31.8
1976	5,857	1,695	31.4	861	271	31.5
1977	5,881	1,654	28.1	855	265	31.0
1978	5,851	1,626	27.8	856	261	30.5
1979	5,842	1,526	26.1	863	270	31.3
1980	5,830	1,504	25.8	862	269	31.2
1981	5,813			861	267	31.0
1982	5,801	1,405	24.2	860	261	30.4
1983	5,783			846*	257	30.0
1984	5,759			846*	249	29.4
1985	5,732	1,191	20.8	846*	250	29.6
1986	5,678			843*	254	30.0
1987	5,611			843*		
1988	5,533	1,040	18.8	840*		
1989	5,455			840*		
1990	5,384			835*	191**	22.9
1991	5,342			842*		
1992	5,292	855	16.2	833*		

[a] Source: American Hospital Association, *American Hospital Association Hospital Statistics, 1993–94 Edition* (Chicago: American Hospital Association, 1993), Table 1, p. 7. This statistic, used by the Alan Guttmacher Institute as the universe of hospitals with capacity to do abortions, is based on those reporting to the AHA that they are "community hospitals," which includes all non-government not-for-profit investor-owned, as well as state and local government hospitals.

[b] Source: Alan Guttmacher Institute, New York City. The number of hospitals is based on its survey of known abortion providers. The surveys were irregular after 1980 so this statistic is not available for 1981, 1983, 1984, 1986, 1987, 1898, 1990, and 1991.

[c] Source: Statistics Canada, Institutional Care Statistics Section, *Some Facts About Therapeutic Abortions in Canada 1970-1982*, October 1984, p. 20, The statistics since 1983 (*) were obtained directly from Statistics Canada and reflect the Fiscal Year (April 1 and March 31) rather than the calendar year. Hospitals performing abortions are those reporting Therapeutic Abortion Committees and those with "capacity" are "public general hospitals" and include voluntary, provincial, and municipal (not-for-profit) hospitals that usually have obstetrics/gynecology and medical/surgical units. Incomplete 1990 (**) data collected by author directly from provinces or territories (see Table 3). The 1990 statistic *assumes* the same number of hospitals as 1986 for Northwest Territories *(1)* and Newfoundland *(5)* performed abortions in 1990 since neither jurisdiction responded to our request for updated information.

beds existed in each province and compared that list with those hospitals reporting that they had established a therapeutic abortion committee (TAC). Overall DRAL found that only 32.9 percent of all Canadian hospitals with capacity had established TACs, a statistic close to the calculation made by Statistics Canada some years later (see Table 2).

A 1986 replication of this study on the provincial level (Table 3) shows that except for New Brunswick and Quebec, the percentage of hospitals with capacity having therapeutic abortion committees (TACs) declined between 1975 and 1986. In both years the majority of British Columbia hospitals with obstetrics or surgical units had TACs. In Ontario, there was a marked decline from 56.8 percent in 1975 to 46.1 percent in 1986. In Quebec, there was an increase in TACs in eligible hospitals from 23.0 percent in 1975 to 29.6 percent in 1986. The combined percentage for the four Maritime provinces (New Brunswick, Newfoundland, Nova Scotia, and Prince Edward Island) was 21.2 percent. For the three prairie provinces (Alberta, Saskatchewan, Manitoba) it was even lower: 11.5 percent.

Since the last year that Statistics Canada obtained abortion data before the *Morgentaler* case was 1986, we collected more recent data in 1990, which showed that the total number of Canadian hospitals performing abortions declined further (see Table 3). Even though the *Morgentaler* case did not affect hospitals directly, that decision, coupled with the failure of Parliament to enact new regulations, presumably sent a welcome signal to the health-care community that, legally at least, they could safely perform abortions. However, increased abortion availability has come almost exclusively from the growth of clinics.

These data are consistent with information from Brodie (1994), who argued that three distinct abortion delivery systems operate in Canada. The most liberal is in Quebec, where presently 19 of the 30 clinics in Canada are found. fifteen are units within the provincial health-care system, which means that abortions are publicly funded. Elections in 1990 and 1991 that brought the New Democratic Party (NDP) to power in Saskatchewan, Ontario, and British Columbia resulted in greater access to abortion services, especially in the latter two provinces. British Columbia introduced regulations within its Health Act to require certain hospitals within each region of the province to provide abortion services, and Ontario is the only provincial government that fully funds abortions by either hospitals or free-standing clinics.

In the remaining provinces, the issue of access is more problematic, if not moot. In the prairie provinces, access is largely confined to one clinic and a handful of urban hospitals, some of which en-

force local residency requirements. In the Atlantic provinces, provincial governments have taken an active role in regulating abortion. In New Brunswick, for example, there are no free-standing clinics and the government is against their introduction. Prince Edward Island passed legislation opposing clinics and only funds-out-of-province abortions when they are performed in a hospital and approved by a five doctor panel. Similar restrictions apply in Newfoundland, where access is limited to one hospital, and approval from a gynecologist, a psychiatrist and a social worker is required. (Brodie, 1994:132,134)

TABLE 3
PERCENT OF HOSPITALS WITH CAPACITY THAT ESTABLISHED TACs
IN 1975/1986 AND NUMBER OF HOSPITALS WITH TACs IN
1970/1974/1986/1990, BY PROVINCE

	PERCENT OF HOSPITALS WITH CAPACITY		NUMBER OF HOSPITALS			
	1975	1986	1970	1974	1986	1990
	TACs[a]	TACs[b]	TACs[c]	TACs[c]	TACs	TACs
Province	(Obst or Surg)	(Obst or Surg)	(Obstetrics or Surgical Units)			
Newfoundland	22.2%	16.1%	4	6	5	5[d]
Pr. Edw. Is.	28.5%	14.3%	2	2	1	0
Nova Scotia	34.3%	24.4%	6	12	12	11
New Brunswick	22.5%	23.3%	7	8	8	4
Quebec	23.0%	29.6%	16	27	38	22
Ontario	56.8%	46.1%	48	110	95	77
Manitoba	14.0%	10.3%	4	9	8	6
Saskatchewan	10.1%	6.2%	8	10	8	8
Alberta	20.1%	17.9%	18	25	22	17
B. Columbia	56.5%	55.1%	29	54	55	39
Yukon	50.0%	50.0%	1	1	1	1
NW Terr.	16.7%	0	1	1	1	
CANADA	32.9%	28.4%[e]	143	265	254	191[f]

[a] Source: Doctors for Repeal of the Abortion Law, *Survey of Hospital Abortion Committees in Canada* (December 4, 1975), Library of Parliament, Ottawa, Canada.

[b] Data for 1986 provided to author by Statistics Canada.

[c] Source: Committee on the Operation of the Abortion Law, *Report of the Committee on the Operation of the Abortion Law* (Ottawa: Ministry of Supply and Services Canada, 1977), p. 446.

[d] Data for 1990 collected by author directly from provincial authorities.

[e] Four hospitals with therapeutic abortion committees in 1986 were not listed in the *Canadian Hospital Directory*, vol. 39, September 1991. If they are included in this calculation, the exact percentage would be 28.8%.

[f] See explanation in footnote c to Table 2 about how the 1990 data were tabulated.

These variations are reminiscent of the United States. Differences in state policies are longstanding and can be traced back to pre-*Roe* liberalized abortion policies. Tatalovich and Daynes (1989: 83) found an average of 34.5 percent of hospitals with capacity offered abortion services in 1986, but that percentage rose to 49.2 percent for the eighteen states which had pre-*Roe* liberal abortion policies and dropped to 23.9 percent for the thirty-two states that either did not change their abortion laws or, in Louisiana's case, barely extended the legal grounds for abortion at all (Mooney and Lee, 1995). Halva-Neubauer (1993: 186–187) examined states enacting nineteen types of anti-abortion regulations between 1973 and 1989. Among the most popular restrictions were "conscience clauses" (35 states) for health-care institutions or personnel, post-viability requirements or post-viability standards of care (29 states), limits on public funding of abortions (25), and controls on fetal experimentation (23 states). On average, each state enacted 6.1 anti-abortion laws at some time over that period, but the mean rose to 7.8 among the sub-group of thirty-two states and fell to 3.1 for the eighteen states with pre-*Roe* liberal abortion laws. Meier and McFarlane (1993) analyzed the data on states that funded abortions for poor women. States that were more Catholic, more conservative, and less party competitive were less inclined to fund abortions, though the strongest and only positive predictor was the relative number of residents who were members of the National Abortion Rights Action League. This would seem to suggest that politics are more important than the socioeconomic milieu. Data for 1990 (Meier and McFarlane, 1993: 250–251) showed that thirty-two states funded at least one Medicaid abortion. California and New York provided for 81 percent of the total. By adding five more states with pre-*Roe* liberal abortion policies (Hawaii, Maryland, North Carolina, Oregon, and Washington), this group of seven accounted for 91 percent of all Medicaid abortions.

If the definition of abortion capacity is limited to hospitals with obstetrics and gynecology (not surgical) units, then the percentage for Canada in 1986 was virtually identical to the figure for the United States. By that criterion, 35.0 percent of Canadian hospitals and 34.5 percent of United States hospitals were providing abortion services. The use of this index of capacity (obstetrics/gynecology units) allows for a comparison of regional variations in both countries. Tatalovich and Studlar (1995) have concluded that in both countries the most liberal region was the West Coast and the most conservative the Great Plains and mountain regions, consisting of the three prairie provinces in Canada and the thirteen states spanning the territory between California and the Midwest in the United States. Access to abortion in the United States Midwest was close to that in the Canadian mountain states, while Ontario was decidedly more supportive of abortion services than the midwestern states of Michigan, Wisconsin, Illinois, Indiana, Iowa, Minnesota, and Ohio. Quebec and the southern states fell somewhere in the middle in terms of available hospital abortion services. Comparisons of the range of abortion services among the fifty states and the ten Canadian provinces for 1986 gave similar results. For the United States in 1986 (Tatalovich and Daynes, 1989: 83), the percentage of hospitals with obstetrics/gynecology capacity ranged from a high of 75.0 percent in Hawaii to a low of 2.5 percent in South Dakota. In the provinces it ran from 64.0 percent in British Columbia to 9.4 percent in Saskatchewan. Thus, there was considerable variation among both states and provinces in the availability of abortion services.

The degree to which different types of hospitals have implemented abortion policy in both countries was close despite their dissimilar health-care systems (Tatalovich and Studlar, 1995). About a quarter of government hospitals in both countries in 1986 provided abortion services, with a slightly higher proportion in the United States. Church-affiliated hospitals did 10 percent of abortions in Canada, 6 percent in the United States. Private non-religiously affiliated hospitals provided about half of the total in each country; 57 percent in Canada had established TACs, while in the United States 45 percent reported doing abortions (Tatalovich and Studlar, 1995).

A 1992 Alan Guttmacher Institute survey (Henshaw and Van Vort, 1994: 103) found that 94 percent of non-metropolitan counties and 51 percent of metropolitan counties had no abortion provider. There was a clear urban-rural cleavage in the availability of abortion services across the United States, and the same was true in Canada. Tatalovich and Studlar (1995) showed that about three in ten hospitals that perform abortions were located in cities, towns, and villages with a population below 100,000. For all cities above that size, the majority of hospitals with the capacity did abortions in the United States, compared to two-thirds in Canada. Thus there was an urban bias to the availability of hospital-based abortion services in Canada despite its universal health-care system (McDaniel, 1985; Brodie, 1994).

In sum, despite structural differences in political regimes and health-care systems, the implementation of abortion policy has followed similar lines of development in both Canada and the United States. American states that liberalized or repealed their abortion laws before *Roe* continued, generally speaking, to support more access to abortion services. In Canada, similarly, the three most populous and urban provinces—Quebec, Ontario, and British Columbia—had complied more fully with the 1969 abortion reforms and represented the most liberal provinces in terms of access to abortion services (Brodie, 1994). In assessing policy developments after *Webster* and *Morgentaler*, the past was prologue; disparities in abortion services among the Canadian provinces and the American states continued along predictable lines. There has been a long-term decline in the number of hospitals with the capacity to perform abortions in Canada, and especially in the United States, and only recently have clinics begun to provide a significant percentage of abortions in Canada, now approximately one-third of the total. In the United States, abortion clinics accounted for the majority of those procedures as early as 1974. Thus, there appear to be parallel developments in the two countries in terms of federalism making a difference in how decisions are carried out. To date, the more decentralized federalism of Canada has not generated greater variations in abortion implementation than in the United States.

ABORTION POLICY: CONVERGENCE OR DIVERGENCE?

As many observers have noted, after the adoption of the Canadian Constitution Act of 1982, especially its provision for a Charter of Rights and Freedoms, the judiciary, and especially the Supreme Court of Canada, began to take a more active political role. Since 1988 abortion has been strongly, but not securely, situated in the Canadian judicial arena. In that sense Canada, like the United States, has moved toward judicializing its politics and at the same time has moved away from the dominance of a parliamentary system. The *Morgentaler* decision was a clear example of where the judiciary acted to change the outcome of legislative policy. The federal executive and legislative branches could have chosen to enact a new abortion law under the court guidelines, but such a new law, like several provincial regulations, would probably have been challenged in court.

Discussion of abortion policy in Canada and the United States invariably raises the question: Why was there no backlash in Canada? After the defeat of the abortion bill in 1991, there was a dearth of non-judicial federal political activity on the issue. Opinion polls indicate that although Canadians were somewhat more supportive of legal abortion than were residents of the United States, there were no vast differences in attitudes toward abortion between the two countries (Chandler, Cook, Jelen, and Wilcox, 1994: 137; Nevitte, Brandon, and Davis, 1993). Public opinion in both countries is relatively moderate, with a majority supporting abortion within certain limits. Each has sizable religious groups that might be expected to be less supportive of abortion: Catholics and Fundamentalist Protestants. Nevitte, Brandon, and Davis (1993) have found that, although Canadians grew more tolerant of abortion over the decade of the 1980s than Americans, social group opinions in the two countries were similar. Religiosity, as measured by church attendance, was the single best indicator of anti-abortion attitudes rather than specific denominational affiliations, a finding confirmed by Chandler, Cook, Jelen, and Wilcox (1994). Since Canadians were somewhat less religious than citizens of the United States, the differences in public opinion might be largely attributable to social structure.

Despite these similarities in attitudes, however, there was a backlash in the United States that impelled the federal executive and legislature to act. Strongly mobilized interest groups exist on both sides of the abortion issue in Canada, as in the United States, but the debate in Canada has been more restrained. The degree of violence and intimidation against abortion providers has been much lower in Canada. Incidents such as the arson of the Morgentaler clinic in Toronto in 1992 and the shooting of a physician in British Columbia in 1994 are rare, compared to such episodes in the United States. Recently, however, the government of British Columbia felt compelled to enact a "clinic access" law, similar to those in the United States. In contrast, in the United States abortion has been an issue in electoral and party politics. Both pro-choice and pro-life groups have attempted to exercise influence by mobilizing financial and voting resources for and against appropriate candidates, ranging from the president to local officials. Evidence has suggested that abortion is becoming a more critical factor affecting the voting behavior of some women (Wattier, Daynes, and Tatalovich, 1996). The Republican Party, which solicited support from the anti-abortion movement, now finds that the issue permeates various facets of public policy, ranging from welfare reform to reducing government regulations. Some observers have gone so far as to predict that abortion could be the issue that fractures the party coalition of free-market suburbanites and religious conservatives.

One could hardly imagine such a scenario in Canada, where abortion has been of minimal importance in election campaigns. In the 1988 election an anti-abortion group, Campaign Life, supported identifiable pro-life candidates of any political party, but this had no discernible effect on the outcome (Kay, Lambert, Brown, and Curtis, 1989). The lack of an abortion law was not an issue in the 1993 Canadian parliamentary election campaign. Although the Canadian party system was transformed by the election of 1993, which featured the meteoric rise of the Reform Party and the Bloc Quebecois and the precipitous decline of the Progressive Conservatives and the New Democrats, abortion played no discernible role in this shake-up.

What accounts for this difference between the two countries? Stewart (1993) has argued that the almost fetishistic embrace of party discipline in Canada has meant that individual federal legislators cannot respond to interest-group demands. In the case of abortion, even allowing a limited number of free votes has not meant that the parties gave up their capacity to structure debate and outcomes on the issue entirely (Tatalovich, Overby, and Studlar, 1993). Then too, the parties themselves have not been firmly wedded to a particular position on abortion. Aside from the New Democrats, no Canadian party took a firm stand on abortion. As Bashevkin (1994) pointed out, feminist groups fared relatively well on policy in Canada under a Conservative government in the 1980s and 1990s compared with their sisters in Britain and the United States. One reason may have been that, unlike the United States, no Canadian party was strongly oriented toward conservative positions on social and moral issues. Even the most right-wing party, Reform, limited its policy on abortion to advocating that its candidates should consult with their constituencies and attempt to develop a consensus on the issue. Furthermore, Canadian interest groups have been left with little room to maneuver at election time because parties stand on a unified platform, which has not included abortion. Additionally, the campaign finance laws in Canada have limited the ability of interest groups to influence election outcomes. Even targeting certain races, as Campaign Life did in 1988, does not guarantee success because many constituencies in Canada are multi-party competitive, not two-party competitive. Since the government controls the legislative agenda, abortion, which has been perceived as a divisive issue, has rarely been the subject of a parliamentary debate. Interest groups then have turned to lobbying provincial governments and the judiciary.

In the United States, the absence of party discipline in Congress and campaign financing has given interest groups a wider scope for their activities. Unlike Canada, the issue of abortion has shown no sign of receding in importance in the political arena or being defined once again as a health-care issue. On the contrary, abortion makes other issues, such as health-care reform, welfare reform, and regulatory reform, more difficult to deal with because it injects moral concerns into the discussion. For instance, Tatalovich and Daynes (1994) found that, in both the judiciary and legislative branches, women's rights groups have increased as lobbyists in the pro-choice coalition since the 1970s, while health-care providers have decreased (Tatalovich and Daynes, 1994).

In some respects though, there has been an institutional and policy convergence on abortion in the two countries over the years. There were similarities in implementation even before the judicial decisions in each country in the late 1980s gave sub-national levels of government the opportunity to write their own regulations. As Brodie (1994) has pointed out, abortion implementation has been decentralized in both countries, and this has limited the formally declared policy. At the same time, there are differences. Although a principal formulator of policy in both countries, the judiciary's role in Canada is *de facto* rather than *de jure*. Canadian federal policy on abortion is now, if anything, less restrictive than in the United States, whose policies had previously been seen as perhaps the least restrictive in Western Europe and North America (Lovenduski and Outshoorn, 1986; Glendon, 1987). Also, the abortion controversy in Canada has remained less moralistic and confrontational because it retained elements of the original impetus for reform legislation: health care rather than entrenched "rights," whether they are those of women or of the fetus.

Federalism has affected policymaking and implementation in the two countries. National government structures have, too, although here the consequences are ironic. In the Canadian parliamentary system, the executive and legislature have great power to change abortion policy, but they have declined to use it. Apart from cases brought before the court, abortion has dropped off the formal policy agenda since 1991. In the United States, the Supreme Court established abortion as a constitutional right to privacy in the *Roe v. Wade*, a decision that subsequent, more conservative Courts have failed to overturn. Perhaps this has left the federal executive and legislature with fewer policy options. Yet abortion has become a more prominent part of the formal political agenda in the 1990s as pro-choice and anti-abortion groups attempt to mould secondary decisions to their advantage.

In the wake of the *Morgentaler* decision, formal abortion policy in the two countries has not differed appreciably, except in the matter of public funding for the procedure. Implementation has been similar and, with rise of clinics in Canada, may be expected to become more so. What has differed most in the two countries has been the politics of abortion. In the United States it is moralistic, confrontational, partisan, and electorally divisive. This is much less the case in Canada.

Abortion has become a potent symbol for groups in the United States, but only a weak one in Canada. These differences, we suggest, may be attributed to the existence of strongly disciplined political parties in Canada, which operate within the institutional framework of a parliamentary system. In such a setting, parties can contain an issue that they see as peripheral to their interests in gaining and successfully holding power.[4] However, if the Canadian judiciary were ever to assume the role played by United States Supreme Court and attempt to impose a sweeping policy which frustrated the will of the legislature, then the potential for rancorous, moralistic conflict might appear in Canada as well.

NOTES

1. At issue in the *Webster* case was a Missouri statute that imposed various restrictions on the right to abortion. After declaring in a preamble that the "life of each human being begins at conception" and that "unborn children have protected interests in life, health and well-being," the law proceeded to (1) require that all abortions from sixteen weeks be performed in a hospital, (2) require physicians to determine "if the unborn child is viable" by conducting

examinations and tests for gestational age, weight and lung maturity, and (3) prohibit public funding, the use of public facilities, or any counseling by public employees for abortion, unless where necessary to save the life of the mother.

2. In the British Parliament, a free vote means that members of Parliament are not directed on how to vote by their party whips, but may instead vote on the basis of their own conscience.

3. Ironically, Morgentaler had lost another appeal of an abortion conviction before the Supreme Court in 1976. At that time, before passage of the Canadian Charter of Rights, the Court had refused to overturn the 1969 law (Mezey, 1983).

4. Similar observations have been made in comparing the abortion controversy in Britain and the United States (Soper, 1994).

REFERENCES

Bashevkin, Sylvia. 1994. "Confronting Neo-Conservatism: Anglo-American Women's Movements under Thatcher, Reagan and Mulroney." *International Political Science Review* 15: 275–96.

Brodie, Janine. 1994. "Health versus Rights: Comparative Perspectives on Abortion Policy in Canada and the United States." In Gita Sen and Rachel Snow, eds., *Reproductive Options in the 1990s*. Cambridge, MA: Harvard School of Public Health.

Brodie, Janine, Shelley A.M. Gavigan, and Jane Jenson. 1992. *The Politics of Abortion*. Toronto: Oxford University Press.

Chandler, Marthe A., Elizabeth Adell Cook, Ted G. Jelen, and Clyde Wilcox. 1994. "Abortion in the United States and Canada: A Comparative Study of Public Opinion." In Ted G. Jelen and Marthe A. Chandler, eds. *Abortion Politics in the United States and Canada*. Westport, CT: Praeger.

Committee on the Operation of the Abortion Law. 1977. *Report of the Committee on the Operation of the Abortion Law*. Ottawa, Canada: Ministry of Supply and Services Canada, National Library of Canada, Ottawa.

Craig, Barbara Hinkson, and David M. O'Brien. 1993. *Abortion and American Politics*. Chatham, NJ: Chatham House.

de Valk, Alphonse. 1974. *Morality and Law in Canadian Politics: The Abortion Controversy*. Montreal: Palm Publishers.

Doctors for Repeal of the Abortion Law. 1975. *Survey of Hospital Abortion Committees in Canada*. Ottawa, Canada: Library of Parliament.

Dunsmuir, Mollie. 1991. "Abortion: Constitutional and Legal Developments." Library of Parliament, Research Branch, Law and Government Division (Current Issue Review, 89-10E), revised 3 September 1991, Ottawa, Canada.

Gibbins, Roger. 1982. *Regional Politics in Canada and the United States*. Toronto: Butterworths.

Glendon, Mary Ann. 1987. *Abortion and Divorce in Western Law*. Cambridge, MA: Harvard University Press.

Glendon, Mary Ann. 1989. "A Beau Mentir Qui Vient de Loin: The 1988 Canadian Abortion Decision in Comparative Perspective." *Northwestern University Law Review* 83: 569–91.

Halva-Neubauer, Glen. 1993. "The States After *Roe*: No 'Paper Tigers.'" In Malcolm L. Goggin, ed., *Understanding the New Politics of Abortion*. Newbury Park, CA: Sage.

Henshaw, Stanley K., and Jennifer Van Vort. 1994. "Abortion Services in the United States, 1991 and 1992." *Family Planning Perspectives* 26: 100–106, 112.

Jelen, Ted G., and Marthe A. Chandler, eds. 1994. *Abortion Politics in the United States and Canada: Studies in Public Opinion*. Westport, CT: Praeger.

Kay, Barry J., Ronald D. Lambert, Steven D. Brown, and James E. Curtis. 1989. "Single-Issue Interest Groups and the Canadian Electorate: The Case of Abortion in 1988." Paper presented at Canadian Political Science Association, Quebec City.

Lovenduski, Joni, and Joyce Outshoorn, eds. 1986. *The New Politics of Abortion.* London: Sage.

McDaniel, Susan A. 1985. "Implementation of Abortion Policy in Canada as a Women's Issue." *Atlantis* 10: 74-91.

Meier, Kenneth J., and Deborah R. McFarlane. 1993. "Abortion Politics and Abortion Funding Policy." In Malcolm L. Goggin, ed., *Understanding the New Politics of Abortion.* Newbury Park, CA: Sage.

Mezey, Susan Gluck. 1983. "Civil Law and Common Law Traditions: Judicial Review and Legislative Supremacy in West Germany and Canada." *International and Comparative Law Quarterly* 32: 689-707.

Mooney, Christopher Z., and Mei-Hsien Lee. 1995. "Legislating Morality in the American States: The Case of Pre-Roe Abortion Regulation Reform." *American Journal of Political Science* 39: 599-627.

Morton, F. L. 1992. *Morgentaler v. Borowski: Abortion, The Charter, and the Courts.* Toronto: McClelland and Stewart.

Nevitte, Neil, William P. Brandon and Lori Davis. 1993. "The American Abortion Controversy: Lessons from Cross-National Evidence." *Politics and the Life Sciences* 12: 19-30.

Pal, Leslie A. 1991. "How Ottawa Dithers: The Conservatives and Abortion Policy." In Frances Abele, ed., *How Ottawa Spends 1991-92.* Ottawa: Carleton University Press.

Riker, William H. 1964. *Federalism: Origin, Operation, Significance.* Boston: Little Brown and Company.

Schwartz, Mildred. 1981. "Politics and Moral Causes in Canada and the United States." *Comparative Social Research* 4: 65-90.

Segers, Mary C., and Timothy A. Byrnes. 1995. *Abortion Politics in American States.* Armonk, NY: M.E. Sharpe.

Soper, J. Christopher. 1994. "Political Structures and Interest Group Activism: A Comparison of the British and American Pro-Life Movements." *Social Science Journal* 31: 319-34.

Statistics Canada. *Therapeutic Abortions.* 1992, p. 15, Table 10.

Stewart, Ian. 1993. "No Quick Fixes: The Canadian Central Government and the Problems of Representation." In David M. Olson and C.E.S. Franks, eds., *Representation and Policy Formation in Federal Systems.* Berkeley, CA: Institute of Governmental Studies.

Tatalovich, Raymond. 1988. "Prochoice versus Prolife." In Raymond Tatalovich and Byron W. Daynes, eds., *Social Regulatory Policy: Moral Controversies in American Politics.* Boulder, CO: Westview Press.

Tatalovich, Raymond, and Byron W. Daynes. 1981. *The Politics of Abortion.* New York: Praeger.

Tatalovich, Raymond, and Byron W. Daynes. 1989. "The Geographical Distribution of U.S. Hospitals with Abortion Facilities." *Family Planning Perspectives* 21: 81-84.

Tatalovich, Raymond, and Byron W. Daynes. 1993. "The Lowi Paradigm, Moral Conflict, and Coalition-Building: Pro-Choice versus Pro-Life." *Women and Politics* 13: 39-66.

Tatalovich, Raymond, L. Marvin Overby, and Donley T. Studlar. 1993. "Patterns of Abortion Voting in the Canadian House of Commons." Paper presented to Canadian Political Science Association, Ottawa.

Tatalovich, Raymond, and Donley T. Studlar. 1995. "Abortion Policy Implementation in Canada and the United States." *American Review of Canadian Studies* 25: (forthcoming).

Wattier, Mark, Byron W. Daynes, and Raymond Tatalovich. 1996. "Abortion Attitudes, Gender and Candidate Choice in Presidential Elections: 1972 to 1992." *Women and Politics* 16: (forthcoming).

Weaver, R. Kent, ed. 1992. *The Collapse of Canada?* Washington: Brookings Institution.

CHAPTER 5

ABORTION POLICY TRIADS AND WOMEN'S RIGHTS IN RUSSIA, THE UNITED STATES, AND FRANCE

DOROTHY McBRIDE STETSON

Abortion is legalized in many countries today. Does this mean that women have achieved reproductive rights? If by reproductive rights we mean the access of women to services that will help them terminate their pregnancies safely then we must look beyond formal legalization to the way policies affect women's access to abortion services. This chapter examines the question of women's reproductive rights in Russia, the United States, and France. Although these countries have different political histories and cultures they have very similar abortion laws: abortion is legal in the first trimester of pregnancy without condition.[1] In France and Russia the laws set up universal administrative hurdles for women seeking abortion, and in the United States such administrative hurdles may be enacted by various states (see *Planned Parenthood v. Casey* (112 S.Ct. 2791 [1992]).

Ever since the professionalization of health care over a century ago, the interests of two groups are present in every abortion debate: doctors who have the expertise to perform safe abortions and women who seek abortions. If there were no laws on abortion, physicians would have exclusive control of the resources for safe abortions and women would be at the mercy of physicians. By enacting laws regulating the circumstances under which physicians may perform abortion, governments may either retain physicians' monopoly or act to guarantee such resources to women. There is a third alternative: policymakers may limit the autonomy of both doctors and women to further other goals relating to pronatalism, religious beliefs, or economic issues. The particular pattern of resource distribution among government, physicians, and women is the *abortion policy triad.*

Abortion laws with apparently similar texts and provisions produce various outcomes for women's rights depending on the abortion policy triad, that is, how the government distributes the resources necessary for providing safe abortion services. The particular triad in turn depends on the way conflicts over the direction of policies are resolved. Policy debates over abortion involve a complex interplay of competing values and interests. Both physicians and women seeking abortions are likely to have representatives in the political debates that affect the enactment and administration of abortion laws. Advocates for women's reproductive rights, called feminists in this study, represent the interests of women seeking abortions. Medical associations express the interests of physicians. Policymakers in legislatures, courts, and bureaucracies may articulate other priorities that affect abortion services. The abortion triad, which determines the access of women to abortion services, is affected by the political interplay among physicians, feminists, and policymakers.

The goal of this chapter is to describe the abortion policy triads in Russia, the United States, and France in order to compare women's reproductive rights. Each country will be treated separately. For each, there will be a brief description of the abortion triad. This will be followed by a description of how the triad developed and the patterns of participation of medical associations and feminists and their interactions with policymakers. The chapter's conclusion compares women's reproductive rights, based on variations in the policy triads, in the three countries.

RUSSIA

The contemporary abortion policy in Russia dates from the legalization of abortion in 1955.2 From 1955 to 1991 under the command economy of the Soviet Communist regime, the law and administrative practice established an alliance between the state and the bureaucratized medical profession to control women's access to abortion. The policy worked to favor the power of individual doctors vis-à-vis women patients. Doctors were not, technically speaking, allowed to deny women abortions. But they were empowered to make all efforts to talk them out of it (Savage, 1988: 1065). Women had few safe alternatives to state-controlled abortion practice. When the Russian Federation became an independent state in 1991, the 1955 law remained on the books. Changes in the administration of medicine as a result of the economic transition have altered little in the way the physician-favored triad works with respect to Russian women's reproductive rights.

DEVELOPMENT OF THE ABORTION POLICY TRIAD

Before legalization in 1955, Soviet Russia had two different abortion laws, a 1920 law permitting abortion and a 1936 law prohibiting abortion. Despite these apparent flip-flops, policymakers never wavered in their official view that abortion was a social evil and that the primary duty of the socialist state must be to eradicate it. In Russia, before 1955, the state used the medical profession to achieve its own, largely pronatalist, goals, paying little heed to either physicians' interests or the needs of women for the procedure. Thus, rather than distributing resources, the state retained a monopoly on them.

For doctors and women, the difference between the more liberal 1920 law and the restrictive 1936 law depended on the political leaders' views of the demand for abortion and the condition of women's health. In enacting the 1920 law, policymakers recognized that many women confronted a social catastrophe. Driven by the dreadful conditions of war, famine, and social revolution, they sought abortions at any cost, "making them victims of greedy and often ignorant abortionists" (1920 Decree, Commissariats of Health and Justice, quoted in Goldman, 1993: 255). Giving doctors permission to perform abortions was a necessary health measure, while the state sought to remedy what policymakers saw as the causes of abortion: poverty, illness, large families, and poor housing.

During the 1920s, despite legalization, the state closely regulated women's access to abortion, which could only be performed in state hospitals by licensed doctors. To gain admission to a hospital, a woman had to apply to a local commission and set forth which particular state-acceptable social conditions had driven her to this act. The commissions had a list of priorities for approval: first preference went to single unemployed women with no jobs; second, to single women with at least one child and a job; and then married women with several children and no means of support. At the bottom of the list were married women with no children or one child. Meanwhile, the government pledged to fight against the abortion evil through information or, as the Communist Party called it, propaganda, about birth control in clinics, protection for mothers and infants, and the dangers of abortion to the health of women.

During Stalin's rule in the 1930s, the state officially declared that efforts to fight the circumstances that drove women to abortion had been successful, thus allowing the state, once again, to ban abortion for women's protection. The leaders also stated that the "woman question" had been solved (Buckley, 1989). With the 1936 decree "On the Prohibition of Abortions," the government asserted that abortion was harmful and would interfere with women's "great and responsible duty of giving birth and bringing up citizens" (Savage, 1988: 1048, n. 115). This was not an unconditional prohibition. Whereas under the 1920 law commissions allowed both social and medical conditions as justification for abortion, after 1936 they would permit abortion only for a limited list of medical and eugenic indications: saving the life of the mother; hereditary diseases; or diseases of the child. Policymakers declared that the goal of this law was to promote women's right to maternity in good conditions. To prove their good intentions, the decree outlawing abortions also contained provisions for expansion of support services for families such as child care, maternity homes, and enforcement of child support and alimony decrees.

In the period between 1920 and 1955, the Russian government kept a tight rein on the physicians' practice of and women's access to abortion services. Most observers of Russian laws in this period conclude that strong pronatalism was part of both the ideological direction and practical concerns of Lenin and Stalin (Buckley, 1989: 128–36; Savage, 1988: 1049–53). Social conditions following the Revolution and Civil War led to an increase in underground abortions that the government could not prevent but that greatly threatened the health of large numbers of potential mothers. The capacity of the state administration to prevent underground abortion had improved by the 1930s, enabling Stalin's government to take direct action to increase the birth rate by prohibiting most abortions.

In 1955, three years after Stalin's death, policymakers quietly repealed the 1936 law—so quietly, in fact, that many women did not even know that abortions were permitted once again. The official justification for liberalization repeated themes from both the 1920 and 1936 laws (Dyl'tsin, 1960). The Presidium of the Supreme Soviet explained that it was time to permit abortion again because of the rise in clandestine abortion and the consequent threat to women's health. (These were the same motives as in 1920.) Leaders asserted that because the state had reached its goal of providing adequate services for maternal-infant protection, and because women's consciousness and cultural development was at a sufficiently high level, it was safe to allow the procedure. Both doctors and women could be trusted not to abuse the law (identical issues as in 1936—but used then to criminalize abortion!). The Presidium decree went on to list one new motive for the law: "In order to give women the opportunity to decide for themselves the question of motherhood" (Savage, 1988: 1053, n. 135).

Under the 1955 law, any abortion performed outside a government hospital or clinic was illegal (Field, 1956). The state further ordered doctors and other health professionals to dissuade women from having abortions by pointing out the dangers to health and fertility. Policymakers promised to fight against the need for abortion by providing contraceptive information and services, along with health education. These pledges were not kept. Despite continued rhetoric from all sides about birth control, the vast majority of Russian women still have to rely on withdrawal and abortion for family planning (Allenova, 1990; Ramennick, 1991).

Market reforms have brought contraceptives and private clinics to Russia. But costs and ignorance about new methods mean that most women still rely on state hospitals and clinics or unlicensed abortionists and still use abortion as the chief method of birth control. The dislocations of economic and political transition have undercut all areas of public health, and the health-care system is disintegrating. Birth rates have dropped dramatically, rekindling pronatalist fears. Since the 1950s, the government has given physicians, through the public-health bureaucracy, the control of access to abortion services for most women. This physician-favored abortion triad continues to characterize post-Soviet Russian abortion policy.

POLITICS OF ABORTION POLICY: PHYSICIANS

Before the Revolution, leaders of the medical profession had called for a liberalization of the repressive laws of the tsars, a position related to their overall anti-tsarist political stance (Engelstein, 1991). After legalization in 1920, doctors began to lose their autonomy from the state, yet continued, until the 1930s, to discuss the desirability of the 1920 law. Evidence that the medical profession took an interest in abortion debates is found in public-health publications and journals of obstetrics and gynecology (Schlesinger, 1949). As consolidation of Communist rule incorporated all medical practice into the centralized state public-health bureaucracy, many practitioners began to reinforce the official view that improving the social conditions women endured was the key to combating abortion. They did not give up on the medical aspects of the issue, however, and vividly pointed out the danger of even hospital abortions to the "female organism." "The operation is performed in the dark and with instruments which, so far as their effect on so tender an organ as the womb is concerned remind one of a crowbar" (Malinovsky, reprinted in Schlesinger, 1949: 265).

Before the Revolution, many doctors, especially women, had argued for an alliance between doctors and women against state repression of a procedure that closely affected them both. However, after the Revolution, doctors were likely to adhere to official interpretations with respect to what sort of law would be best for women. In the 1920s, these arguments reflected the Leninist theory that because women would be equal participants in all aspects of society, they should not be helpless before their function as mothers, but retain some choice. By the 1930s, however, the idea of what was good for women had shifted to emphasize the maternal function exclusively, so much so, that defenders of the 1936 abortion restriction could claim it was a victory for women's rights under socialism. "The superior right enjoyed by Soviet women was the right to maternity in good conditions" (Buckley, 1989: 131).

In the 1950s, the process of establishing a policy of legalized abortion in Soviet Russia involved a reassignment of resources from the pronatalist state monopoly to the medical profession in the health-care institutions. The 1955 law gave doctors control over the granting of abortion services to women. The Russian medical profession's role in the politics of legal abortion arises from its overall organization and position in the political system. Until perestroika, the practice of medicine was a part of the bureaucracy of the centralized command economy. The strict stratification of health care and the medical profession meant that doctors were accustomed to carrying out the orders of the central administration. Yet, at the same time, they wielded nearly total authority over their patients. "In the Soviet scheme, the customer or patient is rarely right" (Field, 1988: 190).

This position made physicians the official experts on the issue. Doctors are most likely to discuss the abortion issue in the Russian journals and even newspapers today, as in the past (Popov, 1991). Their concern is with the continued high incidence of abortion, both legal (in hospitals and clinics) and illegal (outside hospitals and clinics). Research on motives for abortions has produced an appreciation for the complexity of the abortion decision (Popov, 1982; Krasnenkov, 1991). Doctors still refer to conventional social and economic conditions, but also recognize women's personal desires not to have a child, to complete their studies before starting a family, or their reluctance to give birth in "the absence of a husband." Nevertheless, many physicians prefer to focus on the immediate cause of unplanned pregnancies: lack of contraceptive information and services.

POLITICS OF ABORTION POLICY: FEMINISTS

Advocates for women seeking abortions participated in discussions of abortion law in the 1920s. But the voices of women and their advocacy organizations were rarely loud or in unison. Often, the perspective of women's rights was voiced by others, such as members of the medical profession. The issue had divided leaders of the pre-revolutionary women's movement, and many had agreed that with the proper social conditions women would not need abortions. They did not see access to the procedure as a fundamental or emancipatory right for women. After 1917, Zhenotdel, the Women's Section of the Communist Party, lobbied for a liberal law and won the right to appoint one member of the local abortion commissions. They reported that women were "thirsty" for information about contraception and abortion (Goldman, 1993: 259).

Before the final enactment of the 1936 law, the policymakers invited a public discussion of the draft. Among the various letters from this discussion that have been studied, there are only a few pleas from women to keep abortion legal (Goldman, 1991; Schlesinger, 1949: 251–79). These women tied the law to their own ability to finish their educations, find jobs, and locate housing before starting a family. Their voices lost out, however, to the emerging official view of women's rights and abortion: that women had achieved equality with men; that they would now have the right to have children without any worry about social and economic conditions; and that women needed the state's protection against the ravages of abortion on their "delicate organisms" and from being forced into abortion by men seeking to escape their parental responsibilities.

During the period between 1920 and 1955, despite the 1936 prohibition, women in substantial numbers terminated pregnancies through abortion. While the overall rate of abortion was steady, the ratio of illegal to legal abortions varied. Illegal abortions declined dramatically between 1920 and 1936, only to rise rapidly a few years after the 1936 prohibition. Doctors were in the best position to observe the effects of the pronatalist abortion policy as they witnessed the deaths and diseases from botched and incomplete abortions.

The *Soviet Medical Encyclopedia* reported in 1956 that it was women who had proposed legalization of abortion immediately after World War II ("Avort," 1956). In fact, the 1955 law did, in part, define legal abortion as a woman's right. However, evidence of the place of organized advocates for women's rights in the abortion debate remains sketchy. There were few official, let alone unofficial, women's advocacy organizations until the mid-1980s. In their comparative study of the United States and the Soviet Union, Ershova and Novikova gave the abortion issue a brief reference, emphasizing only the dangers of abortion and consequences for health and sterility, not the right of choice (1988). When the Soviet Women's Committee convened under Gorbachev's invitation in 1987, it ignored reproductive issues in favor of labor and family questions. Even the new informal women's groups have yet to place the issue on their agendas. Anastasia Posadskaya, head of the Russian Center for Gender Studies, has indicated that serious public discussion of any sexuality issue remains difficult (Molyneux, 1991). Throughout the period under study, Russian women have had more success in exerting power by the "abdication of reproductive and economic responsibilities" than by direct action (Sanjian, 1990: 630). Thus, their most effective part in abortion politics in Soviet Russia has been their demand for the procedure. This demand persists despite official efforts to persuade them otherwise and despite the well-documented degrading and often painful aspects of legal hospital abortions (Popov, 1991; Witt, 1989). The procedure promises to be less trying with the advent of "mini-abortions," as the vacuum aspiration method is called. Urban clinics now provide this method as a less painful alternative to hospital D & C's without anesthesia (Katkova and Koshovskaya, 1989). The problem of access to these expensive services continues the limitation on Russian women's reproductive rights.

THE UNITED STATES

In the United States, the framework of national policy on abortion is set by the Supreme Court's interpretation of the constitutional limits on states' powers to regulate it. *Roe v. Wade* (410 U.S. 113 [1973]) laid down the outlines for the policy; subsequent rulings have begun to fill in the design. This national policy framework distributes some resources to women and some to physicians. Within this distribution, individual states have the authority to tip the balance one way or another to advance pro-choice or pronatalist interests. The national abortion policy triad leaves the state governments, physicians, and women seeking abortion to find solutions, within the limits of the framework, to problems created by unwanted pregnancies. Within each state, the participants confront each other. In some states the government may use all of its constitutional powers to limit women's access to services. In others, the state may take a laissez faire approach, leaving the field to a struggle between pro-choice and pro-life interests over control of medical services.

DEVELOPMENT OF THE ABORTION POLICY TRIAD

The early laws in the United States, based on English common law, had divided pregnancy into "unquickened" and "quickened" periods, allowing abortion of an unquickened fetus. This placed the decision about abortion in the hands of the pregnant woman, because she alone could determine whether the fetus had reached the quickened state or not. In the latter half of the nineteenth century, after a successful campaign to combat rising rates of abortions, every state changed its criminal abortion law to prohibit all those that were not required for one medical reason—when pregnancy threatened the life of the mother. By permitting only such therapeutic abortions, states empowered licensed physicians to determine which conditions met the therapeutic requirements, thereby driving midwives out of the health-care business. In most states, the individual physician alone could make this determination. These laws allowed physicians to assess the rights of the embryo versus the rights of the woman carrying it. In practice it also permitted doctors to perform abortions for a variety of indications both physical and psychological (Luker, 1984: 35).

It wasn't until the 1970s that the Supreme Court stepped in to establish the framework for a national abortion policy. The issue had returned to the political agenda a decade earlier, through demands from both physicians and the women's rights movement (Lader, 1973; Imber, 1990; Sheeran, 1987). Campaigns for reform offered two models to the states: a proposal from the American Law Institute to expand the conditions of pregnancy under which doctors could perform abortions; and a proposal from feminists for a complete privatization through repeal of all criminal abortion laws. The first would have shifted some resources to women, while maintaining the physician-favored triad. The repeal option would have created conditions for a free market in abortion resources. Some feminist groups adopted the slogan "Free abortion on demand." These groups did not, however, propose a comprehensive policy package that would allocate public funds to provide abortion services.

By its ruling in *Roe v. Wade* in 1973, the Supreme Court began setting forth the outlines of a national abortion policy. In *Roe*, the Court defined abortion as a medical matter. It placed the decision of whether to perform an abortion in the realm of physicians' and patients' privacy, greatly expanding the prerogative of physicians to respond to women's requests (Asaro, 1983). Since *Roe*, private doctors have been free of state interference in performing abortions in the first trimester; they have been equally free not to perform them.

Soon after *Roe v. Wade*, however, the Supreme Court moved away from the official definition of abortion as a medical matter. In the Medicaid cases in the mid-seventies, the court upheld the right of states and Congress to refuse to pay for abortions because they were not "medically necessary."[3] Had these rulings gone the other way, they would have laid the foundation for a women-favored abortion policy triad. As it turned out, the effect was to relieve states and the federal government of the responsibility to provide abortion services for women. Recently, in *Webster v. Reproductive Health Services* (492 U.S. 490 [1989]) and *Planned Parenthood v. Casey*, the Court (112 S.Ct. 2791 [1992]) retreated further; in the *Casey* decision, doctors are not mentioned at all. Instead, the states may now serve other goals, such as pronatalism, in setting up administrative barriers for women and doctors to overcome.[4] However, the Court's opinion in *Casey* made the strongest statement to date that deciding to terminate a pregnancy through abortion is a woman's right and that the Constitution thus limits states from placing "undue burdens" in her path to realize this right. Thus, the national framework requires states to distribute some resources between doctors and women: they must not prohibit abortion, but they can restrict access to services. Within this national policy triad, states are now free to establish mini-policy triads that further their own pronatalist interests, women seeking abortions, or enhance doctors prerogatives.[5]

POLITICS OF ABORTION POLICY: PHYSICIANS

Whenever the abortion issue has been on the public agenda, the representatives of the medical profession have been active participants in the debate (Mohr, 1978; Smith-Rosenberg, 1985; Imber, 1990). In the mid-1800s, progress in knowledge about the gestation of the human fetus combined with firm convictions of morality and social order relating to childbirth and family fertility drove elite doctors to enlist the government to stop the increases in abortions. They argued that women were ignorant of the fact that in aborting an unquickened fetus they were committing the same moral crime as if they had killed their newborn infant. They held that the fetus was a "living being" from the moment of conception (Mohr, 1978: 157).

Beginning in 1857, the American Medical Association (AMA) passed a series of resolutions condemning abortion and calling for its criminalization. In presenting themselves as champions of human life, doctors used the abortion issue to strengthen their claim to self-regulation and autonomy (Luker, 1984: 11–39). In 1871 the AMA declared that it was the duty of every physician to "resort to every honorable and legal means to rid society of this practice" (quoted in Sheeran, 1987: 74). They also expressed some concern about the dangers of illegal abortion to women's health, although this was not the major theme at medical association meetings. The campaign succeeded, according to Smith-Rosenberg, because "physicians convinced the male bourgeois public and male politicians that abortion constituted a threat to the social order and male authority" (1985: 235). Laws that made abortion a criminal act were a victory for the AMA.

When abortion reform once again became a subject of national debate in the 1960s, physicians joined the calls for reform that led to *Roe v. Wade* (Imber, 1990: 30–31). At first, they did not seek total discretion over abortion decisions. Instead they wanted laws that expanded the list of conditions under which therapeutic abortions could be performed. In the 1860s, the dominant concern in ordering a therapeutic abortion had been threats to the life of the mother. By the 1960s, due to progress in treatment, pregnancy rarely threatened maternal life. Doctors had begun to look more carefully at the effect of pregnancy on the mental and emotional health of the woman, especially when the pregnancy was the result of incest or rape. In addition, doctors became interested in the health of the child, specifically the quality of its life. Some doctors were using the relative privacy under the old laws to perform abortions on the basis of fetal deformity caused by rubella and genetic factors. The publicity surrounding the Sherry Finkbine case exposed such practices, which, strictly speaking, criminalized abortion laws did not permit.

Doctors were driven to seek legal support to expand the area of discretion. In 1967, a new AMA resolution urged permitting legal abortion when pregnancy would result in the physical or mental deformity of the child, when pregnancy was the result of rape or incest, or when pregnancy "constitutes a threat to the mental or physical health of the patient" (Sheeran, 1990: 74). Then in 1970, the AMA House of Delegates dropped support for such conditional legalization, affirming that abortion was a medical procedure that should be determined by physicians according to the "merits of each individual case," implying that there should be no governmental involvement as long as the abortion was performed by a "duly licensed physician and surgeon in an accredited hospital only after consultation with two other physicians." They affirmed that "no physician or other professional personnel shall be compelled to perform any act which violates his good medical judgment . . . [or] . . . is violative of personally held moral principles" (AMA,1970: 359).

    Roe v. Wade seemed to grant physicians the full discretion over the abortion decision in the first and second trimester. Since then the medical profession has had little to say, formally, on the subject of abortion.[6] Rather, doctors have acted individually and through their hospitals and health organizations to move abortions from mainstream obstetrics and gynecology to specialized clinics.[7] They have left the abortion debate to women's rights organizations and religious anti-abortion activists. The latter, perhaps taking a page from the history of the medical profession, now seeks to enlist the state in empowering them to control access to safe abortion.

POLITICS OF ABORTION POLICY: FEMINISTS

For contemporary United States feminists, the abortion issue has been central to the campaign for women's rights. This situation is quite different from the way their forebears related to nineteenth-century abortion politics. Then, women's rights advocates had little interest in or were opposed to legalization of abortion (Petchesky, 1990). In general, women's movement leaders supported the AMA's campaign to criminalize the procedure. Some, especially those allied with the social purity movement, saw abortion as part of the overall exploitation of women by uncontrolled male lust (Gordon, 1976; Pivar, 1973; Powell, 1976). Male sexuality was blamed for rape, prostitution, and for driving desperate women to abortion. Later, birth-control advocates like Margaret Sanger claimed strong opposition to the practice of abortion in order to gain support of the medical profession for contraceptive information and services. Unorganized women, on the other hand, continued to defy the law and seek abortions through illegal means. By their actions, they contributed to the debate, showing that the demand for abortion persisted, regardless of formal laws. Many doctors learned firsthand the place of abortion in women's lives by dealing with the effects of botched illegal abortions.

    After 1960, women's rights advocates sought control of the abortion issue, both formally and informally. The ideology of radical feminism—that women's liberation required control of sexuality and reproduction—provided a foundation for a campaign to repeal the laws. When feminists joined the twentieth-century abortion debate, the reform movement was already moving toward an expansion of the conditions for abortion without disturbing the control by physicians or the medicalization of abortion. The feminist perspective changed the debate and directly challenged doctors' control of the abortion. By focusing on a woman's right to choose to terminate an unwanted pregnancy, the advocates revealed that the demand for abortion would be little satisfied by therapeutic abortions. Health collectives set up networks of alternate abortion services that clearly showed the futility of trying to enforce restrictive laws. Instead, they demanded repeal of the law; some activists sought to give health workers other than licensed physicians the right to do the procedure. Feminists succeeded in changing the terms of the reform debate away from expansion of existing laws toward a decriminalization and overall repeal.

Because, since *Roe v. Wade*, the government has refused to assign abortion resources to either doctors or women, feminists have been locked in a struggle with anti-abortion forces over access to safe affordable abortion services. Each group has sought to win over government and medical resources to promote their goals. The effect has been that while abortion remains legal within the Supreme Court national guidelines, there can be a severe limitation of facilities for performing safe abortions. From 1981 to 1992, the anti-abortion point of view dominated federal action. Even when that power limited doctors' professional rights, as in *Rust v. Sullivan* (111 S.Ct. 1759 [1991]), the medical profession failed to respond in an organized way. Further, "abortion remains stigmatized in private medical practice largely because of lingering public perceptions that those who perform them have been or will be discredited among their professional peers" (Imber, 1990: 32). Abortions sought for personal reasons are handed over to clinics and considered dirty work; only those performed for serious medical or eugenic reasons are considered integral to medical practice. The main abortion debate is now a contest between women's rights advocates and family planners on the one hand and religious fundamentalists on the other to win state resources to serve their goals.

FRANCE

The abortion policy triad in France distributes resources in favor of women seeking safe procedures. At the time of initial legalization in 1975, however, such a pattern was not at all in evidence. The 1975 law was provisional, to be reviewed by Parliament after 5 years. The formal version of the law framed abortion as a medical act, explicitly for women in "distress" from pregnancy. To answer conservative critics, the state erected several administrative hurdles that women and their doctors had to cross before the procedure could be performed. The government has cautioned that abortion should not be considered an ordinary means of family planning.

Subsequent policy developments reveal the shape of a women-favored abortion policy triad. The concept of "distress" was initially seen by feminists as a limit to women's rights. On the contrary, it has turned out that, by using the concept of distress that refers to the woman's relation to her pregnancy rather than conditions of health or fetal deformity, the state placed the decision about abortion squarely in the hands of women. Whereas medical conditions must be certified by physicians, only women can determine if their pregnancies have produced the condition of distress. Further, in 1979, when Parliament made legal abortion permanent, government ministers emphasized strongly that access to safe abortion was essential to women's rights. Since 1979, successive governments of both right and left have taken action to shift the balance of resources to empower women to obtain abortions. The government has provided services for abortion and contraception, extended the national health insurance to cover the costs of abortion, and used state power to ensure that the new abortion pill, RU 486, which provides an alternative to surgical abortion for women in the earliest stages of pregnancy, remain available to French women despite pro-life opposition (Mossuz-Lavau, 1986; Beaulieu, 1990). A French sociologist described the relationship between the state, physicians, and women as follows: with the role that the legislator entrusts to him or her, "the doctor becomes the privileged agency for framing the power that women have today to decide whether or not to give birth" (Ferrand-Picard 1982: 395).

DEVELOPMENT OF THE ABORTION POLICY TRIAD

The state now takes an active role in securing women's rights to safe abortions. At one time, however, it was equally active in promoting pronatalist interests. When abortion was criminalized by the Napoleonic Code in 1810, the government was very clear about its purpose: childbearing was a duty to the state. By 1920, what had been a general pronatalist motive became a dramatic plan for repopulation. Laws in 1920 and 1923 outlawing abortion, contraception, and all information about either were consciously designed to prevent French women from having the means to practice birth control. Although these laws reduced severe penalties for abortion in the hopes of achieving a more effective and enforceable law, family limitation remained a crime against the national interest. Under the Vichy regime (1940–45), the government reclassified illegal abortion into a major crime warranting, in one case, the death penalty (Dhavernas, 1978).

Despite these draconian measures, women continued to seek abortions. The more affluent traveled abroad; the poor visited the *faiseuses d'anges* (literally, angel makers, the equivalent of "back-alley" abortionists). The rates of illegal abortion soared in the 1950s and 1960s. Widespread publicity about the ineffectiveness of the 1920–23 laws in preventing abortions or in increasing the birth rate brought the issue, long ignored, to the public agenda. An active family-planning movement proposed bills for conditional abortion. A strong feminist campaign demanded that the government guarantee free safe abortion as a woman's basic right.

Initially, policymakers agreed to permit abortion in a limited way, intending the procedure to be used only in extraordinary circumstances. To this end, the state sought to empower doctors to take charge of the abortion issue, but they refused to be recruited for such a purpose. The 1975 Loi Veil, named for its chief sponsor, Minister of Health Simone Veil, included a number of measures intended to dissuade women from terminating their pregnancies: requirements that doctors inform patients of the risk of abortion and that patients submit to counseling, followed by a seven-day waiting period. These administrative hurdles were the product of a political compromise in the center-right coalition of President Valery Giscard. Although these remain in the law, subsequent actions under the fourteen-year presidency of François Mitterrand—the result of continued pressure from abortion-rights activists— have shifted the balance of resources in the triad to favor women.

POLITICS OF ABORTION POLICY: PHYSICIANS

Some physicians have been interested in the abortion issue, but on the whole the profession has never played an active part in the debates relating to abortion-law reform. In the early 1900s, the medical profession was certainly in a position to restrain pronatalist zealots, who vowed to use state resources to force women to bear children. The medical profession had prestige, close ties with the republican elite, and a monopoly over medical and health practice (Nye, 1984: 39–48; Willsford, 1991: 84–117). The prevailing ideology of *la médecine libérale* stressed the autonomy of physicians from control by the state. A variety of local groups and individuals had taken up some issues relating to birth control. In the late nineteenth century, some health officials made public warnings about the effect of back-alley abortions on maternal health and fertility. Others supported the neo-Malthusian efforts to spread birth control information. No national professional associations to transmit these views were formed, however, until 1928. The elite of the field, who were based in Paris and thus in a position to influence the national policy agenda, supported the pronatalist motives of republican politicians and made few efforts to oppose the official ban on abortion.

When abortion reform came back to the national agenda in the 1960s, doctors were again divided on the issue (Berger, 1975). The Ordre des Médecins, a small conservative organization, favored abortion only for limited therapeutic conditions, such as fetal deformity or a threat to maternal health. The two national professional associations, La Confédération des Syndicats Médicaux Français and La Fédération des Médecins de France, generally favored liberalization of the law, but opposed abortion solely on the demand of women. At the same time, some physicians openly defied the old law and their professional organizations and performed illegal abortions to force liberalization.

Proposals to make abortion a medical matter and to give full discretion to doctors met with firm opposition. The spokespersons for the major medical organizations opposed giving the responsibility to doctors to determine whether a patient had the grounds for an abortion. They preferred strict guidelines for when abortions would be permitted. Finally, in 1975, when faced with a law that addressed a woman's "distress" in pregnancy, they demanded a conscience clause: If the state insisted that only a woman could determine whether she was in distress, then a doctor should not be forced to perform an abortion for her if he or she disagreed.[8] Administrative hurdles in the French abortion law also reflect the compromise between the state and conservative leaders of the medical profession (Ladrière, 1982). As a result, in the first years after legalization, few hospitals offered services to women. To overcome the medical profession's reluctance to respond to women's demands for abortion, the Ministry of Woman's Rights took direct action in the 1980s to increase the number of establishments offering abortion services (Stetson, 1987: 67–74). As a result, the French state has used its resources to engage the often reluctant medical establishment in providing services sought by women.

POLITICS OF ABORTION POLICY: FEMINISTS

Feminists deserve most of the credit for the shift in the abortion policy triad away from state pronatalist goals in favor of women. In this, they made up for the ineffectiveness of their predecessors in the early 1900s. Then, activists for improving the status of women were divided over abortion, as were the physicians. Mainstream bourgeois feminists tended to avoid issues of birth control and abortion. However, individual feminist writers and activists linked women's rights to *la libre maternité* (Movement français pour le planning familial; Pelletier, 1982). Madeleine Pelletier, a physician and feminist, went from writing about the need for legal and safe abortion to openly defying the law and performing the procedure. Further, although the state officially used the abortion law to achieve ambitious pronatalist goals, the laws had scant effect on birth rates and did little to dissuade women from seeking abortions. Efforts to control doctors and women failed as individuals in both groups rebelled against centrist control—doctors continued to perform illegal abortions for a fee and women performed abortions on themselves in even larger numbers (Halimi, 1973). It was the embarrassment over the inability of the state to enforce its own laws against contraception and abortion that brought the government to introduce reforms in the 1960s.

The feminist role in abortion politics has been dramatically different since the late 1960s. Feminists have been united, vigilant, and active in abortion politics. The campaign to legalize abortion was the first successful political activity of the contemporary feminist movement. Tactics varied, from the radical to the moderate, but feminists remained determined to gain access to abortion with the state's assistance. The feminist abortion reform campaign emphasized women's "Right to decide *for themselves* whether to have children" (Jenson, 1982: 82). This way of framing the issue became part of official rhetoric for the *Loi Veil* and again in 1979 when Parliament made it permanent.

From 1981 to 1986, feminists were most effective working within the state ministerial system, led by Yvette Roudy, the Minister of Woman's Rights. The activist Ministry of Woman's Rights strengthened the state's commitment to women by convincing the government to include abortions under the public health insurance system. It also took action to increase the number of hospitals that would perform abortions. However, Roudy's efforts to gain financial support for abortion were stymied until mass action by feminists in street demonstrations broke a deadlock. Many advocates of women's rights remain critical of the persistence of administrative hurdles. However, in comparison with the Russia and the United States, French women have the most state-supported autonomy in exercising their reproductive rights.

CONCLUSION

There is no guarantee that legalized abortion will further women's reproductive rights. This review of the abortion policy triads in Russia, the United States, and France shows that, although the formal aspects of legalized abortion are similar, the particular pattern of distribution of state resources to physicians and women seeking abortions diverge. The result is that women's reproductive rights vary across the three systems. In Russia during the period since legalization in 1955, policymakers, continuing to profess pronatalist goals, have assigned the control of resources to physicians. Until perestroika, this policy meant that state-employed physicians of the enormous health-care bureaucracy determined which women would get abortions and under what conditions. In establishing a physician-favored triad, the government had made a shift from the Stalinist period, when the state closely regulated doctors to limit access to abortion and thus to further its pronatalist goals.

In the United States, the Supreme Court has established a framework for a laissez faire abortion policy triad. The resources for safe abortion are a subject of continuing conflict among doctors, feminists, and pronatalist activists. The result is that across the fifty states, various policy triads are possible, each subject to change as the pattern of conflict shifts. This laissez faire approach marks a change from the pre-legalization period, when the state allowed doctors to perform abortions within very narrow limits.

In France, the state has acted to shift the balance of resources for state abortion in the direction of women seeking the services. While the formal law retains administrative hurdles, the government has directed health agencies to provide services. And, when pro-life activists threatened to force the manufacturer of RU 486 to remove this "abortion pill" from France, the government ordered that it remain available, declaring it the "moral property of women." The establishment of a women-favored abortion policy triad shows a remarkable change from the state's pronatalist restrictions of the pre-legalization period.

These variations in the distribution of resources coincide with the different political roles of physicians and feminists in the three systems. In Russia, where the state has been so dominant in policy debates, the physicians have become the official public experts on the subject. Feminist activity has been intermittent or unseen. This inactivity has continued into perestroika and the transition politics of the new Russian Federation. In contrast, in the United States, both physicians and feminists have been very active in the public debate and conflict over abortion policy and its implementation. Since legalization, however, medical associations have tended to retreat from the struggle that has arisen within the laissez faire triad, leaving the battle over abortion services to the feminists and pro-life activists. Individual doctors, however, continue to be involved in these conflicts over clinic access and safety. In France, there is a third pattern: a divided and generally inactive medical profession and a very activist feminist presence on the issue of abortion services.

These different abortion policy triads and patterns of political conflict are associated with variations in the exercise of women's reproductive rights. The physician-favored abortion triad in Russia, accompanied by an absence of feminist voices from the debate, tends to reinforce the low reproductive rights for Russian women. Until perestroika, and at the mercy of the rigid health bureaucracy, where doctors performed assembly-line abortions and rationed the use of anesthesia, abortions were available, but the state did little to respond to women's needs, and rates of illegal abortions remained high. Since 1991, safe abortion services, while available, are too expensive for all but the newly rich; affordable abortion procedures in the crumbling public health system are of dubious safety. When reproductive issues are publicly discussed it is usually in pronatalist, rather than feminist, terms.

The United States laissez faire abortion policy triad where medical and feminist groups have been active in the political debate coincides with a mixed pattern of reproductive rights. Some states help women obtain abortion services by reducing administrative hurdles, sustaining open clinic access, and providing public assistance to poor women. In others, however, governments use their resources to restrict access, within Supreme Court guidelines, and remove all public assistance. Another pattern is found in states where the government leaves the field and the feminists and pro-life activists battle it out in the courts.

The women-favored triad in France, with an inactive medical profession and feminist activism in favor of women's access, has led to a comparatively high standard of women's reproductive rights. While doctors may legally refuse, on the basis of conscience, to perform abortions, the state requires that they still provide assistance to women to find a provider. Public health insurance pays for the procedure. It is striking to note that the overall rate of abortion is highest in Russia with the lowest level of reproductive rights, while it is lowest in France where access to safe services is highest. This points to the fact that the abortion policy triad and the services that result take place in a social and political context that affects reproductive behavior. Access to contraceptives and sex education have an influence on abortion rates. There is one more ingredient to the abortion-politics mix that must always be taken into account, and this factor does not vary across the three systems. Women who seek to terminate their pregnancies will act to do so, despite the states' efforts to prevent them. In Russia, the United States, and France, when abortion is prohibited or when safe abortion is difficult to get, women have always sought other means to obtain them, and abortion rates have soared. That certainty is the foundation upon which policymakers, physicians, and feminists establish abortion policy triads.

NOTES

1. Abortion has been legal since 1955 in Russia, 1973 in the United States, and 1975 in France.

2. Although Russia was the first country to legalize abortion in 1920, Stalin banned it, except for rare cases, in 1936.

3. *Maher v. Roe*, 432 U.S. 464 (1977); *Beal v. Doe*, 432 U.S. 438 (1977); *Harris v. McRae*, 448 U.S. 297 (1980).

4. In *Casey*, the Court ruled that the following administrative regulations were not undue burdens: 24-hour waiting period and the definition of medical emergency.

5. As of early 1995, 7 states required 24-hour waiting periods; 17 other states provided funds for indigent women seeking to terminate unwanted pregnancies; 26 required minors to notify parents with judicial bypass (Sollom, 1995; for analysis of state variations, see articles in Goggin, 1993).

6. Several medical associations filed briefs in *Webster v. Reproductive Health Services* (109 S.Ct. 3040 [1989]): (1) reaffirming support of the reasoning in *Roe v. Wade*; (2) opposing the ban on abortion counseling by physicians; and (3) affirming the right of privacy for the physician-patient relationship (AMA, 1989).

7. The result of the marginalization of abortion from mainstream medical practice has led to a shortage of practitioners and limits on services. Efforts to reverse the trend were revealed in early 1995, when the accreditation council for graduate medical education set the requirement that prospective obstetricians be taught abortion skills in all teaching hospitals (see "Group Requiring Abortion Study," 1995).

8. Although no doctor is required to perform an abortion, they are required, on the initial visit, to provide the woman with complete information about the law and give her a list of hospitals offering services.

REFERENCES

Allenova, I. A. 1990. "Deyatel'nost' Zhenskikh Konsul'tazii Po Profilaktike i Neplaniruemoi Beremennosti (Activities of Women's Consultation Clinics in the Prevention of Unwanted Pregnancy)." *Sovetskoe Zdravookhranenie* (7): 52–56.

AMA. 1970. "Amagrams." *Journal of the American Medical Association* 213 (July 20): 359.

———. 1989. "*Webster v. Reproductive Health Services*, the AMA Position." *Journal of the American Medical Association* 262, 11 (September 15): 1522.

Asaro, Andrea. 1983. "The Judicial Portrayal of the Physician in Abortion and Sterilization Decisions: The Use and Abuse of Medical Discretion." *Harvard Women's Law Journal* 6 (Spring): 51–102.

"Abort (Abortion)." 1956. In *Bol'shaya Meditsinskaya Entsiklopediia*, col. 22–47.

Beaulieu, Etienne Emile. 1990. *The "Abortion Pill."* In collaboration with Mort Rosenblum. New York: Simon & Schuster.

Berger, Henry. 1975. *L'avortement: Histoire D'un Débat.* Paris: Flammarion.

Buckley, Mary. 1989. *Women and Ideology in the Soviet Union.* Ann Arbor: University of Michigan Press.

Dhavernas, Odile. 1978. *Droits Des Femmes, Pouvoir Des Hommes.* Paris: Seuil.

Dyl'tsin, Ya. A. 1960. *O Vrede Aborta* (On the Pain of Abortion). Leningrad: Medgiz.

Engelstein, Laura. 1991. "Abortion and the Civic Order: The Legal and Medical Debates" In *Russia's Women: Accommodation, Resistance, Transformation*, ed. Barbara Evans Clements, Barbara Alpern Engel, and Christine D. Worobec, 185–207. Berkeley: University of California Press.

Ershova, E. N., and E. E. Novikova. 1988. *SSSR-SShA: Zhenshchina I Obshchestvo; Opyt Sravnital'novo Analiza* (USSR-USA: Woman and Society: A Comparative Analysis). Moscow: Profizdat.

Ferrand-Picard, Michele. 1982. "Médicalisation et Contrôl Social de L'avortement, Derrière la Loi, les Enjeux." *Revue Française de Sociologie* 23(3): 383–96.

Field, Mark. 1956. "The Re-Legalization of Abortion in Soviet Russia." *New England Journal of Medicine* 255 (August): 421–27.

———. 1988. "The Position of the Soviet Physician: The Bureaucratic Professional." *The Milbank Quarterly* 66 (suppl. 2): 182–201.

Goggin, Malcolm L., ed. 1993. *Understanding the New Politics of Abortion.* Newbury Park, CA: Sage Publications.

Goldman, Wendy. 1993. *Women, the State and Revolution: Soviet Family Policy and Social Life, 1917–1936.* New York: Cambridge University Press.

Gordon, Linda, ed. 1990. *Women, the State, and Welfare.* Madison: University of Wisconsin Press.

"Group Requiring Abortion Study." 1995. *New York Times* (February 15): 1.

Halimi, Gisele. 1973. *La Cause Des Femmes.* Paris: Bernard Grasset.

Henshaw, Stanley K. 1995. "Factors Hindering Access to Abortion Services." *Family Planning Perspectives* 27 (March/April): 54–59, 87.

Imber, Jonathan B. 1990. "Abortion Policy and Medical Practice." *Society* 27 (July–August): 27–34.

Jenson, Jane. 1987. "Changing Discourse, Changing Agendas: Political Rights and Reproductive Policies in France." In *The Women's Movements of the United States and Western Europe: Consciousness, Political Opportunity, and Public Policy,* ed. Mary Fainsod Katzenstein and Carol McClurg Mueller. Philadelphia: Temple University Press.

Katkova, I. P., and T. V. Koshovskaya. 1989. "Sotzial'no-gigienicheskie Aspekty Provedeniya Mini-abortov V Zhenskikh Konsyl'tatziayakh (Social-hygienic Aspects of Problems of Mini-abortion in Women's Consultation Clinics." *Sovetskoe Zdravookhranenie* 9: 53-57.

Lader, Lawrence. 1973. *Abortion II: Making the Revolution.* Boston: Beacon Press.

Ladrière, Paul, ed. 1982. "La Libéralisation de L'avortement." *Revue Française de Sociologie* 23(3): 351–48.

Luker, Kristin. 1984. *Abortion and the Politics of Motherhood.* Berkeley: University of California Press.

Mohr, James C. 1978. *Abortion in America.* New York: Oxford University Press.

Molyneux, Maxine. 1991. "Interview with Anastasya Posadskaya, 25 September 1990." *Feminist Review* 39 (Winter): 127–48.

Mossuz-Lavau, Janine. 1986. "Abortion Policy in France Under Governments of the Right and Left (1973–1984)." In *The New Politics of Abortion,* ed. Joni Lovenduski and Joyce Outshoorn, 86–104. London: Sage Publications.

Mouvement français pour le planning familial. 1982. *D'Une Revolte a une Lutte, 25 Ans D'histoire Du Planning Familiale.* Paris: Editions Tierce.

Pelletier, Madeleine. 1982. "Feminism and the Family, the Right to Abortion." Trans. Marilyn J. Boxer. *The French-American Review* 6 (Spring): 3–26.

Pivar, David J. 1973. *Purity Crusade, Sexual Morality, and Social Control, 1868–1900.* Westport, CT: Greenwood Press.

Powell, Aaron M., ed. 1976 (1896). *The National Purity Congress, Its Papers, Addresses, Portraits.* New York: Arno Press (orig. American Purity Alliance).

Remennick, Larissa I. 1991. "Epidemiology and Determinants of Induced Abortion in the U.S.S.R." *Social Science and Medicine* 33(7): 841–48.

Sanjian, Andrea Stevenson. 1991. "Social Problems, Political Issues: Marriage and Divorce in the USSR." *Soviet Studies* 43(4): 629–49.

Savage, Mark. 1988. "The Law of Abortion in the Union of Soviet Socialist Republics and the People's Republic of China: Women's Rights in Two Socialist Countries." *Stanford Law Review* 40 (April): 1027–65.

Schlesinger, Rudolf. 1949. *Changing Attitudes in Soviet Russia.* London: Routledge & Kegan Paul.

Sheeran, Patrick J. 1987. *Women, Society, the State and Abortion: A Structural Analysis.* New York: Praeger.

Smith-Rosenberg, Caroll. 1985. "The Abortion Movement and the AMA, 1850–1880." In *Disorderly Conduct: Visions of Gender in Victorian America,* 217–44. New York: Knopf.

Sollom, Terry. 1995. "State Actions on Reproductive Health Issue in 1994." *Family Planning Perspectives* 27 (March/April): 83–87.

Stetson, Dorothy McBride. 1987. *Women's Rights in France.* Westport, CT: Greenwood Press.

Wilsford, David. 1991. *Doctors and the State, the Politics of Health Care in France and the United States.* Durham: Duke University Press.

Witt, Kerstin. 1989. "Abortion in the Soviet Union." *World Press Review,* August.

CHAPTER 6

ABORTION AND REPRODUCTIVE CHOICE: POLICY AND POLITICS IN JAPAN

JOYCE GELB

For feminists, demanding abortion and reproductive rights has been part of the campaign to eradicate "gender injustice." In most Western nations, reproductive freedom has been viewed as central to the right to bodily self-determination; it is reflective of a larger societal struggle in which the meaning of motherhood, family, and other social relationships, sexuality, and the challenge to patriarchical state ideology has been drawn (see Yishai, 1993: 209). And in most Western democracies, abortion has been high on the policy agenda within the last several decades. This chapter examines practices and policies related to abortion in Japan, a non-Western democratic nation, and draws some comparisons with the United States. In Japan, while access to abortion has been virtually unrestricted in the post-war period, there is almost no public debate regarding the issue and discussion of other aspects of reproductive choice, and freedom has been circumscribed (see Oaks, 1994: 511). By way of comparison, both the United States and Japan have high rates of abortion, with close to two-thirds of Japanese women having an abortion by age 40 (see Buckley, 1988: 206; Shrier, 1988: 157). This figure may be compared to the 46 percent of all American women who have had abortions by age 45 (Brotman, 1990: 5). Despite this apparent similarity, in most respects, abortion and contraceptive practices differ significantly in each nation.

Operationally, abortion and reproductive-rights policy has been construed by feminists as having two dimensions. The first is the legalization of abortion and the right of an individual choice to make reproductive decisions. The second reflects the extent of accessibility to abortion for all women, through state provision of funding and/or health facilities, so that individual choice is implemented without regard to economic level (see Yishai, 1993: 210). In a useful comparative analysis, Yael Yishai argues that the examination of abortion policy with regard to individual choice and state commitment yields four different state policy models. The enabling model provides both choice and means of implementation; the restrictive model prohibits both; the hindering model provides choice but no implementation; and the intrusive model limits choice, but provides implementation for those abortions viewed as legal (Yishai, 1993: 210).

Another perspective on abortion policy examines the decision-making processes leading to changes in reproductive policies and the motives of the state in dealing with reproductive-rights issues. Are feminists accorded a voice, decisive or otherwise, in determining reproductive-rights policies? If their role is limited, what other value or ideological imperative underlies national policy regarding abortion and reproductive policy? (Yishai, 1993). The social approach perceives abortion as a service provided by the state within the context of other societal goals, particularly infant and maternal health and social welfare provisions. Some religious perspectives oppose abortion as a form of infanticide, incompatible with values related to death and life. The libertarian view places the entire decision in the hands of the individual. And finally, abortion may be seen as a means to demographic or population control (Yishai, 1993: 217).

Several additional key background variables may help to expand the framework through which reproductive policies and practices in Japan may be understood. The first is an examination of the alternating relationship between abortion and other aspects of state policy, including pronatalism and population control. The second is an approach that traces the relationship between abortion and other reproductive policies, particularly those related to contraception, as sanctioned by state policies and individual practices. In addition, there is the role played by normative beliefs and the value system in structuring attitudes about abortion. These include religion and culturally approved sexual mores and practices. The pressures and constraints placed on reproductive choice by groups opposing abortion and free access to contraception based on religion and other factors will also be examined.

The central question to be addressed is the role of women's groups in determining policy outcomes in Japan with regard to reproductive choice. An attempt will be made to apply criteria of policy origins, scope, and implementation to a non-Western nation whose values and political systems are distinctive. At the outset, it may be hypothesized that the Japanese case lies somewhere between Yishai's enabling and hindering models, in that abortion is widely and legally available, but in the absence of a state-funded health system, costs must generally be paid by individual women. Japanese women have rarely been accorded a place at the decision-making table with regard to abortion and other reproductive policies. Rather, state policy has focused primarily on demographic concerns. In contrast to the United States, religious antagonism to abortion in Japan has been more muted, although it cannot be completely discounted either in the policy arena or in shaping values and attitudes toward abortion.

THE PARAMETERS OF ABORTION POLICY IN JAPAN

For Japanese women, despite widespread use of abortion since its legalization in the mid-1940s, long in advance of the second wave of feminism, reproductive-rights options are limited. In Japan abortion is relied upon even though it is widely disapproved of and it often serves as a backup for failed contraceptive attempts. Japan is the only nation that has legal abortion but no legal contraceptive pill (*Washington Post Weekly Edition*; November 19–25, 1990: 10). Japan ranks among the leaders in the developed world in the number and rate of abortions for women. At the same time, there is little knowledge of and choice regarding contraceptive alternatives for women in Japan. The concept of reproductive rights as a mechanism to eradicate "gender injustice" and as a means to radically transform the prevailing sexual division of labor has been largely absent from public discourse and even from the political agenda of most women activists. While some women's groups have been active in supporting and defending abortion rights, they have been reluctant to press for other choices, particularly birth-control pills. Religious antipathy and sexual mores have served to limit options as well, and unlike the United States, discussion of abortion and birth control is not encouraged in either public campaigns or even private, familial conversation (Ashino; 1990; *Japan Times, Weekly International Edition*, June 15–21, 1992: 8). The policy of the state has alternated between population control and pronatalism, with abortion and other reproductive choices for women redefined accordingly. The major emphasis of state policy has been to preserve women's role as a mother rather than ensure her health and options as an individual. Policy regarding abortion and access to reproductive choice has been given "from above," and has most often not been fought for by a women's movement, or even recognized widely as an issue relevant to sexual politics. In this society with a strong tradition of government regulation of social behavior, individual rights are seen as subservient to the national ideal of femininity and the family system (*New York Times*, March 19, 1992: A3). Nonetheless, on at least two occasions during the past several decades, women activists and their allies have successfully mobilized against those who sought to limit continued access to abortion.

THE SHAPING OF JAPANESE ABORTION POLICY

As in the United States and other nations, abortion practices and reproductive policies have followed an uneven course in Japan, depending on perceived needs for population growth and stability. Government population policies have been tailored to specific economic and social needs. Prior to the Meiji Restoration in 1868, abortion and infanticide were widely practiced in Japan (Ogino, 1994: 1). However, at the beginning of the "modernizing" era, when more workers were required by the developing economy, abortion was forbidden. Abortion by a pregnant woman and others was declared a crime in 1880, with even stronger penalties adopted in the 1907 Law of Abortion. These laws still persist, although they are largely unenforced at the present time (Ogino, 1994). In the 1920s and 1930s, a feminist movement showed interest in issues of abortion and contraception, and fueled by Margaret Sanger's visit in 1922, contraception clinics were opened in Osaka and Tokyo in 1930. However, by the later 1930s, as the war effort gained momentum, information on birth control and abortion was removed from magazines, clinics closed and movement leaders were arrested, including Baroness Ishimoto Shuzue, who had founded the first birth-control clinic in Tokyo. As women were urged more and more to bear children, a Nazi-like National Eugenic Law was promulgated in 1940, eliminating abortion and sterilization, now branded as "traitorous" acts (Ogino, 1994: 3; Bingham and Gross, 1987: 220).

In the post-war period in Japan, abortion was utilized to enhance and accelerate economic growth (Domoto, 1994: 4). Abortion was recognized as a serious criminal offense until the passage of the Eugenic Protection Law in 1948 that legalized it. The law's stated purpose was "to enhance the quality of the gene pool" of the Japanese population, with a liberal abortion policy adopted to "eliminate undesirable genes" (Koizumi, 1991: 6). The first section of the law (Article 1) thus retained the approach of the 1940 law, which sought to prevent the birth of inferior descendants from a eugenic perspective.

Japan was the first country in the world to allow legal access to abortion (Domoto, 1994: 4). The law's passage was favored both by women's groups organized at the grassroots level, who were fighting for expansion of legally sanctioned birth control, and the physicians who, as Diet members, were its primary sponsors. The law's approval was prompted by the post-war baby boom. Fears of overpopulation, starvation, and confusion in the post-war devastation, as well as problems of women who had been raped by foreign soldiers after the Japanese surrenders in Korea and Manchuria, fueled concern for abortion reform (see Iwamoto, 1992: 37; Oaks, 1994: 513). Under these conditions illegal abortions were conducted under filthy and unsafe conditions, causing physicians to be among the primary sponsors of the new legislation. Finally, concern about interracial birth due to the American occupation was probably another factor in the law's passage (Robbins-Mowry, 1983: 124; Condon, 1991: 86). The law specified that physicians might perform abortions until the twenty-third week of gestation, with the consent of the woman and of the father of the fetus, if known and present. The criteria for abortion included mental illness, possible deformity of the fetus or retardation, health of the mother by reason of physical conditions, and pregnancy as a result of rape. The law was passed without heated debate (Oaks, 1994: 513).

Economic conditions were also added to the criteria for legal abortion and in 1952, a previous requirement that a local committee had to screen applications for abortion was abolished; now only the consent of the attending physician was required (Koizumi, 1991: 5). As the concept of "economic criteria" necessary for physicians to agree to perform abortions was not spelled out, Japanese women were in practice given almost a free hand in procuring abortions on request. The vast number of abortions—between 90 and 99 percent—are performed today for "economic" or health reasons (Condon, 1991: 87). While the Law of Abortion promulgated in 1907 was never repealed, it became virtually forgotten and has rarely been used to abrogate individual rights (Ogino, 1994: 72; Koizumi, 1991: 7).

Although the number of abortions reported skyrocketed from 489,111 cases in 1950, which represented a doubling from the previous year, to a peak of almost 1,200,000 cases in 1955,[1] abortion rates have fallen since then. While the rate of abortion was reported as 50.2 per 1,000 cases in 1955 for ages fifteen through forty-five, by 1989 it had fallen to 14.9 per 1,000 or over 450,000. In contrast, in the United States with somewhat more restrictive laws, the rate is twice as high, with 28.5 per 1,000. (Koizumi, 1991: 8; Iwamoto, 1992: 37) What accounts for the lower rate, despite the legal and social availability of abortions in Japan?

CURRENT ABORTION POLICY AND PRACTICE IN JAPAN

There is widespread agreement that in Japan, abortion is vastly under-reported, perhaps by half or one-third of the actual number performed and probably also with regard to incidence among unmarried women (Coleman, 1983: 31).[2] Some of the under-reporting is related to the intense desire of Japanese women for privacy regarding abortion. And since most insurance does not cover abortion, patients pay doctors directly and the latter under-report the number to avoid payment of taxes (Bumiller, Elizabeth. Japan's Abortion Agony". *Washington Post*, October 25 pages 1 and 6). Despite the absence of a national health-care system to support access to abortion, the Mainichi newspaper surveys conducted nationally since 1950 have provided an important source of information regarding Japanese patterns to fertility control. These surveys, indeed, reveal that the rate of abortion has remained almost constant; 32.8 percent in 1965, 39.8 percent in 1984, and 28.9 percent in 1992 (quoted in Ogino, 1994: 76).

National health insurance generally does not cover abortion costs in Japan. Fees tend to range from $470 to $625 for the first trimester (*Japan Times, Weekly International Edition*, June 15–21, 1992: 8). Thereafter, fees increase to the equivalent of $1,000. Despite the absence of a national health-care system to support access to abortion, and perhaps because of a more egalitarian class system in which income differentials are less exaggerated than in the United States (Verban et al., 1987: 9), many Japanese observers feel that abortion is widely accessible regardless of ability to pay. This calls into question the role of the state in implementing access to abortion, suggested by Yishai's "hindering" model, at least in the Japanese case.

However, despite the widespread view among most of this author's interviewees and in the popular press that access to abortion is quite easy for all groups of Japanese women regardless of income, some feminist writers and abortion supporters express considerable concern about the cost (see Iwamoto, 1992: 33). The cost of 50,000–100,000 yen for an abortion as well as the 3 percent consumption tax that is levied on abortion, but not on childbirth, is seen as an obstacle for indigent women (Iwamoto,1992). In 1991, there was little public discussion of the failure of the Ministry of Finance to lift the 3 percent surcharge on abortion as opposed to other health services. In a society in which discussions about sex are limited, even among husband and wife, abortions are often performed in secret, without a husband's knowledge, making money for the procedure potentially difficult to raise even for more affluent women. At present, national health insurance pays only for abortions for poor women on welfare and the abortion must be health related, not for "economic" reasons. These constitute about 1 percent of the total and must be certified by a caseworker.

A major contrast with the United States is to be found in the ages and marital status of those who have abortions, although in all comparisons, we must be cautious about inexact Japanese data. In Japan, it has been estimated that somewhere between 24 percent and 29 percent of all abortions are likely to be performed on those 30–39 years old who are married mothers with one or two children (Koizumi, 1991: 8; Ogino, 1994: 75–6). In 1993, according to official statistics, over 40 percent of abortions were performed on women aged 30 through 39, virtually all of whom were married (Ministry of Health and Welfare, 1993, supplied by Yuriko Ashino). Relatively few teenage women have abortions, unlike the United States; only 6.6 percent of women compared to 26.3 percent in the United States for those under 20-years-old (Ogino, 1994). The Japanese rate for teen abortion, though on the increase, was only 3.3 percent per 1,000, in contrast to 63.0 percent in the United States and 22 percent in Sweden (Ogino, 1994.). However, one in five Japanese teenagers, perhaps out of shame, ignorance, or fear, applies for a mid-term abortion in the second trimester, which is potentially more dangerous and life threatening (Ogino, 1994: 75–76).

The differences in abortion practices in Japan and the United States appear to reflect different problems related to birth control in each nation. In the United States, teenagers are probably more sexually active and lack education regarding contraception. In Japan, older women appear be using abortion as a backup for contraception (Ogino,1994: 76). In 1990, 29.4 percent of women reported that they had an abortion according to a family survey; over 25 percent said that they had had two abortions. As in the United States, almost all abortions are performed before the eleventh or twelfth week—over 90 percent performed in each case (Ogino, 1994: 9). The vast majority of Japanese women list the mother's health as the reason for their abortion. This may be related either to physical or economic causes; only 1 percent refer to genetic problems (Ogino, 1994: 10).

OTHER REPRODUCTIVE RIGHTS

In contrast to women in other highly developed modernized political systems, Japanese women are heavily reliant on condoms and a uniquely Japanese form of the "rhythm" method, the "Ogino" method, to control unwanted births. In other areas of the world, a greater variety of methods, including the IUD, sterilization, and particularly the pill are more widely available and used. All of these approaches are actively or tacitly discouraged in Japan. While close to 80 percent of Japanese women report using condoms and between 15 and 20 percent the rhythm method, only 1 percent use the pill. Condoms are viewed as safe, simple, and readily available in vending machines, supermarkets, door-to-door sales, and mail orders (Ogino, 1994: 76–77). In 1994, 77.7 percent of women used condoms; 7 percent used the rhythm method; and 0.6 percent used the pill (Mainichi Survey on Family Planning, 1994). Despite the privacy with which matters pertaining to sexuality are viewed in Japan, condoms are commonly advertised in the Japanese media and even in public places—they are widely viewed as "women's products" (Oaks, 1994: 515). Condom use has been promoted by Japanese family-planning organizations; they have relied on condom sales as a source of income, and this has limited their willingness to endorse other forms of contraception. Even today, perhaps one-fourth of the revenue of family-planning groups is derived from condom sales (Ashino, 1995). Japan leads the world in condom production (Ogino, 1994: 77).

The combined use of condoms and the rhythm method frequently proves unreliable. However, Japanese couples apparently find the subject of sex embarrassing and rarely consult physicians regarding appropriate contraception (Ogino, 1994: 79).

The limited use of alternative contraceptives appears to be related to cultural constructions of appropriate behavior for women as well. Fear and ignorance of one's own body inhibit effective birth control. Japanese women apparently dislike handling their genitals, and reject diaphragms, IUDs, and other techniques, as well as tampons, which would create discomfort (Oaks, 1994: 513). Coleman reports that in the 1970s, only 10 percent of Japanese women used tampons, in comparison to 56 percent in the United States (1983, 158). Surgical contraception is also rejected as a means of fertility control, and sterilization, also legalized by the 1947 Eugenic Protection Law, is becoming quite rare. However, in what appears to be a contradictory practice, most sterilizations are performed on women, as opposed to men (Coleman, 1983). In 1989, 99.2 percent of all sterilizations were performed on women, while only 0.8 percent were performed on men (Koizumi, 1991: 11). Vasectomy is frowned upon; it is viewed as a facilitator of male promiscuity, as it will relieve men of responsibility for birth control. In contrast to the Japanese sterilization rate of almost 100 women to 1 man, in the United States, while sterilization is on the rise for women, the ratio is much lower, with only twice as many sterilizations performed on women as men (Koizumi, 1991; see also *Newsweek,* March 13, 1995: 60–61, for a finding that of the 60 percent of American women who used contraception, sterilization was now slightly ahead of the pill in preference).

Japanese women appear to be submissive sexual partners and rarely break out of the Confucian tradition that requires women not be "self-assertive." They treat men as "*otto o tateru*" or "husbands first,"–i.e., the leaders of the household (Ogino, 1994: 80; see also Bingham and Gross, 1987: 221). The result is passivity regarding sexual practices and male responsibility for choice of contraception, especially among the majority of wives economically dependent upon their husbands, who appear to be powerless to intervene in contraceptive matters (Ogino, 1994). As Oaks points out, opposition to sterilization and other birth-control methods is based on the contention that their adoption will make it easier for men to engage freely in extramarital sex. With apparently contradictory logic, arguments against permitting the pill, a female means of exerting birth-control, contend that this liberalization might corrupt women's morals (Oaks, 1994: 514).

OTHER TYPES OF CONTRACEPTION

In addition to these social practices and socialization regarding sex, Japan is exceptional in the world as a country in which oral contraceptive pills are not approved for general use; they cannot be advertised or dispensed for contraceptive purposes (Ogino, 1994: 21). Similarly, research on the acceptability of the IUD dragged on for seventeen years and finally efforts to get official approval for its dissemination were abandoned. Information on the low-dosage birth-control pill, which is the most used contraceptive worldwide, is difficult to come by, preventing women from demanding access (Domoto, 1994). In the

1950s efforts were introduced at the national level to substitute contraception for abortion (Coleman, 1983: 17; Ogino, 1994: 73). The use of midwives as contraception counselors proved unwise; they opposed practices that might limit their role in delivering babies. By 1965 the national family planning budget was dismantled in response to pronatalist opposition from midwives and other pronatalist forces (Coleman, 1983: 34).

While in 1960 the pill appeared in Japan as an over-the-counter drug, in 1972, it was withdrawn. It is currently available only by doctor's prescription for therapeutic uses, primarily in cases relating to menstrual disorders. The decision by the government to treat the pill as harmful has been reinforced by media and government publicity regarding adverse side effects. This concern is not without foundation, because the pill used in Japan is the older "first-generation" type that contains a large amount of hormones and may have a more adverse impact and side effects than the low-dose pill used widely elsewhere.

In 1989, the Ministry of Health and Welfare conducted preliminary tests on the pill, with over four thousand women authorized to take it for one year. The tests were concluded in 1991 and showed the pill to be highly effective (Domoto, 1994: 4). Then information related to the vastly lowered birth rate appeared to herald a new national crisis, in the eyes of many. In 1992, the Ministry of Health and Welfare refused, somewhat unexpectedly, to permit manufacturing and prescription by physicians of the low-dose pill. Putting off the decision, the Ministry cited "harmful, yet unprovable side effects" and the "danger of corrupting women's morals" (*New York Times,* March 19, 1992: A3). In addition to fears of promiscuity and health danger, fear of AIDS was suggested as a factor as well, as the Health and Welfare Ministry cited "public hygiene" as a reason for continuing to ban the pill, meaning that the condom can prevent the transmission of AIDS while the pill cannot (Oaks, 1994: 514). In the view of most feminists, the linking of AIDS with the lifting of the pill ban was a deliberate effort to join two separate issues in order to mislead the public (Iwamoto, 1994).

As suggested above, government officials were also clearly motivated by the decline in the Japanese birth rate, which had fallen to a record low (below 1.50), and which was viewed as a trend dangerous to the nation. They may also have been influenced by the pressure of physicians to keep oral contraceptives illegal in order to continue their lucrative abortion practices (Oaks, 1994: 514). At the same time, the Ministry did lift a ban on home pregnancy tests, which have hormones similar to the low-dose pill and are made by the same manufacturers. Iwamoto argues that a "deal" was made in order to compensate the pharmaceutical industry (Iwamoto, 1994).

Countering the bureaucratic arguments were the Japan Family Association, the Family Planning Federation of Japan, the Maternal Protection Association, and various women's groups who argued that individuals should be permitted to weigh health risks for themselves and that the low-dose pill should be approved immediately (Iwamoto, 1994). However, the Japanese public in general, and many groups in the women's movement as well, remain unconvinced of the pill's value. Unlike the protests that have surrounded government attempts to restrict access to abortion—with the exception of a controversial group, Chupiren, whose confrontational tactics in the early 1970s were shunned by most feminists—there has never been an organized effort by women to make the pill more available. Still, while many Japanese feminists don't view the pill as the best form of contraception, they believe that women should be given as many alternatives as possible so that they may make their own decision.

Despite the ban, the pill is available, but most Japanese women disdain its use. In the Mainichi family planning surveys mentioned earlier, 75 percent of respondents indicated that they had no interest in the pill, while only about 3 percent said they did (Ogino, 1994: 84). When asked to consider legalization of the pill, nearly half of the respondents indicated they were "not sure" about it and fewer than one-third thought it would be a good idea (Ogino, 1994). The numbers of pill supporters are declining steadily. Over 53 percent of married women and 38 percent of unmarried women said they did not want to try even the low-dose pill; fewer than 10 percent of each group said they did (Ogino, 1994). Even among those survey respondents who support the pill's legalization, over 60 percent say they would not use it themselves! Reasons given for not liberalizing dissemination of the pill included "unnaturalness," fear of side effects of even the low-dose version by over three-fourths of respondents, and fear of immoral sexual activity by close to one-third. (These views prevail despite surveys that show that premarital sex is the norm in Japan: see Bumiller, Elisabeth. "Japan's Abortion Agony". *Washington Post*, November 25, 1990: 10). Among those who do support the pill's wider use, the reason most frequently cited is that it will lower the abortion rate (Ogino, 1994: 84). Despite the antipathy to the pill described and documented here, according to one source, there may be upwards of 350,000 to 800,000 women in Japan using the pill illegally as a contraceptive —even though the more dangerous form of the pill is still being utilized there (Iwamoto, 1992: 37). No official discussions on RU 486 have been undertaken there, and there is little pressure to introduce the drug (*Japan Times, Weekly International Edition*, May 31–June 6, 1993: 18).

SOCIETAL VALUES AND THE ROLE OF WOMEN'S GROUPS
AND OPPOSITION GROUPS IN REPRODUCTIVE CHOICE

While women's groups in Japan have strongly advocated on behalf of continued access to abortion, they have been unlikely to seek to increase options increasing the availability of the pill and other forms of reproductive choice.
Although in the early 1980s women's groups participated in a successful public campaign to retain the existing law, public discussion of abortion is
almost "taboo" (*Japan Times, Weekly International Edition,* April 6–12, 1992:
14), and there is a lack of information regarding other forms of contraception.
Akiko Domoto, of the Upper House of the Diet, contends that with pressure
from women on issues related to reproductive rights, some of the outcomes related to policy might be different, but at present, women lack the information
and perhaps the will to protest publicly (Domoto, 1994: 4). The policymaking
process in Japan consists of the Ministry of Health and Welfare, which has as
its advisory council (or shingikai) the Eugenic Protection Section of the Public
Health Council and the Diet. The latter body consists of representatives from
the health, judicial, and welfare communities. There are none from women's
groups, although a member of the Maternal Protection Association does serve
on the council (Iwamoto, 1992, 38).

In contrast to the United States, abortion has never become a significant
electoral issue in Japan, even when revisions in the existing law have been
proposed. However, threats to abortion rights have arisen on several occasions. Vocal and visible opposition to abortion has occurred at least twice;
once in the early 1970s and again in the 1980s, spearheaded by the Seicho no
le (Home of Infinite Life, Wisdom, and Abundance), a religious organization
founded in 1930. This group, comprised of right-wing nationalists with
alleged links to the United States–based Moral Majority and "Right to Life "
movement, attempted to bring back the pronatalist Emperor-based policies
that they saw as strengthening the nation. Together with conservative Diet
members of the Liberal Democratic Party, they sought to remove the "economic reasons" clause from the Eugenic Protection Act. During the second and
more significant attack in 1982, they launched a national campaign with the
slogan "Reverence for Life" through television and various publications. They
also made an effort to gather ten million signatures for repeal. They were
joined by three hundred Diet members, organized as the "Federation of Diet
Members Who Revere Life" (Ogino, 1994: 88).

On both occasions, women's groups fought to retain their abortion
rights and were successful. In 1972, they coined a counterslogan, "It is Women
Who Decide to Bear or Not to Bear." In August 1982, feminist activists were
joined by a broader coalition: citizens' groups, traditional women's organiza-

tions, trade unionists, and politicians, including female Diet members, as well as family planners and physicians (Condon, 1991: 87; Steinhoff, 1989: 181). The "82 Anti-Abortion Law Reform Coalition" gained the support of over sixty groups (Ogino, 1994: 28). In March 1983, women students conducted a hunger strike before the Health and Welfare Ministry. A national assembly as well as a demonstration of more than two thousand people in Tokyo's Yoyogi Park was held the same month. The feminist movement had made it possible to discuss the abortion issue in a more public fashion, as women's issues had gained more legitimacy (Steinhoff, 1989). A split in the ranks of the then-politically dominant Liberal Democratic Party in a pre-election period, when there was some concern about opposition from women voters, prevented the restrictions from being enacted (Ashino, 1995).

However, at the end of 1989, the Ministry of Health and Welfare announced its intention to shorten the period for abortion from twenty-three to twenty-one weeks, citing increased possibilities for fetal survival (*Japan Times, Weekly International Edition*, October 22–28, 1990: 7). The bureaucrats sought to avoid public discussion and potential opposition from women's groups and their allies by making the decision behind "closed doors" (Iwamoto, 1992: 28).[3] A possible factor in the decision of the Ministry to initiate a bureaucratic change in the rules regulating legal abortion was the election of ten new female representatives to the Diet in July 1989; among them, Akiko Domoto, who was committed to the perspective of women's choice (Iwamoto, 1992: 29). A one-year protest campaign by women's groups and their allies included meetings and the issuance of opinion papers *(ishenko)* that stressed the perspective of women's reproductive choice. Their main points were the absence of female leaders in the decision-making process, and their opposition to the idea that mid-term abortions are inevitable. They pointed out that increased regulation would not prevent abortions from being performed in secret and under dangerous conditions and that more information should be available to reduce unwanted pregnancies and abortions. They also stated that the Diet should have a more significant role in the process. Nonetheless, the new rule went into effect on January 1, 1991, shortening the period for legal abortion by two weeks.

The organized action to retain access to abortion led to interest in continuing movements on "women and health" with an agenda about reproduction, sexuality, and women's bodies (Ogino, 1994: 88). However, the only movement that combined opposition to abortion restrictions with support for liberalization of the "pill" was the pink-helmeted Chupiren (Women's Union for Liberalization of Abortion and the Pill), which was viewed as a strident and avowed advocate of women's liberation, in the 1970s (*New York Times,* March 19, 1992, A3). Under the leadership of Misako Enoki, it was ridiculed thoroughly by the media, and the feminist movement was "put at a . . . disadvantage" by its identification with this group's "notoriety" (Ogino, 1994: 85). Apart from this failed attempt, most feminists have never placed the issue of pill liberalization on their agenda (Ogino, 1994). On the contrary, the suspicion surrounding the pill and the possibly exaggerated reports of its harmful side effects persist, and as a result numerous activists oppose it as well. In 1987 the first women's health center in Osaka published a book entitled *The Pill—We Don't Choose It*, a view similar to that expressed in the 1984 edition of *Our Bodies Ourselves*. The Japanese book opposes the pill on the basis of its "unnaturalness" and as a potential contributor to the failure of communication among men and women. Concern exists among students of reproductive rights in Japan that, as many Japanese women are passive and ignorant of sexuality and male-female relations, "the pill may not bring them more control over their own bodies, but . . . further inequality between men and women" (Ashino, 1990).

It should be noted that despite the absence in Japan of a "Right-to-Life" movement such as that which exists in the United States, societal values stress innocence for women and place great value on virginity before marriage. The periodic and well-respected Mainichi survey on contraceptive usage among Japanese women, for example, excludes unmarried women and women below the age of sixteen. This is an indication of the unwillingness to acknowledge widespread sexual practices (see Koizumi, 1991: 5). "Hymen reconstruction" is a popular practice among cosmetic surgeons and is widely advertised on kiosks and in news magazines (Koizumi, 1991: 5).

In Japan, religion tends to shape philosophical and ethical positions and also to be a private affair. Despite easy access to and widespread tolerance of abortion, and the acceptance of the idea that abortion is a woman's choice, the major Japanese religions, Shinto and Buddhism, tend to view abortion as a necessary and regrettable evil (Chamberlain, 1994: 14). The Shinto religion, which celebrates such life-related ceremonies as birth and marriage, holds that abortion places a curse by the aborted fetus on the mother. The major religion associated with death in Japan, Buddhism, holds an anti-abortion stance as well. For Buddhism, the practice of abortion is in opposition to the notion of overcoming one's ego (Bumiller, Elisabeth. "Japan's Abortion Agony". *Washington Post*, November 1990: 11). Fetus's souls are seen to "demand" recognition from the women who have aborted them or else women risk the possibility of misfortune or illness for their family (La Fleur, 1992: 174–75). In a climate of general tolerance toward abortion, Buddhism and Shintoism have sought to create constraints related to fetal spirithood, rather, than as is the case among United States pro-lifers, fetal personhood (Oaks, 1994: 520). In Japan there is no concept of the fetus as a person who has a right to life.

While the origins of ritualized memorials to aborted spirits may date back several centuries, in the post–World War II period many Buddhist temples and new religious cults have begun a new business targeting women who have abortions. They have provided a culturally condoned release for women's grief, particularly significant in a society placing such a high value on the mothering role and acknowledging fetal spirits (Oaks, 1994: 515). Large statues of Jizo, guardian of children, and stone memorial monuments for babies have been constructed. The religious sects have also induced women with abortion experiences to visit temples and pay money for services (*kuyo*) and small statues of Mizuko Jizo, the guardian deity of unborn children. They warn that failure to do so will bring misfortune to the woman and her family, thus supporting and encouraging a lucrative profit-making activity (Ogino, 1994: 83; *Washington Post,* November 1990: 10).

Recently, several Western observers have contended that the ritualized memorials common in Japan provide an object lesson regarding an approach that may avoid the intense feelings and passions surrounding abortion in the United States (see Oaks,1994; La Fleur,1992; and Chamberlain, 1994). Others, however, point to the high prices charged for these rituals, ranging from $300 to $2,100, their increased popularity since media publicity in the 1970s, and the feelings of fear of retribution as well as loss that these rites have created for women (Chamberlain, 1994). Regardless of one's interpretation, it is difficult to see how extrapolation of a cultural practice rooted in different values could transform the contentious abortion debate in the West.

CONCLUSION: REPRODUCTIVE RIGHTS POLICIES IN THE UNITED STATES AND JAPAN

In both Japan and the United States, as in other nations, abortion and the politics of reproductive choice reflect a compromise between competing interests including the perceived needs of the state, as well as moral, religious, and ideological values and medical and health factors. Abortion laws often have "the character of a provisional compromise," while continuing reanalysis and policy changes appear inevitable as the balance of interests is altered (Ketting and Van Prang, 1985: 155–58; Randall, 1987: 266). During the current era, in both nations, the "provisional compromise" reached regarding abortion may be undergoing changes detrimental to women's right to choose.

In contrast with Japan, abortion has been a controversial issue in the United States during the past several decades. It has played a central role in campaigns and has been in the forefront of public discussion. Partisan and pressure group conflict around the issue has escalated, pitting women against each other and resulting in the mobilization of two diametrically opposed social movements. Abortion has been viewed as "the most politically divisive domestic legal issue of our time" (Yishai, 1993: 216).

The United States increasingly lacks a national policy with regard to abortion, as states are more free to restrict abortion rights as long as they do not place an "undue burden" on women or outlaw all abortions—an issue that will need to be reexamined by the courts and/or legislative bodies. In 1992, only thirteen states funded abortions for poor women; in Japan, abortions without restrictions are available primarily to those who can pay private doctors. As in Japan, in the United States, first trimester abortions can often be had for as little as $200–300; in later months costs may increase to $2,000 or more (*New York Times*, March 15, 1992). Access to clinic and hospital-based abortions has been increasingly restricted for American women; 83 percent lack such access, although private doctors continue to perform abortions in some areas (*New York Times*, March 15, 1992). Public hospitals perform only 13 percent of all abortions, and where they are available, they are utilized more by African American than by white women (Yishai, 1993: 213). Publicly subsidized abortions dropped almost by half from 1977 to 1985 to 187,000 (Yishai, 1993: 10). Increasingly, in the United States, abortion has become isolated from traditional medical practice; fewer doctors are trained in and willing to perform abortions (*Newsweek*, July 13, 1992: 18). As of 1995, the number of counties with doctors willing to perform abortions had shrunk to just 16 percent (*Newsweek*, March 13, 1995). In Japan, doctors who perform abortions undergo rigorous training of up to thirty months (Coleman). In the United States, the use of the pill has decreased to 28 percent down from 38 percent in 1973, and sterilization for women has more than doubled (38 percent) during the same period (*New York Times*, March 19, 1992: A3; *Washington Post Weekly Edition*, November 19–25, 1990: 11). In Japan, sterilization for women has also increased, tripling to close to 10 percent from 1973 to 1990, and although statistics are probably vastly under-reported, only a fraction of male sterilizations are reported in contrast to women's (Ogino, 1994: 81). In contrast, in the United States, teenage abortions, particularly among African American women, are common and they have increased for the under-fifteen year olds as well (Bianchi and Spahn, 1986: 60–62). In the United States also, the notion of abortion for economic reasons appears to be less favored than for health reasons (Bianchi and Spahn, 1986). Among Japanese teens, second-trimester abortions are a cause for concern. However, the vast majority of abortions are performed on married women, as a result of unwanted pregnancy due to the failure of ineffective fertility control.

Finally, in the United States pro-choice groups seek vigorously to advance their position politically through a variety of means, including litigation, national, and state-level legislative efforts, and protest. Issues of reproductive freedom have been central to the feminist political agenda. In 1989 and 1992, women and their allies held mass rallies in Washington, DC, among the largest on record, to demonstrate their support for abortion rights. Pro-choice women have stepped up activism, particularly since the *Webster* decision in 1989, and increasingly have donated money and other types of support (Yishai, 1993: 222). Nonetheless, they face difficulty because of opposition within the women's constituency and due to the extraordinary activism of the pro-life movement. The latter has adapted a variety of strategies to oppose abortion, including harassment of clinics and violent, life-threatening attacks on doctors performing abortions and on women seeking to obtain them. Under the Clinton administration, the state has increased access to RU 486, the pill that induces abortion, which is being tested for future licensing. Meanwhile, the introduction of a new "pill" in Japan seems unlikely, given the resistance to similar forms of contraception. In the United States, despite widespread support for feminist approaches to abortion and reproductive rights, the federal commitment to providing abortion to all economic groups of women has steadily eroded and, at present, access to reproductive freedom for all women appears to be at risk in many states.

In Japan, the Eugenic Protection Law remains in effect, as it has since 1947. Japan was among the first nations to permit legal abortion, far in advance of the second wave of the feminist movement. Because the law was legislated from above for reasons other than reproductive freedom for women and with a minimum of controversy and public opposition in the post-war period, it did little to galvanize a women's movement, as was the case in most other nations. Abortion virtually on demand is widely available in Japan, although it is not subsidized through a free national health-care system. However, abortion remains most important as a means of contraception; it is the third most popular form of contraception after condoms and the Japanese version of the rhythm method. The women's movement and other supporters have fought for retention of the "economic reasons" clause of the Eugenic Protection Act and have successfully beaten back attacks on it in the Diet. In this sense, feminists and their supporters have challenged societal precepts that limit public and private discourse regarding reproduction. However, women as a group and individually have been unenthusiastic about supporting alternate means of contraception. To the extent that the "availability of a contraceptive pill must be seen as an important precondition of the women's movement," and as a key to reproductive control and health (Kaplan, 1992: 13), this has not occurred in Japan. Japanese women have remained passive in their relationships with sexual partners, and have found it difficult to accept the idea that they can claim rights over when, how, and whether to bear children (Ogino, 1994: 26–27). The concept of "reproductive freedom" as a key feminist demand has rarely been recognized in a public manner. Even today, the language of choice endorsed by Japanese feminists supports reproductive health, not rights. The Japanese government has viewed matters concerning reproduction as related to population control and motherhood; the concept of women's health linked to reproductive choice has been totally absent from state consideration.

As in the United States, there is concern about the potential for changing Japanese policies toward abortion. In 1991, when the Japanese Health and Welfare Ministry shortened the time period for legal abortion from twenty-three to twenty-one weeks; the voices of women activists and their allies protesting this change were ignored and little public support or interest in this administrative change was aroused (Ogino, 1994: 87). In 1994, however, a small group of Diet-based women representatives sought to break precedent and create a cross-party coalition on the issue of pill legalization (Domoto, 1994: 4). A new Japanese women's movement for sexual and reproductive health and rights, Japan's Network for Women and Health, was formed prior to the 1994 Cairo UN conference on Population and Development, but by the winter of 1995 it was all but defunct due to monetary difficulties (Ashino, letter to the author, August 29, 1994; Ashino, 1995). Support for reproductive health and choice thus continues to rest on several small, relatively weak feminist groups. Allies in the cause of reproductive choice are generally few, except during the successful defense of access to abortion in 1982. Even the Family Planning Association of Japan, a strong supporter of abortion as a woman's right, continues to use maternalist symbolism in its slogan, "protect mother's health, build happy homes," and stresses infant care and childbearing safety as primary themes in its campaigns. It also has a stake in the existing contraceptive system due to its reliance on condom sales as a source of revenue (Coleman, 1983: 45). The medical lobby, which was largely responsible for the adoption of the 1947 abortion law, and which has continued to support it, apparently also wishes to limit access to other forms of choice. The failure of Japan to implement its pro-abortion policy through national health insurance may be attributable to the interest of physicians in maintaining a monopoly over abortion. A continuation of the present policy will ensure a continuation of their lucrative practices in private clinics.

At present, there is no proposal for a revised abortion bill before the Diet. However, in response to public criticism of the Eugenic Protection Law's underlying precepts, there is some consideration being given by the Japanese government to its revision (Ashino, 1995).

In recent years, the unprecedented decline in the Japanese birth rate has occasioned great attention from government, the corporate sector, and the media. Pronatalist rhetoric has been much in the air, and policies have been advanced that seek to encourage women to have more children. These policies include increased child allowances, the Ministry of Health and Welfare's "Welcome Baby Campaign," the shortened period for legal abortion, and the abolition of the consumption tax for childbirth expenses but not for abortion, contraceptives, or contraceptive advice. Anti-abortionists are promoting a "quiet" campaign to undermine existing rights by distributing videotapes to schools with the message that "abortion is murder." Under these circumstances, there is reason to fear that continued access to abortion rights and further efforts to attain meaningful reproductive freedom for Japanese women may be challenged in the future.

NOTES

1. The actual number was probably far greater at both times.
2. Coleman alleged that the actual number of abortions is one-and-a-half to four times that of the official number.
3. In 1976 the period was shortened from 28 to 24 weeks by the bureaucracy with minimum controversey.

REFERENCES

Ashino, Yuriko. January 1990; February 1995. Deputy Director, Family Planning Federation of Japan.

Bianchi, Suzanne, and Daphne Spahn. 1986. *American Women in Transition*. New York: Russell Sage.

Bingham, Marjorie Wall, and Susan Hill Gross. 1987. *Women in Japan*. St. Louis Park, MN: Glenhurst Pub. Co.

Brotman, Barbara. 1990. "The Abortion Maze." *Chicago Tribune*, January 14: 5.

Buckley, Sandra. 1988. "Body Politics: Abortion Law Reform." In Gavan McCormack and Yoshio Sugimoto, eds., *The Japanese Trajectory: Modernization and Beyond*. Cambridge: Cambridge University Press, 205–17.

Bumiller, Elisabeth. "Japan's Abortion Agony". *Washington Post*, October 25, 1990, pages 1 and 6.

Chamberlain, Gary. 1994. "Learning from the Japanese." *America*, September 17: 14–16.

Coleman, Samuel. 1983. *Family Planning in Japanese Society: Traditional Birth Control or Modern Urban Culture*. Princeton: Princeton University Press.

Condon, Jane. 1991. *A Half Step Behind: Japanese Women Today*. Tokyo: Charles Tuttle Co.

Domoto, Akiko. 1994. "Network." Summer 1994, Tokyo: Author, 1994.

Iwamoto, Misako. 1992. "Reproductive Rights and the Policy Making Process in Japan: The 1990 Reduction in the Term Limit for Abortion by Two Weeks." (Seishoku no Jikoketteiken to Nihonteki Seisaku Kettei: 1990-nen Ninshln Chuzetsu Kano Kikan Nishukan Tanjuko o Megutte). *Joseigaku 1*, 4.20/92, Z7–48. (Translations by Dawn Lawson and Tiana Norgren.)

Iwamoto, Misako. 1994. "Reproductive Self-Determination Today—the Freeze on Lifting Japan's Pill Ban." (Seishoku no Jikoketteiken no Ima—Nihon ni okeru Kaıkın Toketsu o Megutte), *Joseigaku*, 2, 2/5/94. (Translated by Tiana Norgren.)

Japan Times, Weekly International Edition, 1989–1995.

Kaplan, Gisela. 1992. *Western European Feminism.* New York: New York University Press.

Ketting, Evert, and Philip Van Prang. 1985. "The Marginal Relevance of Legislation Relating to Induced Abortion." In Lovenduski and Outshoorn, eds., 154–69. *The New Politics of Abortion.* Beverly Hills, CA: Sage Pub.

Koizumi, Kiyoka. 1991. "Reproductive Health of Women in Japan." Unpublished paper, presented at Founders Day Conference, City College of New York, October.

La Fleur, William. 1992. *Liquid Life: Abortion and Buddhism in Japan.* Princeton: Princeton University Press.

Mainichi Shimbun Sha. Family *Planning in Japan.* Tokyo: The Mainichi Newspapers, 1992.

Muramatsu, Minoru. 1988. "Japan." In Paul Sadchev, ed., *International Handbook on Abortion.* New York: Greenwood Press, 293-301.

Newsweek. 1994. "Abortion Revolution," December 12, 37-40; 1995, "Still Fumbling in the Dark," March 13, 60-62.

New York Times. 1989–1995. March 19, 1992, A3; June 16, 1994, D23.

Oaks, Laury. 1994. "Fetal Spirithood and Fetal Personhood." *Women Studies International Forum* 17, 5: 511–23.

Ogino, Miho. 1994. "Abortion and Women's Reproductive Rights: The State of Japanese Women 1945-1991." In Joyce Gelb and Marian Palley, eds., *Women of Japan and Korea.* Philadelphia: Temple University Press, 69-94.

Randall, Vicky. 1987. *Women and Politics: An International Perspective.* Chicago: University of Chicago Press.

Robbins-Mowry, Dorothy. 1983. *The Hidden Sun—Women of Modern Japan.* Boulder, CO: Westview Press.

Shreir, Sally, ed. 1988. *Women's Movements of the World.* London: Longman.

Steinhoff, Patricia. 1989. "Protest and Democracy." In Takeshi Ishida and Ellis Krauss, eds., *Democracy in Japan.* Pittsburgh: University of Pittsburgh Press, 171-200.

Verba, Sidney. 1987. *Elites and the Idea of Equality.* Cambridge: Harvard University Press.

Washington Post Weekly Edition. November 19-28, 1990: 10.

Yishai, Yael. 1993. "Public Ideas and Public Policy: Abortion Politics in Four Democracies." *Comparative Politics* 2, 25: 207-228.

PART III

RHETORIC, REALITY, AND RIGHTS:
The Implications of the
Policy Environment

INTRODUCTION

Much has been written about the effects of European integration on national sovereignty, the emergence of the "new European," and the evolution of common policies. To what extent, if any, has the European Community/Union affected abortion policy in its member states? Has ease of travel among countries in the European Union spurred policy convergence? Both chapters in this section explore these questions by discussing the policies of individual Western European countries within the framework of a policy environment that transcends national boundaries. The implications of the European Community/Union for policy convergence in individual countries are then analyzed.

Chapter 7 begins with an examination of the factors that contributed to the emergence of abortion law reform in Western Europe and of the types of reforms that were subsequently enacted. In the discussion of these reforms, the point is made that variations were often the result of the ways in which the issue of reform was initially framed and the compromises that political elites made when they were confronted by such a disruptive issue. Generally speaking, the legislation that was passed can be classified as falling within either the term limit or the indication model. These models, Outshoorn argues, reflected the pressures exerted by some for limiting availability and by the women's movement and more radical traditional groups, such as family planning associations, for more liberal reform. In responding to these conflicting demands, decision makers negotiated carefully worked-out compromise solutions, opting for a term limit or indication policy as circumstances required. As time went on, however, the indication model proved unworkable, and physicians operating under ambiguous guidelines felt especially vulnerable to legal challenges. Hence, indication models have been largely replaced by some form of term limit.

Outshoorn emphasizes the importance of implementation and notes the conditions that limit availability: time limits, the kind of consent required to perform the procedure, the number of facilities and doctors willing to perform abortions, and cost. Outshoorn argues that easy availability leads to a decrease in doctors' fees and hence greater accessibility for less affluent women. Inter-regional discrepancies in availability have contributed to abortion tourism, but this phenomenon, in turn, has promoted more liberal reform at home. The ability to travel freely among member states of the European Union has eased the burden of restrictive abortion policies in countries like Spain, Portugal, and Ireland, and has acted as a stimulus to press for more liberal policies in those countries.

In assessing the stability of Western European abortion policy, Outshoorn points out that there has been a trend toward more liberal abortion policy, and that this tendency has remained remarkably constant over time. Even in those countries that have not adopted abortion reform, public opinion supports a more liberal position than that which currently exists.

To what may this stability be attributed? Chapter 7 makes the argument that in Europe policy has been largely made by parliament, often after a long and difficult battle. This battle focused public attention on the issue of abortion and created a solid base of support for the reforms. In the battle waged in parliament, political parties were forced to work out compromises and commit themselves. This has made it much more difficult to reverse liberal policies. In countries, such as Ireland and Germany, where there is a process for judicial review, the chances for abortion reform are more problematic. Judges do not need the same broad-based electoral support required by parliamentary parties and, therefore, do not feel compelled to balance conflicting forces. This leaves conservative forces with an effective alternative route for advancing their position.

Chapter 8 examines one of the exceptions to the trend of liberalizing abortion policies in Western Europe: the Republic of Ireland. This chapter carefully chronicles the debates in that country over the issue of abortion from the adoption of a constitutional amendment in 1983 until the present. Just as chapter 7 focuses on the compromises negotiated by political elites in their efforts to balance conflicting pressures, chapter 8 explores the implications of balancing domestic concerns—including demands by some for a theocratic state—with Ireland's membership in the European Community/Union.

Outshoorn sees a steady drift toward liberal abortion reform throughout Western Europe, even in countries such as Ireland, Spain, and Portugal, and argues that there is a convergence of policy grounded in more liberal attitudes and in the realities of everyday life. Girvin is more guarded in his assessment. He views Ireland's membership in the European Union, as well as the liberalizing abortion trends in the rest of Western Europe, as a catalyst for the formation of an anti-abortion lobby in the 1970s and as an incentive for mobilizing Irish conservatives. It was a fear of liberal values filtering in through the European Community, he argues, that prompted the passage of the anti-abortion amendment to the Irish Constitution in 1983. Efforts to contain influences that would challenge existing abortion policy have continued and have become a major force contributing to the dominant role of moral politics in the current Irish debate over abortion and the distribution of information concerning abortion abroad. In Girvin's opinion, this trend of discussing abortion in terms of "moral politics" is likely to persist for some time to come.

However, Girvin acknowledges that some convergence is occurring. Public opinion polls show that the majority in Ireland favors abortion at least under some circumstances. The ambiguous results of the Supreme Court's decision in the X case and the subsequent defeat of the abortion amendment in 1992 have left Ireland without a clearly defined abortion policy at home. One consequence of this is that doctors are uncertain about when they may perform an abortion. This uncertainty and the legal challenges stemming from it have served as a incentive to enact an abortion law. Ireland's adoption of a policy that permits the dissemination of information about abortion abroad has also served to encourage the adoption of new legislation. Finally, recent scandals have rocked the Catholic Church, and fewer Irish now view the Church favorably. The demand for a theocratic state is now widely repudiated, and the power of the anti-abortion movement has lessened somewhat. All these factors may mean reforms that more closely resemble those of other, more liberal, Western European countries.

In short then, both chapters see the broader European policy environment as a force in the development and implementation of abortion policy, although there is some difference of opinion about the nature of its influence. For Outshoorn, the Western European environment is a positive force on individual states' domestic policies, while for Girvin, the European influence has stimulated a demand for both liberal and conservative reforms.

CHAPTER 7

THE STABILITY OF COMPROMISE: ABORTION POLITICS IN WESTERN EUROPE

JOYCE OUTSHOORN

INTRODUCTION

Abortion politics in Western Europe have become relatively tranquil in recent years. All nations in this part of the world, with the exception of Ireland, have now legalized abortion in some way or other. This contrasts sharply with the period of the seventies and early eighties, when abortion occupied a prominent place on the political agenda and both the women's movement of the second feminist wave and anti-abortion groups forced governments to confront the issue. The relative quiet on the front of abortion policy after the reforms is all the more striking when one takes into account the continuous conflict surrounding abortion in the United States. Opponents of abortion there, following the Supreme Court decision of 1973 (*Roe v. Wade*), have been trying to overturn this decision by all available means, and managing to restrict the access of women to abortion to a considerable extent. In Central and Eastern Europe the situation is also unstable, with anti-abortion groups on the offensive, but to date only Poland has imposed serious restrictions. In Western Europe, however, no "contra-revolution" has occurred; despite vigorous campaigns in a number of nations, anti-abortion groups have not succeeded in turning back the clock. With the exception of Germany, all the reforms of the last decades are still in place; the trend has actually been toward further liberalization, with most subsequent successful policy revisions improving women's access to safe abortions. From a Western European perspective the United States would be the exception to be explained: What accounts for the long period of protracted conflict, and why has no decent settlement been forthcoming?

This chapter aims to explain the stability of the Western European situation, examining the state of recent abortion policy in Western Europe and taking into account not only the legal and political situation but also the access of women to an abortion. For this purpose I have been able to draw on a considerable comparative literature on abortion in which legislation, access, and abortion frequency have been analyzed (Ketting and van Praag, 1985, 1986; Glendon, 1987; Eser and Koch, 1988; Berer, 1993; Blayo, 1993; Rolston and Eggert, 1994a). Less frequent are the studies that take a comparative political perspective on abortion (but see Lovenduski and Outshoorn, 1986; Outshoorn,

1988; Rucht, 1994). Single-nation studies on the politics of abortion exist for most Western European nations, however, not all of them are available in English.[1] In order to address the major question, the reform period will be examined and the types of reform enacted discussed, raising the question of actual abortion practice and the access of women to an abortion. Next, the politics of abortion reform will be analyzed, discussing the various strategies the political elites resort to when confronted by a disruptive issue. The argument will be made that precisely because the reform process was so difficult, it is also very unlikely that reforms will be overturned. Finally the major question will be tackled: why have the Western European reforms, with the exception of Germany (and possibly Spain) proved so stable?

THE ABORTION LAW REFORMS

The Western European abortion situation is relatively stable (Table 1 gives the dates of the Western European abortion reforms). From Table 1 it can be observed that the high tide of the Western European abortion reform occurred in the period from 1970 to 1986. In that period, too, early reformers in Sweden and Denmark readjusted their legislation to guarantee women's control over abortion. France, where the abortion reform was first enacted as a provisionary measure, confirmed the reform in 1979. With the coming to power there of the left-wing coalition in 1982, the final reform took place, ensuring financial support by national insurance for women having abortions (Mossuz-Lavau, 1986). In the mid-eighties only Ireland and Belgium (and the minor states of Monaco and Malta) had failed to liberalize their legislation, leaving intact very restrictive statutes dating back to the nineteenth century. After twenty years of debate, Belgium finally revised its abortion laws in 1990 (Witte, 1990, 1993). As discussed in chapter 8, Ireland has stuck to its extremely conservative position, enforcing the existing prohibitive legislation by constitutional amendment in 1983. With the legal tangles around several Irish and European Court cases, the Maastricht Treaty, and the 1992 referendum, however, the first cracks are beginning to appear in the hitherto impenetrable Irish edifice (Rolston and Eggert, 1994b). In Spain, further reform is pending; the Spanish government sent a new bill to parliament in June 1994 that aims at extending the grounds for abortion.[2]

Until German Unification in 1990, no European nation, except for Ireland, had changed its laws in a more restrictive direction. Prior to unification, West Germany had reformed modestly in 1976, allowing abortion on a limited number of grounds, while East Germany had had an abortion-on-request law. After much controversy, the German parliament finally passed a

TABLE 1
ABORTION IN WESTERN EUROPE: YEAR OF REFORM

NATION	YEAR
Switzerland	1942
Sweden	1960, 1967
Britain*	1967
Denmark	1970, 1975
Finland	1970
Austria	1974
Iceland	1975
France	1975, 1979, 1982
Germany (West)	1976
Luxembourg	1978
Italy	1978
Greece	1978, 1986
Norway	1978, 1979
Netherlands	1981
Ireland	1983, 1992
Portugal	1984
Spain	1986
Belgium	1990

*The 1967 Act does not apply to Northern Ireland, where no reform has taken place.
Sources: Ketting and van Praag, 1986; Outshoorn, 1988; Blayo, 1993.

very restrictive abortion bill in 1995. It allows for abortion until twelve weeks if a woman's mental or physical health is seriously endangered and has a small loophole for social grounds. Counseling for each woman is compulsory with the explicit aim of dissuading her from her intention to have an abortion.

For the purposes of comparison, several authors have endeavored to draw up a topology of laws (Ketting and van Praag, 1985, 1986; Glendon, 1987; Outshoorn, 1988; Rolston and Eggert, 1994a). Most classifications distinguish term models from indication models. Term models have a time limit; up to a certain time, usually twelve weeks, abortion is permitted on request, with or without special requirements, after which another regime is operative, usually only allowing abortion for health reasons or in the case of deformity of the fetus. Term models also differ as to whether they set an upper time limit; several nations have no time limit if health reasons are involved. Sometimes it is hard to distinguish term models from indication models, as some term models allow abortion on request if the woman is in a "state of distress" (France) or in an "untenable emergency situation," which can only be alleviated by an abortion (the Netherlands, Belgium); this is a stipulation close to an indication, enacted with the intent of pacifying parliamentary opponents of abortion law reform.

Indication models allow for abortion on a number of grounds. These can be medical grounds (with attendant debates about whether this also covers mental health), or they can take into account damage to the fetus, or allow for socioeconomic problems. They usually also include cases of pregnancy after rape and incest. "Narrow" types only allow medical indications; the "broader" ones will include the socioeconomic grounds. Much earlier reform in Europe started off as an indication type of law; but generally speaking over the course of time these reforms have proved unworkable. They were not liberal enough to satisfy the demands for reform from the emerging women's movement and the more radical "traditional reformers" such as various family planning and sexual reform groups. Moreover, indications lead to continual controversy over the interpretation of what constitutes a permissible reason for an abortion, resulting in considerable inequality before the law, which undermines the law's legitimacy. Britain, with its very early 1967 Abortion Act, is a clear case in point. Like much early abortion legislation, it was only meant to be a limited reform, allowing doctors to perform abortion without running the risk of prosecution. An indication model was drawn up, leaving the decision and interpretation firmly in hands of the medical profession (Sheldon, 1994). Paradoxically, Britain today has one of the most restrictive regimes in Western Europe, a long cry from the day when women from all over Europe traveled there for an abortion which they could not obtain under their own country's law.

Generally speaking, term models are more liberal than indication models, but further analysis is needed to establish whether abortion on request is possible, how indications are interpreted, and whether women have decent access to an abortion. In addition, the crucial question of control cannot be read off from the above topology. Who actually decides about an abortion? The woman herself, or a doctor or even two doctors? In case of indication types of laws, it will be the doctor (and sometimes, as in Britain, Switzerland, and West Germany before 1993, two doctors) interpreting the permitted indications, in which case women are placed in a dependent position and have to plead their case. Term models score quite well in terms of control up to the time limit, after which the doctors also take over, defining the exceptions allowed under the law. The clauses in the law about the actual decision are often (deliberately) ambiguous, not explicitly allowing an abortion on request, but not ruling it out either. Despite such clauses, in countries like Iceland, Finland (with an indication model!), and the Netherlands, abortion on request is the normal situation. If a woman states she is in a situation of distress because of the pregnancy, and abortion is the only way out of this state of distress, the doctor accepts this and will limit his or her intervention to checking to ensure that the woman is not being coerced into the abortion by her partner or parents. Only in Sweden (since the amendments of 1975), Denmark (since the 1973 revision of its legislation), and Norway (the 1979 revision) is abortion on request explicitly written into the statutes.

ABORTION IN PRACTICE

TABLE 2
TYPE OF ABORTION LEGISLATION IN WESTERN EUROPE

TERM MODEL (UP TO 12 WEEKS)	INDICATIONS (BROAD)	INDICATIONS (NARROW)	ILLEGAL
Austria	Britain	Portugal	Ireland
Belgium	Finland	Spain	Malta
Denmark	Italy	Germany	Monaco
France	Switzerland		
Greece			
Luxembourg			
Netherlands			
Norway			
Sweden			

Sources: Blayo, 1993; Rolston and Eggert, 1994a.

One should bear in mind, though, that legislation is only half the story when examining whether women can obtain abortions on request and in how far they actually have access to abortion facilities. It is generally accepted that the availability of proper medical services and financial support are crucial in going beyond mere *de jure* provision. The differences in access for women in various Western European nations to abortion facilities therefore vary more than just by what the legal provisions may lead one to believe.

From the work of Ketting and van Praag (1985, 1986), in which they compared nine Western European nations and the United States, one can derive several barriers to free abortion. First of all, there is the law itself. Does it allow for abortion on request or is the woman seeking an abortion dependent on others such as medical doctors? Does the framing of the law specify indications? Are there time limits after which abortion is not permitted? Is there a compulsory waiting period between approaching a doctor and the actual medical operation? Is registration of the operation required by statute? Is a second opinion of another doctor required? Is parental consent required in the case of minors? (The consent of the father of the fetus is not required in any Western European statute.[3]) Is counseling required? Is advice on "solutions" other than abortion obligatory? Does it specify where abortions have to take place, for instance, only in hospitals?

Second, barriers to access can be found in the implementation of the legislation. This mainly revolves around the question of whether sufficient hospitals, clinics, and doctors willing to perform abortions are available. Institutional factors such as different hospital systems, the possibility to set up private clinics, and the presence of trained personnel are key factors here. Of extreme importance are the attitudes of hospital and clinic boards and personnel. Most European laws allow for a conscience clause, i.e., that personnel can refuse help in abortion cases for reasons of conscience. Doctors are not always obliged to refer the woman seeking an abortion to a more cooperative colleague; and sometimes these colleagues do not exist. Because of such limitations, in Roman Catholic regions and nations it has proved much more difficult to implement reform legislation. In the seventies, this factor was important in accounting for differences between nations. Relatively liberal laws in France were circumvented by conservative Catholic doctors and nursing staff, but the situation improved after the 1982 reform, which was also an attempt to compel hospitals to provide services. Availability remains a crucial problem in Spain and Portugal after their very limited reforms. Even women who fall under the cases delineated by the law have considerable difficulty in obtaining professional help. Needless to say, clandestine abortions continue to flourish: for Spain, estimates are around 70,000 a year; for Portugal, no figures are available (Rolston and Eggert, 1994a: xxvii).

Interregional discrepancies within nations can also be accounted for by this factor. Germany has had a North-South split in availability for years: the conservative Catholic Lander of Bavaria and Baden-Wurttemberg applied the 1976 regulation in the strictest manner possible, while in the northern (and Protestant) cities of Bremen and Hamburg facilities for abortion are widely available (Ketting and van Praag, 1985). In Italy abortion has remained inaccessible for poorer women from the rural South and in those areas where the Catholic Church has managed to retain control of the hospital services (Caldwell, 1986). In Austria, the Vienna district with its big-city secular tradition provides good facilities, in contrast to the rural and conservative districts of Tyrol and Salzburg (Ketting and van Praag, 1985; Lehner, 1994). French-speaking Belgians found their way into clinics in their own part of the country, traditionally the industrialized and more secularized area, while Dutch-speaking Belgian women crossed over the Dutch border for their abortions for years through lack of similar facilities and an active prosecution policy in Flanders.

Because of these differences a lively traffic, often called "abortion-tourism" by anti-abortionists, has always been part of the European landscape. Before the major reforms of the seventies, Dutch women traveled to London, Austrians to Yugoslavia, and Scandinavians to Poland. From 1972 onward West Germans traveled to the Netherlands, as did the Belgians, the French, and the Spanish. The Irish are still traveling to England. One of the reasons that the incumbent government party, the Christian Democrats in Germany, was keen to develop one new federal law as part of the unification treaty was to prevent West German women traveling into the former Eastern Lander, where a term-law was operative since 1972, making abortion on request accessible for women until the twelfth week of pregnancy.[4]

Although it can be argued that this abortion traffic can work as a safety valve, taking pressure off the necessity for reform, which has demonstrably been the case in Belgium, it is more likely that it has promoted the speed of the reforms. Countries were very much aware of what was going on across the border, and although authorities did try to interfere with women crossing over, in due course they also became convinced that the traffic could only be stopped by reform in their own countries. It also meant that abortion reform was not something distant or abstract happening in a totally different culture, but something going on right on your own doorstep. For this reason, the early reforms of Sweden and Britain had an impact going far beyond the material effect of allowing women from abroad to obtain an abortion. It brought home to other nations' political elites the issue that reform could not be avoided altogether.

At the stage of implementation, the monitoring of the law can provide barriers for women seeking an abortion. Usually the text of the law is in need of interpretation, giving doctors and women some leeway in how the abortion decision is taken. If, however, some form of registration is required of this process, doctors can be called to account for their interpretation. Through this channel, public prosecutors can restrict the workings of the law and limit access. This has been very much the case in Germany, where occasional prosecutions in the South kept doctors towing the line. In Spain a doctor was recently jailed for performing abortions, which, according to the prosecution and the court, were only made possible by his too-liberal reading of the indications allowed under Spanish law.[5]

Finally, the cost of abortion is a potential barrier. In the early period of reform especially, when doctors often had to take risks to perform abortions, fees were high and only more affluent women were able to obtain a medically safe abortion. Today, fees are still high when abortion is taboo and not openly discussed, or when most abortions are *de jure* illegal, as in Portugal, Spain, and also in Switzerland. Doctors are then protected from the workings of the free market and can set their own fees. The demand for the inclusion of abortion in a national health insurance scheme has therefore always been part of the demands of both the women's movements and the various reform groups. It also has been a concern shared by Western Europe's many socialist parties, who have included state funding in their party platforms. Reform groups providing abortion facilities in private clinics have always had reserve funds providing financial assistance to those women who could not afford to pay. They also kept their prices at an acceptable level. Once abortion became legalized, it also became possible to regulate abortion fees and put a rein on doctors' tendencies to use their monopoly to set prices at a profitable level. In most European nations today, national health insurance covers the cost of an abortion on condition of it being performed under the terms of its national legislation. This is not the case in Austria, however (Ketting and van Praag, 1986: 161; Lehner, 1994: 11). In Britain, abortion is only refunded if it is done in one of the hospitals of the National Health Service, but only about half of all abortions are actually performed there (Berer, 1993: 39). Half of all women go to private clinics and pay themselves. This is not only due to the long waiting lists of the National Health Service, but also because these abortions fall under the terms of the 1967 Abortion Act with its paternalistic treatment of women, requiring the consent of two doctors and their assessment of the indications as final.

Given the different barriers, it is very difficult to make an assessment of the access of women to abortion facilities and their *de facto* control over abortion decisions. On the basis of their extensive 1983 study of nine Western European states, Ketting and van Praag (1986: 160–61) defined Sweden as the nation allowing women the greatest degree of self-determination, with Denmark and Austria as second, and the Netherlands, France, and Italy in third place. Assessment is difficult, however, as the weighing of the various factors operating in the matter of self-determination can hardly be done by objective indicators. In Ketting and van Praag's assessment, regional differences were not taken fully into account. This becomes apparent by looking at Austria and Italy, who end up high in this hierarchy, while both countries are characterized by a poor geographic spread of facilities. Traveling for an abortion is both a financial and psychological burden for women and does form a real barrier in a number of cases (especially for young women and poorer women).

Abortion rates are not good indicators of women's access to abortion facilities. They also do not say much about the effectiveness of abortion legislation. They do reflect several other extremely important indicators for women's health, which indirectly contribute to their self-determination. Low abortion figures indicate the level of knowledge about the availability and use of contraceptives and the presence of medical provisions and the level of sex education. In addition, there is the problem of obtaining reliable figures on abortion rates, even for countries where registration is required and illegal abortion is virtually absent. In their recent overview Rolston and Eggert (1994a: xxiv–xxviii) do supply statistics, but these are difficult to compare, as the size of the population is not mentioned and figures per nation are calculated in various different ways. Henshaw and Morrow (1990) indicate that the Netherlands has the lowest abortion rate in the world, less than half of the English rate and one-fourth of the Danish and Swedish rate. It can also be noted that countries with a very low abortion rate, such as the Scandinavian nations and the Netherlands, also have the most liberal abortion regimes in Western Europe and probably in the world. This fact can be attributed to the widespread use of contraceptives and an open climate around sexuality and sex education at all schools. A careful assessment of the degree of self-determination for women in Western Europe today would therefore show that all Scandinavian countries and the Netherlands rate at the top. Falling below the average would be Germany, Britain, Italy, and drawing up the rear Spain, Portugal, and Ireland.

Summarizing the argument thus far, abortion law reform, which was accomplished in the seventies and early eighties, has not been repealed. The adopted legislation conveys that Western European abortion laws reconcile many opposing principles, coming up with different time limits, indications, and stipulations about facilities, to ensure what politicians have labeled "conscientious decision-making." Most of the laws necessitated compromise and much of the legislation was often deliberately drafted in ambiguous terms, so one has to read in between the lines to interpret the intent of the bill in question. Actual practice cannot be deduced from the prevailing laws, but there is a considerable literature that enables assessment of access for women seeking an abortion. For access they are dependent on unequivocal interpretations of the law, cooperative medical personnel, reasonable facilities, and acceptable prices and refunding on state medical insurance.

THE POLITICS OF ABORTION REFORM

The major point to note when discussing the politics of abortion law reform in Western Europe is that all cases are decided in the various national parliaments. On a first examination, this may not seem surprising, as all of these nations have parliamentary systems. Abortion was part of many penal codes and prohibited by parliamentary acts, and their strict formulations allowed little room for legal interpretations to establish exceptions and develop a more liberal jurisprudence. So when demands for reform arise, parliament becomes the natural arena for reform decision making. But when one takes into account the nature of the prevailing party systems, it becomes rather surprising that parliaments and governments were willing to tackle the issue at all, especially when the abortion issue increasingly was becoming defined as a position issue (Outshoorn, 1986) on which parties cannot agree about goals, so that compromise becomes very difficult to develop.

As an issue, abortion cuts across the dominant cleavage of Western European party systems, which are based on the socioeconomic cleavages of these societies. This means that political parties will not easily take a stand on abortion, which touches on the secular/religious divide. In a few nations, this cleavage overlaps with the left-right divide. In such nations, abortion was immediately part of the major cleavage; it was the socialist party, also standing for secular values, which created reform once it had a parliamentary majority, as happened in Austria, Spain, Portugal, and Greece. In other party systems, the secular/religious cleavage is expressed in the existence of substantial religious parties, usually the Christian Democrat parties, who define the abortion issue according to the religious doctrines of the major Christian churches. In that case, abortion aggravates the cross-cutting cleavages, making for complications in the bargaining over coalitions needed to ensure a majority government in multi-party systems. However, openings for a resolution of conflict lie in everyday political life. These parties also tend to let socioeconomic issues dictate their political agenda, as they are fully aware that voters let these issues prevail when marking their ballots. Christian Democrat parties also have to reckon with possible coalition partners for government in those systems where a majority government can only be formed by more than one party (as is the case in the Netherlands, Belgium, Luxembourg, Italy, and often in Germany). In countries where the secular/religious divide has not led to major party formation, abortion reform could take place early.

But even in situations of a clear majority government, political elites will try to prevent the issue from gaining agenda status, as within parties there is often no consensus on the issue.[6] They know abortion has the potential to divide the electoral party. Several strategies will be resorted to in order not to deal with the issue. First of all, governments and party leaders will try to avoid taking a stand. One way of doing so is to deny that abortion is the government's responsibility, requiring action on its part, or to stall by saying that public opinion is not ripe for such an innovation. They can decide to leave it to other institutions, for instance to the medical profession, to develop careful practices or to the courts by instructing the public prosecution to

TABLE 3
ABORTION POLITICS AND PARTY SYSTEMS

NATION	CLEAVAGES	SUBSTANTIAL RELIGOUS PARTY	PARTY SYSTEM AND EFFECTIVE NO. OF PARTIES	NECESSITY OF COALITION GOVERNMENT	YEAR(S) OF REFORM	GOVERNMENT AT TIME OF REFORM	GOVERNMENT BILL OR PARLIAMENTARY INITIATIVE
Iceland	l/r; c/p	no	MP with D3.5	yes	1975	center-right	G
Finland	l/r; c/p	no	MP 5.0	yes	1970	broad center/ experts	G(?)
Sweden	l/r; c/p	no	MP with D 3.2	yes	1960 1967	left coalition	G(?) G(?)
Norway	l/r; c/p	no	MP with D 3.2	yes	1978 1979	soc. minority?	G(?) ?
Denmark	l/r; c/p	no	MP with D 4.3	yes	1970 1973	rad/lib/cons soc. minority	G G(?)
England	l/r	no	two-party 2.1	no	1967	Labour	PI
Germany	l/r; s/r	yes	two-and-a-half** 2.6	yes	1995	Chr. Dem/ liberal	G -
Luxembourg	l/r; s/r	yes	two-and-a-half 3.3	yes	1978	Chr. Dem/ socialist	?
Netherlands	l/r; s/r	yes	MP 4.9	yes	1981	Chr. Dem/ liberal	G
Belgium	l/r; s/r; lb	yes	MP 3.7	yes	1990	Chr. Dem/ socialist	PI
Austria	l/r; s/r	yes	two-and-a-half 2.2	some-times	1974	socialist	G
Switzerland	l/r; s/r; lb	yes	MP 4.3	yes	1942	national coalition(?)	G
France	l/r; s/r; overlap	no	MP 3.3***	yes	1975 1979 1982	center/right center/right left-wing coalition	G G G
Italy	l/r; s/r; overlap	no	MP with D 3.5	yes	1978	Chr. Dem. minority	PI
Spain	l/r; s/r; overlap	no	MP with D 2.5****	no	1986	socialist	G(?)
Portugal	l/r; s/r; overlap	no	MP 4****	yes	1984	socialist/liberal	?
Greece	l/r	no	MP 3****	some-times	1978 1986	socialist socialist	G(?) G(?)
Ireland	on nationalist question	no	two-and-a-half 2.8	some-times	1983 1992	Fine Gael/ Labour Fianna Fail	

Cleavages: l/r = left/right; c/p=center/periphery; s/r=secular/religious;lb=language barriers
MP: multi-party system
MP with D: multi-party system with one dominant party
*score from: Lijphart, 1984: 125–126
**term from: Blondel, cit. in Lijphart, 1984: 118; two big parties and one small party sometimes needed for government majority
***score only for Fifth Republic
****no scores in Lijphart, 1986; my approximation
Sources: Lijphart, 1984; Woldendorp, Keman, and Bunch, 1993; Lovenduski and Outshoorn, 1986; Rolston and Eggert (1994a); author's research.

refrain from prosecuting the most clearly medical and therapeutic cases. But this strategy becomes very difficult to maintain once the reform movement starts mobilizing and groups demand action against emerging abortion practices. But even then the government can refrain from taking a stand, as happened in England. The 1967 Abortion Act was the result of a private member's bill by the Liberal David Steel (thus not a member of one of the two major parties). All later attempts at revising this bill in a more restrictive sense, no less than ten in total, were by private member initiative as well. Indirectly, the incumbent party does give support by allowing for scarce parliamentary time to debate the private member's bill. But abortion has always remained a bipartisan issue, although Conservative MPs are more likely to support restrictive measures.

This policy of avoidance can even be seen once a bill is being voted on in parliament. Then it is often left to the individual conscience of the member of parliament how he or she is to vote. No party discipline is imposed, in order not to aggravate internal party dissent. The only exceptions to this rule have been the vote on the Norwegian and Dutch abortion bills, where, although hotly denied by party spokesmen, whips were imposed (Wiik, 1986: 149; Outshoorn, 1986: 269). Most recently the policy of avoiding a party position could be observed in the new German Bundestag when it voted for a new bill in 1992. As noted, the proposal accepted was drafted by women members of various parliamentary groups and it was also left to a free vote. It split the Christian Democrat Party (CDU), as a number of its parliamentary members supported the initiative bill. This bill was struck down by the Federal Supreme Court in Karlsruhe in May 1993 as unconstitutional, as it was held not to guarantee sufficient protection of the unborn.

When attempts to avoid the issue fail and it is placed on the political agenda, governments deploy various strategies of postponement to avoid really having to deal with it. A time-honored postponement act is to appoint an official commission to study the issue. This commission usually represents divergent views on the issue, so it will take time before it comes up with advice. Commissions can postpone matters endlessly, but they do have the advantage that they can lead to a debate and can contribute to the development of public opinion. Governments in Sweden, Finland, Denmark, the Netherlands, and Belgium all appointed such bodies in the early stages of reform. Another favorite postponement tactic has been to propose a "non-aggression pact" (no debates or voting on parliamentary initiative bills in exchange for no prosecution of abortions likely to fall under the pending reforms). This has been part of Dutch and Belgian abortion politics. Postponement has also been employed in Germany at the time of unification. In the treaty of unification the Bundestag was allowed no less than two years to draft a new bill to replace the divergent legal regimes in the two "old Germanys."

The political elite may also try to defuse the topic by turning it into a matter to be left to experts. This strategy of depoliticizing abortion can be combined with strategies of avoidance and postponement, as in the case of setting up an expert commission. But it is also resorted to in later stages of the policy process. Many early reforms did just that: making abortion a medical issue by leaving it to the doctors, as happened in Switzerland very early on, and later in England. Leaving it to the courts is another tactic. But this strategy became increasingly unfeasible when the women's movement was able to redefine abortion as a lay issue, a matter in which a woman is her own best expert. Once framed as a subject for self-determination, the woman becomes the central person to make the decision. This leaves no room for experts to determine the woman's best interests.

It was the strength of the rising women's movement of the late sixties and early seventies that put an end to stalling governments and the politics of delay. Combined with the already existing reform groups, they radicalized the demand for reform by asking outright for total repeal of earlier restrictions and for abortion on request. Many earlier reform groups had been more prudent in their aims, letting doctors perform abortions on a number of indications without running the risk of prosecution. The subject was placed squarely on the political agenda, and the women's movement and its allies saw to it that new reform bills had to be formulated and taken to the vote in parliament. This happened after considerable mobilization had taken place and public opinion had shifted to a more liberal position. By that time, most political parties and relevant interest groups such as the medical profession, legal experts, and the various churches had had their say. Public demonstrations took place, while heavy-handed prosecutors clamped down on doctors performing abortions and referral services. Sometimes the women's movement occupied an abortion clinic to prevent it from being shut down by the local authorities. When the issue did arrive in parliament, there was high public awareness of the various aspects of abortion and the necessity for some extent of reform.

But because of cross-cutting cleavages and coalition complications, enactment was never a straightforward affair. The high incidence of private member's bills construction has already been pointed out, while in most cases in Western Europe parliamentary systems, governments take the initiative on policy proposals. It must be said that this occurred most frequently at the early stages of the abortion debate, with governments gradually taking over and incorporating parts of these earlier bills into their compromises. But in Britain, Italy, and Belgium, parliamentary initiatives resolved the issue. There is also the question of free voting, another unusual procedure in the time-honored practice of party discipline in parliament. Even when a bill was passed, not all its legislative troubles were over. After the vote has been taken, it has to be proclaimed law and signed by the responsible cabinet minister and the head of state. An unwilling minister can then again postpone implementation or can threaten to withhold his or her signature. The most spectacular example of this has been the enactment of the Belgian abortion reform in 1990. After twenty years of stalemate, parliament finally accepted a compromise bill drafted by MPs. Then the King, a devout Catholic, refused his signature, which meant it could not become law. The Belgian cabinet then devised a creative if debatable novelty to ensure its passing. It based its action on a constitutional provision to be used in case the sovereign is unable to exert his powers. The provision enables the council of ministers (cabinet) to take over his powers. The King was "suspended" for one night; the council signed the bill and parliament approved of the procedure in a special session the next day, after which the King was reinstated (Witte, 1993: 79).

The bills enacted represent a compromise solution, negotiated by the major political parties in parliament and the government of the day. Even when a party had a parliamentary majority, it had to take into account the opinions of others, as parties were well aware that the abortion issue could also split their party and their electoral following. (This led to complaints of reformers and feminists that the party was opting out.) Only in Scandinavia is abortion on request the formal legal situation. In countries where this is in fact the case, legal provisions reflect the bargaining process between the political parties in parliament. Phrases such as the "situation of distress" are a way of defining an indication for abortion to avoid stipulating strict grounds, but also to avoid saying outright that the decision is up to the woman herself. Making enactment conditional on evaluation, as happened in France and Belgium, can also be seen as attempts to pacify the opposition.[7]

Many bills contain a so-called waiting period, for three to five days, between a woman's first consultation with a doctor and the actual operation. It has been introduced to prevent "hasty decision making," a favorite phrase among opponents of reform who perceive women as rushing into irresponsible behavior. Such a clause is not just a symbolic appeasement, however. It is often used to prevent women coming from abroad to obtain an abortion, usually with little success, as clinics have found ways around this clause. It is important to note that no bill in Europe denies women living in another country access to an abortion outright. This would interfere with the free traffic of persons, goods, and services guaranteed by various European international treaties. Similarly, national governments cannot prevent its nationals from going abroad for an abortion, although this was precisely what an Irish High Court tried to do in 1992 in the notorious case of the fourteen-year-old girl who had been raped by the father of her best friend and wanted to go to

England for an abortion. The referendum of 1992 did, however, ensure the right of women to travel abroad (Rolston and Eggert, 1994b: 119).

Glendon has argued that the rhetoric of the various European laws should not be viewed cynically as "mere political compromise," maintaining, rather, that Western European laws reaffirm certain basic values in society, while the 1973 decision of the United States Supreme Court does not (1987: 140–41). While the phrasing of the laws has certainly contributed to the successful pacification of the abortion issue, there is no such thing as "mere political compromise." Compromise, along with conflict, especially in the multi-party context of Western Europe, is the essence of politics.

OUT OF STEP: WESTERN EUROPEAN EXCEPTIONS

If one looks at the two major exceptions to the stability of the Western European scene, Ireland and Germany, it can be noted that in both cases external factors enabled the anti-abortion groups to prevent reform or to reopen the debate and get the issue back on to the political agenda. In Germany this was the factor of unification, in Ireland it was the Maastricht Treaty of 1991.

As mentioned, the Einigungsvertrag gave the legislature two years to come up with a harmonization of the two different abortion regimes. The abortion debate returned in all its earlier vehemence, with both reformers and anti-abortionists remobilizing (Rucht, 1994). In 1992 a parliamentary initiative bill, which stood closer to the East German law allowing abortion on request, acquired a majority. A new phenomenon was that the original version was drafted by an all-women group of Bundestag members who were from all the major parliamentary parties. Also, it split the Christian Democrat vote. The losing CDU (Christian Democratic Union) members and the members of its southern partner CSU (Christian Socialist Union) (which had not split on the vote) then took the bill to the federal Court in Karlsruhe for judicial review. It was suspended by the Court the day before it was to become effective, and in 1993 the Court pronounced it be in contradiction to the constitution, as it was held to be insufficiently protective of the rights of the unborn. In February 1995 the Bundestag opened its debates on an adjusted version. As a result, and because of the Karlsruhe decision, abortion is illegal unless performed on medical grounds, although not prosecuted if it occurs within the first twelve weeks of pregnancy. Because it is illegal, there is no longer refunding from the national health service insurance save for abortions on medical grounds (Klein Schonnefeld, 1994).

The Irish situation was very stable after 1983, but events at the beginning of the nineties have led to stormy debates and may well have led to the end of this stability, with the first openings in the legal situation already emerging. There was the case of the young girl seeking to travel to England for an abortion and the prosecution of women's health centers who provided information about abortion services, which led to several court cases right up to the European Commission.[8] Although the Maastricht Treaty had nothing to say about abortion, anti-abortion groups in Ireland persuaded the government to introduce a protocol to the effect that the European Community would not override domestic law on abortion in Ireland (Rolston and Eggert, 1994b: 166). This would stop any Irish citizen from invoking European law on freedom of information and movement (see chapter 8).

In other Western European nations it has by no means been the case that the anti-abortion groups gave up the fight after liberalization occurred, but it is unlikely they will be successful in these countries. They have been very active and strong in all the nations with a substantial Roman Catholic population. The Church has given both strong moral and material support to various groups. In Italy the anti-abortion groups managed to get enough votes in 1981 to hold a referendum to repeal the reform, only allowing abortion on very restricted grounds, but they gained only 32 percent of the vote. In Britain, a coalition of Catholic anti-abortion groups with the right wing of other churches managed to stage a series of private member's bills to amend the 1967 Act, but each time the bill was either voted down or it ran out of time. The 1990 Human Fertilization and Embryology Act did place an upper time limit of twenty-four weeks to the Act, but it also confirmed the Act in other respects (Sheldon, 1994). In Austria anti-abortion groups took the reform law to the Supreme Court straight after its enactment in 1974, but, contrary to the federal German Court in 1975, it was held to be constitutional (Lehner, 1994). In Scandinavia and the Netherlands anti-abortion groups are active, but they have been marginalized in the course of the debate. In Belgium anti-abortion groups have been very successful in fending off reform, being very closely allied with the Flemish Christian People's Party. The recent draft for reform in Spain is already leading to a concerted counter-campaign, but recent public opinion polls show that a majority of the Spanish population is actually in favor of further reform.

What in effect has happened after the reform is that the natural allies of the anti-abortion groups, the Christian Democrat parties, have given up the fight. They refrain from tackling the issue again for fear of internal dissent; in some cases they have in due course accepted or committed themselves to the compromise reform, often from political realism. Public opinion polls indicate that among Catholic voters in many countries there is by now also a majority accepting at least an indication type of law.[9]

In summary, in no Western European nation was abortion law reform a simple affair, taken care of by routine policymaking at the national level; in the prevailing political systems reform was in the end always enacted by the parliaments. Both the tortuous process of reform and the necessity of parliamentary action are major barriers to any group now wanting to revise the existing compromise. The abortion issue has proved so unsettling for the "normal business of politics" (the usual socioeconomic issues) and so disruptive for intra-party consensus and external coalition formation that political elites have become very unwilling to reopen any debate on the issue. One can actually maintain that the factors that made abortion law reform difficult in the first place are now also the factors inhibiting a renewed place for the topic on the political agenda, and these make it unlikely that the clock can be turned back.

THE STABILITY OF COMPROMISE

How can the relative stability of the Western European situation be accounted for then? The most important reason is undoubtedly that all the Western European reforms have been enacted in parliament, which makes them difficult to undo. In all cases parliamentary decisions were hotly debated over a prolonged period of time, making the public well aware of the issue and leading to a solid front of social movements and interest groups on both sides of the subject. This has also meant that parties had to define the common ground. Compromise was negotiated, in the process of which a majority was formed, however precarious negotiations often were. Politicians and parties have invested heavily in it, making their support more durable.

Moreover, as Rucht (1994) has pointed out in his comparison of the United States, France, and Germany, parliamentary decisions are sustained by political parties, which, in comparison to the United States, are deeply rooted in European society. The political parties have managed to regulate and to pacify the reform process, which in the decision-making stage marginalized the opposition outside parliament. It can be added that, as parties are still well-rooted within society, they have also evolved in their party platforms along with society at large. Since the time of reform, public opinion has shifted generally toward more liberal positions and has been remarkably constant over the last decade. From public opinion research it can also be observed that it was always ahead of parliament. If legislation lagged too far behind public opinion, this has meant sustained mobilization for further liberalization. This is shown very clearly in the case of West German settlement of 1976, which was more conservative than German opinion, leading to a constant level of mobilization of both sides of the issue and to women "voting with their feet," going abroad or to the North for an abortion. The same may be observed in present-day Spain.

Only a few systems provide another channel of political action through the possibility of judicial review, but this can only be resorted to at the national level after parliamentary decision making has taken place. Activists therefore must take the parliamentary route and tackle the relevant political parties. In those countries having judicial review, anti-abortionists, when losing out on the issue in parliament, shifted the arena of the debate and took the case to court (in Austria, Germany, and up to a point Ireland) (Outshoorn, 1988).

Although developments such as the new reproductive technologies touch on abortion, it seems unlikely that they will lead to repeal of the reforms, although anti-abortionists undoubtedly will utilize these to reopen the discussion. The European discussion about RU 486 is a case in point. Propagated by the believers in technological solutions to social problems as the pill that would give women the right to self-determination and also as a way to bypass the whole issue, it was very quickly defused by various governments. Its use was regulated by quickly bringing the pill under medical professional control.[10] The same strategies can be observed by the political elites and governments in handling the issues of the new reproductive technologies. Having learned the lesson from the abortion debate (avoid the political arena), the potential issues arising from these developments are made into medical professional matters. In the long run the medical profession may become more of a threat to women's reproductive self-determination than all the Christian Democrat parties together. It will take the emergence of a new cleavage and coalition in Western European politics to counteract the forms of control and discipline that the new biotechnology is making imaginable and possible.

NOTES

1. For further references, see the contributions in: Lovenduski and Outshoorn, 1986 (covering Belgium, Britain, France, Ireland, Italy, the Netherlands, Norway, and the United States); Rolston and Eggert, 1994a (covering in Western Europe all nations except Iceland, Italy, and Greece).

2. The bill is a term model, allowing for abortion on request until twelve weeks. A woman has to observe a three-day waiting period and undergo counseling about so-called alternatives to abortion. With the socialist majority in uncertainty, the fate of the bill is uncertain.

3. This would also be in contravention to the jurisprudence on Art. 8 of the European Convention of Human Rights, in which the European Commission on Human Rights pronounced the interests of the woman to prevail above those of the potential father. See: *8416/79 x v United Kingdom European Commission of Human Rights, Decisions and Reports,* 19 (October 1980): 244–45.

4. East Germany had a term model; abortion on request up to twelve weeks was possible. A woman was counseled about contreception, and the abortion had to be done in a state clinic. It was also refunded by state insurance. After twelve weeks of pregnancy abortion was only possible on stricter grounds, to be judged by a commission (Klein-Schonnefeld, 1994: 117–18).

5. NRC Handelsblad, May 1, 1995.

6. The discussion of abortion politics is based on Outshoorn, 1986.

7. The Belgian law is to be evaluated by a special Evaluation Commission, whose members will have to represent various views and professions (Witte, 1993: 77) within two years. The Commission turned out its first major report in December 1994, which estimated the Belgian abortion figure to be around 13,000 a year, a decrease in comparison to earlier estimates. This finding gives the anti-abortion groups very little leverage to reopen the debate. There have been some parliamentary questions, but the general opinion is that the issue is now settled. Abortion is not part of the current coalition government's platform.

8. At the time two women's health centers were appealing to the European Courts on Irish courts' decisions against the dissemination of information about abortion services, invoking the Art. 10, freedom of information clause, of the European Convention of Human Rights. The Commission upheld their appeal in 1991 and referred the case to the Court, which upheld this decision in October 1992 (Rolston and Eggert, 1994: 164).

9. For indications of this, see the various contributions in Rolston and Eggert (1994a) and the overview they provide on pp. xxiv–xxix.

10. For France and Germany: Rucht, 1994; for Britain: Sheldon, 1994.

REFERENCES

Berer, M. 1993. "Abortion in Europe from a Woman's Perspective." In K. Newman, ed., *Progress Postponed: Abortion in Europe in the 1990s.* London: International Planned Parenthood Federation Europe Region: 31–46.

Blayo, C. 1993. "Abortion in Europe: Access to Abortion: the Legal Context, Practice and Frequency of Recourse. " *Entre Nous* 22/23: 6–9.

Caldwell, L. 1986. "Feminism and Abortion Politics in Italy." In J. Lovenduski and J. Outshoorn, eds., *The New Politics of Abortion.* London/Beverly Hills: Sage, 105–124.

Eser, A., and H.G. Koch. 1988. *Schwangerschaftsabbruch im Internationalen Vergleich.* Baden-Baden: Nomos Verlag.

Glendon, M.A. 1987. *Abortion and Divorce in Western Law: America Failures, European Challenges.* Cambridge: Harvard University Press.

Henshaw, S.K., and E. Morrow. 1990. *Induced Abortion: A World Review.* New York: Alan Guttmacher Institute.

Ketting, E., and Ph. van Praag. 1985. *Schwangerschaftsabbruch: Gesetz und Praxis im Internationalen Vergleich.* Tubingen: DGVT Verlag.

Ketting, E., and Ph. van Praag. 1986. *The Marginal Relevance of Legislation Relating to Induced Abortion.* In J. Lovenduski and J. Outshoorn, eds., *The New Politics of Abortion.* London/Beverly Hills: Sage, 154–170.

Klein-Schonnefeld, S. 1994. "Germany." In B. Rolston, B. and A. Eggert, eds., *Abortion in the New Europe. A Comparative Handbook.* Westport, CT/London: Greenwood Press, 113–139.

Lovenduski, J., and J. Outshoorn, eds. 1986. *The New Politics of Abortion.* London/Beverly Hills: Sage.

Marques-Pereira, B. 1989. *L'avortement en Belgique. De la clandestine au debat publique.* Bruxelles: Eds. de l'Université de Bruxelles.

Mossuz-Lavau, J. 1986. "Abortion Policy in France under Governments of the Right and the Left." In J. Lovenduski and J. Outshoorn, eds., *The New Politics of Abortion*. London/Beverly Hills: Sage, 86–105.

Outshoorn, J. 1986. *De politieke strijd rondom de abortuswetgeving in Nederland, 1964–1984*. Den Haag: VUGA.

Outshoorn, J. 1988. "Abortion Law Reform: A Woman's Right to Choose?" In: M. Buckley and M. Andersen, eds., *Women, Equality and Europe*. Basingstoke: New York: McMillan, 204–220.

Rolston, B., and A. Eggert, eds. 1994a. *Abortion in the New Europe. A Comparative Handbook*. Westport, CT/London: Greenwood Press.

Rolston, B., and A. Eggert. 1994b. "Ireland." In B. Rolston and A. Eggert, eds., *Abortion in the New Europe. A Comparative Handbook*. Westport, CT/London: Greenwood Press, 157–173.

Rucht, D. 1994. *Modernisierung und Soziale Bewegungen*. Frankfurt: Campus Verlag.

Sheldon, S. 1994. "Into the Hands of the Medical Profession: the Regulation of Abortion in England and Wales." Unpublished dissertation, European University Institute, Florence.

Wiik, J. 1986. "The Abortion Issue, Political Cleavage and the Political Agenda in Norway." In J. Lovenduski and J. Outshoorn, eds., *The New Politics of Abortion*. London/Beverly Hills: Sage, 139–154.

Witte, E. 1990. "Twintig jaar strijd rondom de abortuswetgeving in Belgie (1970–1990)." *Res Publica* 32, 4: 427–487.

Witte, E. 1993. De liberalisering van de Abortus-wetgeving in Belgie (1970–1990). In M. Scheys, ed., *Abortus*. Brussels: VUB Press, 21–103.

CHAPTER 8

IRELAND AND THE EUROPEAN UNION: THE IMPACT OF INTEGRATION AND SOCIAL CHANGE ON ABORTION POLICY

BRIAN GIRVIN

INTRODUCTION

Policymaking within the European Union takes place at many levels. The *Treaty of Rome*, subsequent additions to it, and new treaties establish the parameters for policy formation at the level of the European Union.[1] Insofar as the treaties are applicable, community law is the law for each of the member states. There are other areas, more ambiguous and intermediate, where policy is unclear or where national governments have retained more authority. At the other extreme, there are policy areas that come entirely under the jurisdiction of the individual national governments. This tension between the evolution of the European Union and the authority of the individual state has usually been framed in terms of integration versus sovereignty, presupposing a zero-sum game between the two. This, as recent research has shown, is an inadequate approach to the question. Milward (1993) has argued that integration itself has been a product of the push of "national interest," and the process does not necessarily undermine the authority of the state.

Policy formation and implementation may thus operate at different levels depending on the nature of the subject. In most economic matters, the member states are constrained by the integrationist framework of the treaties, whereas in defense the arrangements remain intergovernmental. Some areas of policy formation may be at a transnational level, but implementation can be left to the individual governments. Thus, the concept of subsidiarity is important in that it insists that the policy of the European Union should be appropriate to the level at which it is aimed. One policy may be appropriately designed to cover all member states, whereas another would be designed by and implemented by a sub-national government (Dinan, 1993; Nicoll and Salmon, 1994).

Comparing public policies alerts the analyst to differences and similarities. Different states approach issues in different ways, taking up some issues and ignoring others. Elites in a particular system may successfully exclude some issues from debate for a considerable time, while others may place the issue at the forefront of debate at a very early stage. After the ratification of the Maastricht Treaty in 1992, and in the run up to the proposed Inter-governmental Conference in 1996, there is considerable evidence to suggest that the European Union sees itself and its institutions as playing a central role in the promotion of a common policy network for the member states. The Maastricht Treaty is certainly considerably more ambitious than anything which has preceded it in the development of European integration. It seeks to introduce new policy areas that would be within the competence of the European Union (EU) institutions, and this includes a common security and foreign policy as a major focus for the first time.

The expansion of the EU involves a considerable lessening of the autonomy of individual states, but it does not involve the end of national sovereignty. Issues that are outside the jurisdiction of the treaties will continue to be handled by the state, especially if these issues are moral and cultural. It may be true that decisions of the European Court of Justice are binding on the member states, but the Court has to operate within the limits imposed by the treaties. Moral and cultural matters are correctly perceived as controversial and best left to the individual state to define. Indeed, the submission of the European Union to the United Nations International Conference on Population and Development in Cairo in 1994 insisted that abortion policy would be determined by the member states and not by the Union.

This is to be expected, given the diversity of opinion within Western Europe. Despite this, abortion policy in Europe lends itself to comparative analysis. By placing the Irish position in context with that of its European partners, it should be possible to determine why the Irish government pursues a specific strategy and what the formative influences on this policy are (Heidenheimer, 1990: 3). The study of abortion policy in this context also highlights a number of unique features about the politics of abortion. It is a relatively new political object, a product of the changes which have taken place since the 1960s. It is also a cross-cutting issue, in that predominant and established voting patterns are not predictable on this subject. It is also an extremely controversial area of debate since it confronts traditional values, beliefs, and processes. It juxtaposes conservatism with liberal or radical politics within a new political and social arena. At a further level, abortion can demonstrate, and this is the case in Ireland, the ability of radical policy initiatives elsewhere generating the momentum for opposition to similar policies in a state where the issue is not salient and where elites and the public have not attempted to raise it. Inaction can bring about a reaction as well as action. The political structure of a society will affect the policy mix favored by a government, and this will determine the outcome of policy in many such circumstances (Lovenduski and Outshoorn, 1986; Girvin, 1986).

THE EUROPEAN CONTEXT

Ireland has been a member of the European Economic Community (later the European Community and now the European Union) since 1973. Its reasons for joining were essentially economic, but the political elites then and subsequently agreed on the need for integration on issues that were not necessarily economic. The focus here will be on the evolution of abortion policy in Ireland, but it will be suggested that Ireland's membership in the EC, as well as liberalizing trends within member states, prompted Irish conservatives to seek the means to prevent abortion from becoming part of public policy in the state. What they sought to achieve was to contain any European influence which would allow abortion to be discussed in terms of public policy rather than as a moral or constitutional issue.

In this respect a number of related factors have to be considered. The first was the availability of abortion in Britain after 1967; this gave relatively easy access to abortion to those who wanted it in Ireland. Second, the evidence from the United States indicated that an activist Supreme Court could have a significant impact on social issues, especially if privacy was the grounds for appeal. In the specific Irish case, the Supreme Court had removed the prohibition on contraception on the grounds that it infringed an individual's right to privacy under the 1937 Constitution. This was further reinforced by the recognition after 1973 that European Law could be appealed to by Irish citizens to protect the individual against the effects of national legislation. In a number of cases the European Court of Justice and the European Court of Human Rights delivered judgments against domestic law, which were of a moral or cultural nature. The most recent of these was the demand by the European Court of Human Rights that Irish laws discriminating against homosexuals be repealed. It is of interest to note that the individual who most obviously promoted the European dimension in Irish law after 1973 became the first woman to be elected president of Ireland in 1990 (O'Reilly, 1992; O'Toole, 1994).

Europe loomed large in Ireland during the 1970s for liberals and conservatives alike. To liberals it promised a secular and tolerant future, to conservatives it threatened permissiveness and evil. In some ways, each side of the debate paralleled the other, while drawing very different conclusions. It is possible to exaggerate the extent of the influence of the EU in the individual states. Notwithstanding the enhanced power acquired by the European Parliament after the Maastricht Treaty, real power continues to rest with the Council of Ministers representing individual sovereignties. At its most succinct, if the Council of Ministers attempted to apply a policy on abortion in 1996 to the Union, then any state would, quite legally and correctly, invoke its sovereign right to veto such proposals.

Convergence can operate at levels other than the institutional. In their report on the 1981 European Values Survey, Harding and Phillips (1986: 213) found that strong similarities existed among opinions across the member states of the EC. While opinion was not uniform, the report concluded that it was possible to locate a common European "civilization" or "culture." The evidence for convergence on some issues can also alert us to the divergences. Some of the widest divergences emerge along the religious and moral dimension, with Ireland (North and South) occupying the conservative end of the spectrum and Denmark the liberal end (Harding and Phillips, 1986; Ashford and Timms, 1992; Whelan, 1994). One of the most interesting aspects of the European Values Studies in 1981 and 1990 is the continuing strength of Irish identification with traditional Catholic beliefs. In both surveys there is a strong correlation between an endorsement of the Catholic Church's right to speak on specific moral issues and the extent to which Irish opinion considers certain moral actions to be unjustified. In matters relating to morality, especially abortion, divorce, euthanasia, and suicide, the Irish differ most strongly from the European average. However, what is also noticeable between 1981 and 1990 is that the Irish trend is toward convergence with Europe in general and specifically in respect to issues reflecting moral and cultural concerns (Whelan, 1994; Girvin, 1993a).

MORAL POLITICS AND ABORTION IN IRELAND

If this is the case, such convergence on opinion gives no guarantee that there will be policy convergence as well (Durham, 1994). In respect to abortion policy this is even less likely. However, it was fear of just such an eventuality that prompted the organization of an anti-abortion lobby at the end of the 1970s, one which successfully orchestrated the referendum that amended the Irish Constitution in 1983. The Eighth Amendment to the Constitution contained in Article 40.3.3, which was passed in 1983 by a two to one majority, reads:

> *The state acknowledges the right to life of the unborn and, with due regard to the equal right to life of the mother, guarantees in its laws to respect, and, as far as practicable, by its laws, to defend and vindicate that right.*

Subsequent Supreme Court judgments effectively enforced this amendment by prohibiting referral, counseling, and the circulation of information. By 1990, it appeared that the activist anti-abortion campaign had successfully implemented its program (Hesketh, 1990; O'Reilly, 1992: 98–126), though it should be added that no legislation was introduced in Parliament to give effect to the amendment or its consequences.

Despite the apparent success of conservatism in Irish moral politics, a number of factors indicated that opinion was changing by the early 1990s. The 1990 European Values Survey found that there had been an appreciable shift in opinion on moral issues over the previous decade. Moreover, there is a detectable shift on the abortion issue, which can be seen from the data in Table 1.

TABLE 1

CIRCUMSTANCES UNDER WHICH ABORTION IS APPROVED, 1981 AND 1990

	1981		1990	
	WOMEN	MEN	WOMEN	MEN
When the mother's life is at risk by the pregnancy	43	49	63	67
Where it is likely that the child would be physically handicapped	24	26	29	35
Where the mother is not married	3	9	7	9
Where a married couple does not want to have any more children	4	6	8	9

Source: Whelan, 1994.

Whereas in 1981, 46 percent agreed that abortion would be acceptable if the mother's health was placed at risk by a pregnancy, by 1990 the percentage approving of this position had increased to 65 percent. In addition to this, as one might expect, those approving of abortion under any circumstances were concentrated in the younger age groups: for example 80 percent of those aged between twenty-eight and thirty-seven approved of abortion if the mother's health was at risk.

However, the most important event occurred in 1992 when the Irish Attorney General successfully sought a High Court injunction against an underage girl to prevent her traveling to England to have an abortion. The appeal to the Supreme Court lifted the injunction, but in its judgment the Court found that Article 40.3.3. of the Constitution actually permitted abortion *in Ireland* (my emphasis):

> *if it established as a matter of probability that there is a real and substantial risk to the life as distinct to the health of the mother, which can only be avoided by the termination of her pregnancy, that such a termination is permissible, having regard to the true interpretation of Article 40.3.3. of the Constitution.*

The Supreme Court interpreted this further to mean that an abortion could be performed in Ireland if the woman's health was endangered by her threatened suicide. In addition, the Court decided that there could be restrictions on the right of travel, independent of the "X" case, if there was a conflict between the right to life of the fetus and that of the mother. The implication of this judgment was that a woman intent on traveling to Britain for an abortion could be prevented from doing so on the grounds that her own life was not threatened, but that of the fetus was (O'Reilly, 1992; *Attorney General*, 1992).

Whatever the legal consequences, the political consequences of the decision were dramatic. The Church and the anti-abortion groups claimed that this outcome had not been their intention, and demanded a new referendum to reinforce a total ban on abortion. Liberal and feminist opinion was mobilized in a new and radical fashion and for the first time in a decade seemed to reflect public opinion. The government declared that it had no intention of curtailing travel, but feared that the issue would complicate the forthcoming referendum to ratify the Maastricht Treaty. The government was placed in a difficult position, because of its previous actions. The Taoiseach (Irish Prime Minister) and the Minister for Foreign Affairs had negotiated a special protocol to the Treaty which read:

> *Nothing in the Treaty of European Union, or in the Treaties establishing the European Communities, or in the Treaties or Acts modifying or supplementing those Treaties, shall affect the application in Ireland of Article 40.3.3. of the Constitution of Ireland.*

The intention of the protocol was to overturn a decision of the European Court of Justice that had declared abortion a service within the meaning of Article 60 to the treaties. As a consequence, information distributed in Ireland on behalf of an abortion clinic in Britain would constitute such a service, and would therefore be legal. There is considerable evidence to suggest that the protocol was included after pressure from anti-abortion groups was brought to bear on the Fianna Fail party in government. The judgment in the "X" case undermined the intention of the protocol, which was to return to a prior ban on distributing information about abortion services abroad. The protocol itself, however, caused considerable controversy with respect to the status of the Constitution, the Supreme Court decision, and more indirectly the European Community itself (Hogan, 1992: 109–21).

The government pursued a dual strategy. In the first place, it reached a consensus with the main political parties agreeing to hold the referendum on the Treaty prior to dealing with the abortion issue. The government for its part guaranteed that a referendum on these issues would be held later in the year.

Second, the government attempted to reopen the protocol issue with the European Community, but was rebuffed on the grounds that matters were already too delicate with respect to the Treaty to do so. However, the European Community did agree to include a "Solemn Declaration" in relation to the Protocol, the main aims of which were

> that it was and is their intention that the Protocol shall not limit freedom either to travel between member States or, in accordance with conditions which may be laid down in conformity with Community law, by Irish legislation, to obtain or make available in Ireland information relating to services lawfully available in member states.
>
> At the same time the High Contracting Parties solemnly declare that, in the event of a future constitutional amendment in Ireland which concerns the subject matter of Article 40.3.3. of the Constitution of Ireland and which does not conflict with the intention of the High Contracting Parties hereinbefore expressed, they will, following the entry into force of the Treaty on European Union, be favorably disposed to amending the said Protocol so as to extend its application to such constitutional amendment if Ireland so requests.

At one level the EC seemed to be saying it was up to the Irish government to deal with the problem in its own way. However, at another there was considerable ambiguity about the protocol and the solemn declaration, and many doubted if it addressed the issues raised by the Supreme Court. At the very least, it might be interpreted as a promise to act, but was probably not legally binding (Hogan, 1992: 120–21). These doubts were also reflected during the referendum campaign. Despite the government's claim that abortion was not an issue, some 39 percent of those polled in June believed that the right to travel or the introduction of abortion were major concerns for them during the referendum. In the end the Treaty was comfortably endorsed, and the available evidence suggests that a majority of those voting were convinced of the government's good faith.

Yet the government was faced with a delicate decision by mid-1992. In effect, abortion was now legal under certain circumstances, and there was considerable pressure to close off this possibility. Alternatively, the government was under pressure from liberals and feminists to act decisively on the issues of travel and information. By November 1992, some 20 percent believed that abortion should never be allowed, about 50 percent agreed it should be allowed under certain circumstances, while just under 20 percent considered it should be available on demand. There was widespread agreement (82 percent) that a referendum on the abortion question should be held. Three amendments were proposed for the referendum which was to take place in November:

> *Travel*: This subsection shall not limit freedom to travel between the State and another state.
>
> *Information*: This subsection shall not limit freedom to obtain or make available, in the State, subject of such conditions as may be laid down by law, information relating to services lawfully available in another state.
>
> *Abortion Issue*: It shall be unlawful to terminate the life of an unborn unless such termination is necessary to save the life, as distinct from the health, of the mother where there is an illness or disorder of the mother giving rise to a real and substantive risk to her life, not being a risk of self-destruction.

The travel and information amendments were relatively uncontentious, but the wording of the abortion referendum which reflected Fianna Fail concerns over the suicide aspect of the Supreme Court decision was drafted specifically to prevent an appeal on this count. The abortion amendment ended up satisfying neither liberals nor conservatives. Liberals were concerned that a mother's life would not be adequately protected if the amendment was passed, while the Church and conservatives believed that it remained too tolerant of abortion. The situation was further complicated by the collapse of the government, which resulted in the general election and the referendum being held on the same day.

The outcome was an ambiguous one. The right to life (abortion) proposal was defeated, while those on information and travel were ratified (see Table 2).

TABLE 2
VOTING IN REFERENDUM, NOVEMBER 25, 1992

	YES	NO
Right to Life	34.6%	65.4%
Freedom of Travel	62.4%	37.6%
Freedom of Information	59.9%	40.1%

The vote on the abortion issue was a clear rejection for the Fianna Fail position, which had sought to present a reasonable approach to a very difficult problem. In the two weeks prior to the referendum, both liberals and conservatives seemed alienated. Whereas at the beginning of November it appeared that all three would be ratified, a shift in opinion had taken place by the last week of the campaign, as indicated in Table 3 (Girvin, 1993b).

TABLE 3
OPINION ON ABORTION ISSUE, NOVEMBER 1992

	YES		NO		DON'T KNOW	
	NOVEMBER	17/18	NOVEMBER 9TH	17/18	NOVEMBER 9TH	17/18
Total	48	33	30	42	22	23
Fianna Fail	50	34	29	47	20	18
Fine Gael	44	28	34	46	22	25
Labour	50	42	34	38	16	20
Prog. Dem.	56	30	33	49	11	19
Other	58	34	22	43	20	21
ABC1	47	35	34	41	18	22
C2D2	51	35	27	41	21	22
F1	39	24	28	51	33	22
F2	46	20	33	42	21	34
Male	49	38	29	38	21	22
Female	48	28	30	46	21	23

ABC1: Middle Class, which includes upper middle, middle, and lower middle classes.
C2D2: Working Class, which includes skilled working class and unskilled working class.
F1: Farms with 50 acres or more.
F2: Farms with less than 50 acres.
In all cases the reference is to the occupation of chief income earner or head of household if not working.
Unfortunately the data available do not allow for more discrete analysis.
Source: *Irish Times/MRBI* Polls, November 9, 17/18, 1992

ABORTION POLICY AFTER THE REFERENDA

Defeat was assured by the decision of both liberals and conservatives to reject the amendment, if for opposing reasons. Conservatives rejected any compromise on the abortion issue, but liberals sensed that a rejection simply reinstated the Supreme Court judgment, thus providing the opportunity for legislation. This assumption proved to be correct and was subsequently confirmed by the Minister for Justice and the incoming government. The failure to endorse the abortion amendment was a considerable embarrassment to the outgoing government, but its impact was going to affect any party which might form a government. At the 1992 election, Fianna Fail, the largest party, provided the most restrictive view on the abortion issue. It had promoted the referendum on the grounds that the Supreme Court decision in the "X" case was too permissive. Fine Gael, which contained a liberal wing, took the view that though suicide should not be a cause for an abortion, the referendum did not adequately provide for the safety of the mother. The Labour party, the main left-wing party, explicitly stated that it was not a pro-abortion party. It, nevertheless, endorsed the Supreme Court decision, warning that the amendment was dangerous to the life of the mother. Two other smaller left-wing parties, the Democratic Left and the Workers Party, both endorsed limited abortion. The right-of-center Progressive Democrats were divided on the issue, but the party as a whole opposed the specific amendment because of inadequate safeguards for the mother.

After considerable discussion, a new government was formed in January 1993 between the outgoing Fianna Fail party and the Labour Party, probably the main victor in the election. If the increase in Labour Party support was an indication of liberalism on moral issues, this is not apparent in the joint document produced for the government. The only reference to the subject in the *Program for Partnership Government* reads:

> *Following the decision of the people in the constitutional referenda in November, arising from the X case, it will be necessary to introduce legislation to regulate the position, recognizing the sensitivity of the issue throughout the community. The legislation will also cover the right to information.*

Although this appears to commit the incoming government to legislate on the conditions under which abortion would take place in Ireland, as well as the conditions for the receipt and circulation of abortion information, the reality was otherwise. The former Minister for Health, just prior to the election, had provided some suggestions concerning the circumstances under which an abortion could be obtained in Ireland. He had recommended that designated hospitals might carry out the operation, and that a committee of medical personnel could be formed to adjudicate on each application. In cases where suicide was threatened, the committee would include a psychiatrist. There is no evidence that the incoming government had any intention of pursuing a policy in January 1993 or subsequently. The statement has to be interpreted as an intention to introduce a policy in the future, but no indication was given of when, and under what circumstances, such a policy would be undertaken by the government.

Cautiousness was the key element among the parties in government and in the opposition. In some ways this was a realistic approach, because after the referendums there was nothing preventing a doctor from performing an abortion in theory; in practice no abortions probably took place. In addition, the Irish Medical Council changed its ethical guidelines after the referendums, the effect of which would lead to a doctor being removed from the medical register if he or she actually performed an abortion within the guidelines provided by the Supreme Court decision. In addition to this, public opinion was fluid. There is little evidence that the rejection of the abortion amendment actually amounted to an endorsement of abortion itself. One poll carried out shortly after the three referendums demonstrated the complicated nature of the public's decision making (see Table 4).

TABLE 4
REASONS FOR VOTING NO IN THE ABORTION AMENDMENT

	WOULD NOT RULE OUT ABORTION	FELT IT WOULD NOT PROTECT RIGHTS OF MOTHER
National	48	48
Dublin	38	59
Rest Leinster	51	42
Munster	43	53
Connacht-Uls	64	35
Urban	46	50
Rural	50	46
Non-manual	42	55
Manual	46	49
Large Farmer	51	44
Small Farmer	56	42
Male	43	54
Female	52	43
Fianna Fail	56	40
Fine Gael	46	50
Labour	39	57
Progressive Democrats	45	55
Other	50	50

Source: Irish Marketing Surveys Poll, December 4, 1992

An analysis of these data carried out by Kennelly and Ward (1993: 130–31) concluded that the right of the mother was primary for those under the age of 50, whereas abortion was the main concern of those over 50. The authors further concluded that in the three referendums about one-third were liberals, another third were fundamentalist conservatives, while the remaining third constituted realists or centrists. In a very real sense it was the combination of polar opposites on the abortion amendment which defeated it, and these extremes were reinforced by mixed considerations among the rest of the electorate (Girvin, 1994; Sinnott, 1995). These data also show that the political parties were seriously divided on the issue: while Fianna Fail supporters took the most conservative position, large minorities taking the conservative position also existed in the other parties, including Labour. As Fianna Fail and the Labour Party were in government after January 1993, the cautiousness of their government program is to be understood in this light.

During 1993 no policy initiative on the abortion issue appeared. The Pro-Life Campaign insisted that a new referendum was required to overturn the decision of the Supreme Court and denied that the decision in the referendums gave the government the right to legislate without consulting the electorate. However, neither party to the coalition government wished to reopen the conflict on the terms dictated by the pro-life and anti-abortion groups. The strategy was to neutralize their influence to the greatest possible extent. However, the anti-abortion lobby was reinforced by the publication of a papal encyclical by Pope John Paul II entitled *Veritatis Splendor,* which reaffirmed the papal condemnation of contraception, abortion, suicide, and euthanasia. This encyclical also insisted that these acts were "intrinsically evil" and therefore contradicted the moral law (Pope John Paul II, 1993), and strongly reinforced both the Irish hierarchy and the anti-abortion groups in their determination to prevent any further erosion of "their" amendment.

Yet public opinion was also moving in other directions. At the same time as the Pope's encyclical was published, a public opinion poll provided new insights into opinion on abortion. When asked whether the government should introduce legislation to provide for access to information on abortion, some 71 percent agreed while 23 percent disagreed. The response to this question did not differ significantly across the parties, though the Labour party did produce the largest support (81 percent) and Fianna Fail the lowest (66 percent). On the specific question of abortion policy the question asked was:

> *Should or should not the Government legislate, as promised, to allow for abortion in limited circumstances, where there is a real and substantial threat to the life and health of the mother?*

Twenty-four percent believed that there should be no legislation for abortion, which can be taken to be the conservative position on the issue. Seventy-one percent agreed that abortion should be introduced, but differed on the limits to be established. Forty-one percent considered that suicide should be included as one of the reasons, while 30 percent believed that the legislation should take account of physical risks to life only. Fianna Fail and Fine Gael were less likely to support the suicide risk and more likely to oppose abortion than the other parties (Jones, 1993).

Public opinion polls do not, of course, make policy but they do provide an insight into the evolution of opinion among the electorate. The evidence available from 1992 and 1993 indicates that while Irish opinion remained anti-abortion in general, it was no longer homogeneous on the issue. In these circumstances it became more possible to frame policy. By the middle of 1994, due to divisions within the government, it was decided not to proceed on abortion legislation as such, but to introduce legislation to regulate the information available on it. The Minister for Health, Brendan Howlin, had prepared legislation that provided that a doctor or other trained personnel could give non-directive counseling and could also make appointments in Britain on behalf of individual women. It was argued privately at the time that the reasoning behind this was that an Irish doctor would not actually be referring a patient for an abortion, but referring her to a clinic where she would be assessed by a British doctor for an abortion. Furthermore, the Department of Health and the Minister insisted that it was not bound by the policy decisions made by a previous government, on the grounds that a new government had been formed with a different program. The reason for this was that during the abortion referendum the minority Fianna Fail government had published an information booklet explicitly denying that the referendum on information would allow referral: "The amendment would permit non-directive counseling but not abortion referral" (Government Information Service, 1992: 13).

This decision to proceed with a policy on information drew the fire of the anti-abortion lobby. They had been mobilizing following the 1992 referenda to organize a new referendum. Prior to the 1994 European elections, it was clear that some Fianna Fail and Fine Gael candidates had agreed to support another amendment to the Constitution, one that would overturn the Supreme Court decision. Furthermore, an estimated fifteen Fianna Fail parliamentary deputies were also thought to support this initiative, while over fifty elected local government authorities had passed motions in favor of such a referendum. The method used by the government to deal with the issue of referral in the proposed legislation was not to mention it. The general provisions of the legislation followed those expected as a consequence of the successful amendment to the Constitution in 1992, but the circumstances where information would be available and how it would be made available were defined closely. The effect of the legislation, as it stood prior to its introduction at the end of 1994, was that doctors or counseling agencies would not be prohibited from making an appointment for a woman at a British abortion clinic, nor would they be prevented from providing the woman with a letter of reference.

These proposals undermined the determined policy of the anti-abortion groups. According to the Pro-Life Campaign:

> *The provision of the names and addresses of abortion clinics, or the referring of women to such clinics, promotes abortion and has no other purpose than to facilitate it. (Sunday Press, November 6, 1994)*

Government sources were quoted as claiming that the Pro-Life Campaign was "now engaged in rewriting history," adding that:

> *The result of the 1992 referendum gave an unqualified constitutional right to travel for an abortion. The information referendum result provided a right to information on abortion subject to regulation by law. A women has an implicit right to have the decision to travel put into effect. It would not be possible in law to frustrate a woman in giving effect to her decision to travel. (Irish Times, November 3, 1994)*

It should be remembered that this was draft legislation introduced by a minister who was decidedly more liberal on the issue than the majority of his cabinet colleagues; and certainly more liberal than the majority of the largest party in the coalition government. In addition, the legislation had not even been brought before the cabinet, where it was expected to be the focus of criticism from conservatives, when the government imploded and collapsed.

A number of events indirectly contributed to the fall of the government, but the direct event concerned moral politics. There was controversy concerning a Catholic priest, Father Brendan Smyth, accused of pedophilia and whose extradition to Northern Ireland had been requested. The individual involved was subsequently imprisoned in Northern Ireland, but considerable confusion existed over the circumstances in which the extradition papers were handled by the Irish Attorney General's office in Dublin. Accusations were made that the Attorney General's office held up the extradition papers because the individual involved was a priest. Although this was denied on a number of occasions, conflict between the two coalition parties led to the resignation of the Taoiseach and to the renegotiation of a new government among the existing government parties. However, as a result of further revelations concerning this issue, the Labour party refused to endorse a new government with Fianna Fail and instead negotiated a government agreement with Fine Gael and the Democratic Left. The new government was slightly to the left of the previous one, with the balance tipped more to the liberal wing of politics than previously. Government formation meant that the proposed information bill fell on dissolution, but it was also uncertain what approach the new government would take to the issue and how active the new Minister for Health, Michael Noonan, would be in the area. Noonan was a member of Fine Gael, the largest and most conservative of the three government parties, and it was understood at the time that he would take a more cautious attitude to the legislation than his predecessor.

One of the revealing factors in the crisis in government at the end of 1994 was how the Catholic Church had suffered as a consequence of the sexual scandals associated with some of its members.[2] In 1990 only 28 percent of those in the Irish Republic reported that they lacked confidence in the Church, as opposed to an average of 49 percent in Europe (Ashford and Timms, 1992: 16). A survey carried out in 1995 found that the association between sexual scandals and the Church tended to undermine the confidence of the public in the Church's position on abortion, divorce, homosexuality, and contraceptives. Some 45 percent of those interviewed believed that the Church had too much influence on government (*Irish Times*, March 2, 1995). While it is too early to draw firm conclusions from these data, it is evident that the short-term impact of sexual scandals within the Church has been to weaken the authority of the Church in public affairs.

This can be confirmed by the handling of the information on abortion legislation by the Minister for Health. In a surprise move in February 1995, Noonan introduced the **Regulation of Information (Services Outside the State for Termination of Pregnancies) Bill**, following quite closely the legislation which his predecessor had drafted. However, in contrast, the Noonan bill was more conservative than that of Howlin, as the former believed that it was necessary to explicitly outlaw referral. The bill prevented a doctor or counselor from making any arrangements for a patient or client with an abortion clinic outside the state; the legislation did not, however, prohibit a doctor from giving a patient phone numbers or addresses of such abortion clinics. The Minister believed that he had got the balance about right, deflecting the criticism that the electorate had not voted for referral in 1992 while at the same time fulfilling the commitment to legislate in the area. At first he appeared to have succeeded brilliantly; there was some disquiet among the coalition partners, but not enough to bring down the government. Furthermore, with the outlawing of referrals it seemed that the Fianna Fail party, now in opposition, would support the bill or at the very least not actively oppose it. The Pro-Life Campaign, as expected, opposed the legislation on the grounds that it "would clearly breach undertakings given to voters prior to the 1992 referenda and would foster an abortion culture directly opposed to the values enshrined in the Constitution." Postponement of the legislation was also urged on the grounds that a case pertaining to the issue was before the High Court and the government should await that outcome prior to acting. The immediate response of the government to this challenge was to ignore it in the belief that the High Court case was not material to the issue, and that there was a wide-ranging consensus in Parliament (*Irish Times,* February 23, 27, 1995).

This was being overly optimistic, as events turned out. If, at first, Fianna Fail was relieved that referral was explicitly outlawed, it soon was put under pressure to reverse its moderate approach to the question. Justice Rory O'Hanlon, a Judge of the High Court, issued a statement on February 28th comparing the current legislation to the horrors of Nazi Germany. He argued against the proposed bill explicitly on Catholic grounds, linking the dedication of the Irish Constitution to Article 6 of the same document, which reads: "All powers of government, legislative, executive and judicial, derive, under God, from the people." While this Article can be construed in a republican and secular fashion, O'Hanlon's view was that this required that legislation be in conformity with Catholic teaching on every issue. He also offered the view that the entire text of the Constitution guaranteed the life of the unborn, as did explicitly Article 40. This led him to conclude that "law making power is derived not from the State or the people of the State but from God" (see *Irish Times* March 1, 2, 1995, for details). In fact, O'Hanlon's view of the Constitution implied a theocratic state, an objective which the author of that document never intended (Girvin, 1986). The Fianna Fail party began to reflect similar views, though they were not expressed as eloquently. Various questions were raised in Parliament about the extent to which a doctor or a clinic could provide addresses or phone numbers of abortion clinics in Britain. Opposition to the Bill centered on this issue, which the Pro-Life Campaign argued was the same as referral, and this position was increasingly taken by Fianna Fail. However, the government was on strong ground in countering this, arguing that in fact referral was penalized in the bill and that the provision of names or addresses was a different matter and did not amount to referral. The most prominent legal adviser to the anti-abortion lobby, Professor William Binchy, rejected the government's claim, asserting that what was involved was abortion on demand (*Irish Times,* March 2, 1995).

The anti-abortion campaign had its first major success when on March 1, at a parliamentary party meeting, Fianna Fail decided to oppose the legislation in Parliament. It was reported that out of forty-two speakers at the meeting, only ten supported the Bill. This was followed shortly afterwards by the decision of a Fine Gael member of Parliament to oppose the Bill on moral grounds. His decision came after a long week of lobbying by the anti-abortion organizations, amounting to harassment on occasions. It was complemented by the Bishop of Cloyne's condemnation of the Bill; he drew specific attention to Article 2272 of the Catechism of the Catholic Church that provided excommunication as the penalty for abortion or for cooperating with one. The political implication here was that those members of Parliament who voted for the information legislation were so cooperating (*Irish Times,* March 2, 1995; *Cork Examiner,* March 2, 1995). Shortly afterwards there was a further condemnation of the Bill by the Archbishop of Dublin who implied, as Judge O'Hanlon and others had done, that Irish law should be compatible with the theology of the Catholic Church. What is of interest here is that the Irish hierarchy, in contrast with previous statements made at the time of the 1992 referenda, were arguing for a strongly fundamentalist position, emphasized by the Pope in his encyclical in 1993, which seemed to preclude Catholics acting in good faith or making up their own minds. One reason for this is that the individual Bishops recognized that their influence in this topic had been eroded and that opinion had shifted; therefore there was a need to take a more pronounced rather than nuanced view on the topic. This was also strongly reflected in the statement issued by the Irish hierarchy on March 8th, while the debate on the Bill was already underway. In contrast to past statements, the tone is dogmatic and conservative, giving no latitude for individual conscience.

These fears were realized once the debate began in parliament. Most government supporters reported the harassment organized by anti-abortion groups, but virtually all successfully resisted. The Minister for Justice, Nora Owen, stated that while the Church was entitled to an opinion on the matter, Church and State were separated in Ireland, and that the 1992 referendum provided the legitimacy for the legislation. The implicit hint here and elsewhere was that the hierarchy, Fianna Fail, and the anti-abortion groups were opposed to the expressed will of the electorate. The Fine Gael member, Alan Dukes, argued openly during the debate on the Bill that Parliament had to assert its authority against what he described as "self-appointed arbiters of what is and is not acceptable in constitutional terms." He accused opponents of the Bill of being anti-democratic, arguing that they should recognize what the electorate had opted for in 1992. Others on the liberal wing of the political spectrum argued likewise, while the Minister made a careful speech commending the legislation to the House. The legislation was passed easily, with only one major amendment involving an opt-out clause for doctors who did not wish to give information on abortion.

However, of more interest were the clear divisions within the Fianna Fail party. All party members voted against the Bill, accepting party discipline. The majority of Fianna Fail members who contributed to the debate reflected the position of the Catholic Church and the anti-abortion lobby. However, a number of Fianna Fail members made it clear that they disagreed with the line taken by the party. One member accepted publicly that he was a hypocrite, adding that "many of my colleagues have been intimidated over the last number of weeks." Others from Fianna Fail openly acknowledged that Parliament would have to legislate on abortion because it was a reality which could not be ignored in the modern world. What seems to have occurred in this, the largest party in Ireland, is that the conservative element gained dominance during the debate on tactics. They grounded their opposition on the nature of Catholic influence in their constituencies, genuine belief in the evil of abortion, and the effective campaign of the anti-abortion lobby. The newly elected leader of the party, Bertie Aherne, was unable to control this backlash against what he personally believed was a moderate measure. This weakened him as a leader, but it also prompted him to state publicly that this was a special issue and that it did not mean that the party would take a similar stand in opposition to divorce. The liberal minority in the party was leaderless and was unwilling to break with the party on the issue. The outcome was one of confusion and embarrassment that worked in favor of the government.

CONCLUSIONS

Although the Bill was passed, it had one more hurdle. The President of Ireland has the right to refer any legislation to the Supreme Court to test its constitutionality prior to signing it into law. After consultation, she did so and it is expected that the Supreme Court has found it constitutional. However, the introduction and debate over the Bill highlights a number of salient features about the Irish political process and about the politics of morality. A majority of political parties, left and right, remain anxious to contain the issue of abortion. In particular, there is a consensus to prevent the anti-abortion lobby from intruding into the deliberation of governments and from intimidating elected representatives. Although the issue was made volatile by the Church and the anti-abortion lobby, the conservatives proved less effective than on previous issues.

Even Fine Gael, in some ways as conservative as Fianna Fail, resisted the pressure in unprecedented fashion. The Ministers of Health and Justice (both Fine Gael members) argued strongly for the superiority of Parliament in the legislative process and rejected the Church's claims that they should obey its teaching. Noonan explicitly rejected the pressure exercised by the Church, the anti-abortion groups, and Judge O'Hanlon, and insisted that the principle for the future would be the primacy of Parliament. He did, however, recognize that further legislation was required subsequent to the Supreme Court decision. He now announced that there would be a review of the Constitution, one which would cover all aspects of that document. He also recognized that the outstanding feature of the Supreme Court decision, that of abortion itself, would require further consideration. In a careful review of the options he concluded that it was not possible to legislate in accordance with the Supreme Court decision, while retaining a narrow interpretation of the conditions under which abortion might be possible in the state. The response might be to promote another referendum to limit the conditions under which an abortion would be permitted, or to legislate in another fashion. Accordingly, he wrote that, "The options are not great, and it is extraordinarily complex."

This will not be the end of moral politics in Ireland, nor will it mark the end of the politics of abortion. Ireland has a non-policy on abortion at the moment; the remarks of the Minister for Health indicate that the government will move with extreme caution. The divorce issue has more salience in the present government than the abortion issue. It may remain for the Supreme Court to prompt the politicians to act. What Ireland does have is a policy on abortion information, one which allows a degree of flexibility to doctors or counselors not available prior to this legislation. It is unlikely that the abortion issue will disappear; privately, some specialists in the area believe that the policy environment remains fraught with danger and their actions open to legal challenge. One of the ironies of the abortion question in Ireland is that an amendment, which was intended to outlaw abortion under every possible circumstance, opened the way for its possible introduction. It certainly has made it easier for those wishing to avail themselves of abortion facilities in other states. A further irony is that during the debate in Parliament on the information bill it was announced that an eleven-year-old-girl was pregnant after rape by a fifty-one-year-old man. As the information bill went back to the Supreme Court the individual convicted in the "X case" had his original fourteen-year jail sentence reduced on appeal to four years. The conditions under which decisions about abortion are taken have not changed, but the debate on policy to address these needs have. This outcome reflects the impact of social change, the nature of constitutional law in Ireland, and the interrelationship between Ireland and the European Union. All of these factors are now dynamic, and future changes should clarify the evolution of policy in the abortion area.

NOTES

1. The narrative is based on a reading of the main daily newspapers and the reports of parliamentary debates. Quotations are normally taken from the *Irish Times*. Various data have been used. I am grateful to Professor C. T. Whelan of the Economic and Social Research Institute, Dublin, for providing me with the European Values Survey data sets. I am also grateful to Mr. Jack Jones of the Market Research Bureau of Ireland for providing me the

      data from the *Irish Times/MRBI* polls. A number of individuals involved in various aspects of this question were interviewed to provide background on issues. Their privacy is respected in the text.

2.   There had, for some time, been considerable concern in the United States about widespread abuse by priests, but in Ireland there was little public discussion of the issue. The Bishop Casey affair in 1992, when he acknowledged fathering a son some years earlier and to using diocesan funds for non-church purposes, was accepted by many as a private matter and an isolated one. The allegations against Father Smyth could not be dismissed as easily; it was admitted that the Church authorities had known for some time about his behavior, but had not acted decisively.

REFERENCES

Ashford, S., and Timms, N. 1992. *What Europe Thinks: A Study of Western European Values.* Aldershot: Dartmouth.

Attorney General v X and Others. 1992. *Irish Law Reports Monthly.*

Dinan, D. 1993. *Ever Closer Union,* London: Macmillan.

Durham, M., ed. 1994. *Abortion Issue: Parliamentary Affairs* 47: 2.

Girvin, B. 1986. "Social Change and Moral Politics: The Irish Constitutional Referendum 1983." *Political Studies* 34, 61–81.

Girvin, B. 1993a. "Social Change and Political Culture in the Republic of Ireland." *Parliamentary Affairs* 43, 3: 380-98.

Girvin, B. 1993b. "Referendums on Abortion 1992." *Irish Political Studies* 8: 118–24.

Girvin, B. 1994. "Moral Politics and the Irish Abortion Referendums, 1992." *Parliamentary Affairs* 47, 2: 203–21.

Government Information Service. 1992. *The Referendums on the Right to Life, Travel and Information: Key Questions and Answers.* Dublin: Stationery Office.

Harding, S., and Phillips, D. 1986. *Contrasting Values in Western Europe.* London: Macmillan

Heidenheimer, A. J., Heclo, H., and Adams, C. T. 1990. *Comparative Public Policy.* New York: St. Martin's Press, 3rd. ed.

Hesketh, T. 1990. *The Second Partitioning of Ireland?* Dun Laoghaire: Bransma Books.

Hogan, G. 1992. "Protocol 17." In P. Keatinge ed., *Maastricht and Ireland.* Dublin: Institute of European Affairs,109–21.

Irish Times, March 2, 1995; *Cork Examiner,* March 2, 1995

Jones, J. 1993. *The Irish Times/MRBI Poll.* Dublin: Market Research Bureau of Ireland.

Kennelly, B., and Ward, E. 1993. "The Abortion Referendums." In Michael Gallagher and Michael Laver, eds., *How Ireland Voted 1992.* PSAI PRESS and Folens: Limerick and Dublin, 115–34.

Lovenduski, J., and Outshoorn, J., eds. 1986. *The New Politics of Abortion.* London: Sage.

Milward, A. 1993. *The European Rescue of the Nation State.* London: Routledge.

Nicoll, W., and Salmon, T. C. 1994. *Understanding the New European Community.* London: Harvestor-Wheatcheaf.

O'Reilly, E. 1992. *Masterminds of the Right.* Dublin: Attic Press.

O'Toole, F. 1994. "Here's to you, Mrs Robinson." *Irish Times,* 21 May.

Pope John Paul II. 1993 *Veritatis Splendor (Splendor of Truth).* Dublin: Catholic Information Office.

Sinnott, R. 1995. *Irish Voters Decide: Voting Behavior in Elections and Referendums 1918 92.* Manchester: Manchester University Press.

Whelan, C. T., ed. 1994. *Values and Social Change in Ireland.* Dublin: Gill and Macmillan.

PART IV

BEYOND ABORTION:
New Reproductive Technologies

INTRODUCTION

The articles in the first three parts of this book offer a comprehensive look at the ways the abortion issue intersects with political institutions and processes in a variety of advanced industrial states. Political scientists have characterized abortion as an "emotive-symbolic" question because it involves conflicts over questions of basic values: life, death, rights, morality, and ethics. Looking at a country's politics through the lens of a symbolic-emotive issue like abortion gives a perspective on institutions and processes that is different from the usual treatment of governmental economic and social policy. With abortion, the resolution of policy conflicts is especially difficult to obtain; the basic values involved defy the standard forms of political give-and-take. When stable solutions have been obtained, as in most of the Western European states, it is usually through a manipulation of symbolic and effective policy elements (see Outshoorn in this volume). In some societies, the prospects of stable solutions seem far off indeed (see Githens in this volume).

The two articles in this final section show politicians and feminist writers contending with the new conflicts raised by rapid changes in technologies of reproduction. The New Reproductive Technology has presented emotive-symbolic questions that greatly challenge the capabilities of democratic institutions to resolve conflicts and make policy. Already in the United States, as the chapter by Merchant shows, there are unsettling legal developments as parents sue physicians for "wrongful life." Even more disturbing for feminists is the growing legal separation between the pregnant woman and her fetus, empowering would-be protectors of the fetus to sue pregnant women for child abuse for failing to obey medical recommendations. Commissions in the United States and France, seeking to provide guidelines to scientists and the courts, have tried to place the use of the new techniques in the conventional framework of family and gender relations by reserving them for heterosexual, preferably married, couples.

Feminist writers have begun to consider the impact of the new technologies on women, but for the most part their perspectives are absent from the policy debates. The use of women's bodies by the medical and scientific community to advance knowledge of all aspects of human reproduction has enormous implications for gender relations. However, the debates are rarely discussed in gendered terms; rather, the discourse is gender neutral, and feminist fears of the disappearance of women from the entire discussion of human reproduction are justified. Yet, as the chapter by Stetson shows, feminists are themselves divided over the use of these technologies, making a unified stand unlikely. And, since new procedures affect relatively few women at this time (in comparison with abortion law) there is little basis on which to build an organized campaign to inject feminist voices into the policy debates.

CHAPTER 9

CONFRONTING THE CONSEQUENCES OF MEDICAL TECHNOLOGY: POLICY FRONTIERS IN THE UNITED STATES AND FRANCE

JENNIFER MERCHANT

INTRODUCTION

It has only been in recent years that public authorities have directed their attention to the social consequences of fundamental and applied scientific research in artificial reproduction and biogenetics. The techniques in question opened up new horizons long before the elaboration of any type of public policy. Only in the 1990s are authorities beginning to explore the question of their regulation. Ensuing legislation will most probably rely on a re-examination of the traditional image of the family and the representation of the sexes throughout history, as well as on philosophical debates over the notions of nature and/or the concepts of "feminine vs. masculine nature."

Unquestionably, public-policy elaboration relative to these specializations sparks more controversy than other scientific/medical fields. Any and all matters linked to human reproduction continue to ignite fundamental conflicts as to what human life and death represent, and as such usually reflect a variety of religious and ethical positions. This chapter examines public-policy questions raised by these technologies and explores efforts of public authorities in the United States and France to cope with the conflicts they present. In the United States, courts are beginning to develop principles for some individual problems, but the question as to what role the government should play remains in large part unanswered. In France, on the other hand, efforts have been made to begin constructing a legal framework.

One central question is to what extent these policies reflect, contradict, or directly prolong previous measures relative to abortion, and to a lesser degree, contraception. Of concern is how new technologies force authorities to redefine the legal status of the fetus and the implications for that status on women, men, and the redefinition of basic gender roles of mother and father. The chapter will begin with a review of the evolving legal status of the fetus, followed by descriptions of some of the new reproductive technologies that constitute *medically assisted procreation* (MAP). The bulk of the chapter will discuss the areas in the United States and France where policymakers confront the social effects of MAP and compare their tentative steps to provide a legal framework to cope with resulting conflicts.

THE EVOLVING LEGAL STATUS OF THE FETUS

Western tradition never conferred legal status on the fetus. Roman law defined the fetus not as *homo* (human) but as *spes animantis* (one who hopes to live and eventually receive a soul). Until its birth, the fetus was part of the mother and did not deserve any special treatment.

Early Christians condemned abortion but never considered it as the murder of a human being, only as an act signifying the selfish refusal to procreate. The idea that the fetus deserved some sort of legal protection was not part of early Christian theological doctrine, and was to remain absent from the Catholic Church's doctrine up to the end of the nineteenth century.[1]

Traditional Anglo-Saxon common law, which forms the basis of United States law, also did not consider abortion as murder, even those illegal abortions that followed quickening (i.e., when the mother felt the first movements within her at approximately four months), nor could a fetus be a civil party in a legal dispute. Under common law, the fetus became a person at birth and only if it lived a short period following birth.

In the United States, a shift from the traditional common law definition of the fetus occurred in the 1946 case *Bonbrest v. Kotz* (65 F.Supp.138 [D.D.C., 1946]). For the first time in United States legal history, the plaintiff in a case was a newborn suffering from serious injury incurred during delivery. The court declared that the fetus was alive and well during delivery, but because of its contact with the obstetrician (the defendant) it had been severely damaged. As a consequence, it deserved full legal protection because: "The law is meant to keep abreast of scientific progress and medical science has certainly progressed."[2] The *Bonbrest v. Kotz* decision laid the foundations for a new judicial domain in the United States that related to changes in the medical technology of reproduction.

In *Roe v. Wade*, the Supreme Court declined to define the fetus as a person according to the Fourteenth Amendment, regardless of its embryonic/fetal development state. Nevertheless, Judge Blackmun's trimester framework used the developmental state of the fetus to determine the point when the state could intervene to protect "potential life," thereby specifying the moment when a woman no longer had a fundamental right to make decisions about childbirth. Considered by many as a necessary initiative, the *Roe v. Wade* trimester framework nonetheless ignited the contemporary debate surrounding the question of when life begins. This framework was based on advances in medical knowledge of fetal development. The *Roe v. Wade* decision constituted a judicial precedent that has had the strange effect of serving women's rights as well as obstructing them.

On the other hand, France is one of several European countries whose laws are part of the Romano-Germanic family of code law. When the French government criminalized abortion in the early nineteenth century, it did not suggest that the fetus had any sort of legal interest; rather the motive was the state's desire to increase the birth rate. Similarly when abortion was legalized in the 1970s, the law did not refer to the legal status of the fetus. In 1975, the *Loi Veil* did not balance women's right with that of the state's right to intervene. The notion of an individual woman's *détresse* (distress) is emphasized, and though abortion becomes illegal after the twelfth week of pregnancy, it is not because the state has a sudden interest in the "potential life" of the fetus.

TECHNOLOGIES OF MAP

Medically assisted procreation (MAP) dates back to at least the eighteenth century, when the first artificial insemination was recorded in Great Britain. But it was the technology of *cryogenic preservation*, the successful freezing and subsequent thawing of human sperm (in 1940), then of fertilized embryos, and finally ova, that gave physicians powerful tools to affect fertility through *in vitro* fertilization (IVF).[3]

Progress in hormonal stimulations of women patients had allowed for the increase in the number of ova collected during the punction phase of IVF (when ova are extracted from ovaries). A pregnancy is more likely when three inseminated embryos are transferred to the uterus of the gestational mother instead of just one. The question arose: What to do with surplus embryos, since the punction procedure, as well as the subsequent fertilization with spermatozoa, often produces more than three embryos? The answer appeared obvious to many, that is, to utilize the same technique in operation since 1940 for the conservation of spermatozoa, i.e., freezing.

Cryogenic preservation thus allows for the use of surplus embryos in a subsequent attempt to obtain a pregnancy; that is, they are thawed, treated with nutrients, and transferred to the uterus of the gestational mother. Obviously, this practice still does not resolve the question of the future of left-over or "abandoned" embryos due to definitive IVF success or failure, the death of genetic parents, or other reasons.

The cryogenic preservation technique has not only raised questions relative to surplus embryos, but it has also provoked severe controversy when it is employed along with prenatal genetic analyses. The origin of an increasing number of hereditary diseases has now been located in certain genes. In addition, it is possible to determine the sex of an embryo through early prenatal genetic analysis. Given that, a couple and/or individual desirous of a child could pursue these genetic analyses in order to select embryos with a particular genetic predisposition before uterine transfer.

Another very recent technique used in IVF, discovered by a Belgian team, involves injecting a single spermatozoid into the ovum. This procedure is prescribed in the case of poor spermatozoa mobility and motility. From a purely scientific standpoint, numerous geneticists have pointed to significant dangers, notably genetic damage and/or subsequent transformation of the genotype involved, since the injecting procedure can have adverse effects on the development of the ensuing embryo. From a more "bioethical" standpoint, the same arguments employed in the case of cryogenic preservation have been reiterated, that is, what will prevent couples or individuals from selecting the most "performant" spermatozoa or the one that carries a certain number of desired characteristics prior to insemination?

ASSESSING MAP APPLICATIONS

By 1989 in France, more than 30,000 children had been born following MAP with the use of anonymous-donor sperm.[4] In the United States, this figure hovers around *500,000* children born to women fertilized by a variety of artificial insemination methods.[5] However, in both countries (indeed, in all countries where IVF is employed) approximately 50 percent of the women who undergo ovary punction do not become pregnant. A third to a half who do either have miscarriages or give birth to stillborn children. (This figure does not include births of severely deformed or seriously ill children.) At present, success rates are estimated at 25 percent; however, this figure refers only to obtained pregnancies and does not include the rate of subsequent miscarriages, stillbirths, or births of severely handicapped children. To say the least, the very notion of success remains a contested concept.[6]

When inflated success rates are put forth, they are often derived from ambiguous definitions of sterility. According to many in the medical profession, it has now become the *mal du siècle*. Hence, fervent MAP advocates conclude that: "Soon 15 to 20 percent of couples in their procreating age . . . will sooner or later have to turn to IVF techniques because of their sterility."[7] These predictions contradict studies that point to a maximum of 3 to 5 percent who suffer from physiological, and thus, irreversible, sterility. The problem appears to be one of semantic interpretation. Ardent advocates of MAP often confuse the term *sterility* (medically diagnosed incapacity to procreate, e.g., blocked fallopian tubes, severe sperm deficiency) with the term *infertility* (delays in conceiving due to a variety of factors).[8] Many couples seek MAP because of perceived delays in conceiving. According to a recent study, only 20 percent of French couples requesting IVF were diagnosed as being irreversibly sterile; the remaining 80 percent were diagnosed as experiencing delays linked to unexplained infertility.[9] As a general rule in Western industrialized societies, at least 20 percent of couples do not conceive naturally within two years of their initial attempts.

Delays in conceiving are very often the result of the birth-control method used by the individual and/or couple (hormone methods may delay conception); individual physiological tolerance or intolerance to external environmental factors (recent hypotheses regarding sperm deficiency point to exposure to pollution, poor diet, and alcohol or drug abuse);[10] and psychological factors, which quite obviously entail a variety of origins.[11]

Sterility and/or problems of infertility have yet to be defined as a disease, yet curiously they are progressively being perceived of as an illness that is to be treated by the medical community.[12] The fact that so many couples who experience delays in conception consult doctors for a "quick cure" is the consequence of the medicalization of childbirth over one hundred years ago.

UNITED STATES POLICY: THE COURTS

Under the federal constitution in the United States, issues of family law and medical practice are the province of the fifty states rather than of the central government. When state legislatures fail to set limits, the private sector is given free reign. When conflicts arises between doctors and their patients, the state courts settle the cases. The accumulation of cases results in the articulation of legal principles based on precedent. These cases take place in the context of pro-life and pro-choice debates and the relentless demand of couples for assistance with fertility problems.

One may analyze initial judicial responses to the consequences of scientific progress in the field of what is called maternal-fetal medicine. Progress in this discipline has indirectly contributed to the advent of two new legal concepts that conflict yet also complement each other: *torts for wrongful life/wrongful birth* and *fetal negligence/prenatal abuse.* In the first case, a medical agent is accused of negligence in his or her diagnosis of a future child's normalcy, or a child is a civil party opposing the parents for the same reasons. In the second case, a pregnant woman is accused of failing to contribute to, or of acting to threaten, her future child's normal development. In both cases, the legal status of the embryo/fetus is enhanced in comparison to its former juridical status as "potential" life in *Roe v. Wade.* In these cases the fetus attains separate status in juxtaposition to the woman carrying it.

The timid development of these concepts serves as a springboard for anti-abortion groups in their struggle to confer to the embryo/fetus the status of a person (or as they would put it a human being). It is important not to condemn these new juridical concepts categorically, for in many cases they provide retribution for couples, women, or children who are victims of medical negligence during pregnancy or delivery. Nevertheless, the translation into tort law of these legal concepts has contributed to the expanding notion of fetal rights.

THE NOTION OF WRONGFUL LIFE

Prenatal genetic analysis, as well as artificial procreation techniques, allow couples to avoid the birth of a fetus whose future existence could be hampered by serious physiological handicaps. Wrongful life suits permit them to sue medical agents for not having sufficiently detected fetal deformity or informed patients of its potentiality. A wrongful life accusation posits that life evolved contrary to what was hoped for: the child should never have been born but was. As a consequence, the child or the parents can receive compensation, since the child is now required to live with handicaps.

Before the 1980s, state courts systematically refused to take into consideration wrongful life suits. This trend was reversed with *Curlender v. Bio-Science Laboratories* (165 Cal. Rptr. 477 [1980]), in which a California appeals court ordered compensation in the name of wrongful life to a child afflicted with Tay-Sachs, a fatal hereditary disease. In a decision that recalls the 1946 *Bonbrest v. Kost* case, the court recognized the effect of changes in medical knowledge:

> *The reality of the wrongful life concept is that such a plaintiff both exists and suffers due to the negligence of others. It is neither necessary nor just a retreat into meditation on the mysteries of life. . . . . The certainty of genetic impairment is no longer a mystery.*[13]

Despite an ensuing series of similar decisions, some courts show a reluctance to consider such cases or to rule in favor of the plaintiff. However, it is important to note that it is not the concept *per se* that is rejected, rather the circumstances of the specific case, such as the age of the plaintiff or the fact that the handicap involved is not easily detectable through fetal genetic analysis.[14]

Scientific advances, coupled with the fear of being dragged into court for wrongful life charges, have contributed to the embryo/fetus becoming the object of unprecedented medical recognition. New technologies (ultrasound, amniocentesis, MAP, genetic analysis, alpha-fetoprotein analysis) encourage physicians and other gynecological and obstetrical specialists to confer to the embryo/fetus the status of a patient.

Indeed, anti-abortion groups proclaim that potential wrongful life suits encourage doctors to prescribe an abortion at the slightest hint of fetal deformity. These activists have encouraged public officials—mulling over the need for policies relative to maternal/fetal medicine, artificial procreation, and bio-genetics in general—to direct their attention elsewhere than the medical community. They urge authorities to hold the mother responsible for what is called *fetal negligence.*

Maternal/fetal medicine distinguishes between direct fetal therapy (DFT) and indirect fetal therapy (IFT). DFT would consist, for example, of intra-uterine surgery. IFT consists of preventive measures voluntarily undertaken by the pregnant woman, for example, that she eats properly and no longer smokes or drinks during pregnancy. The responsibility of a physician failing to provide sufficient DFT, given improvements in treatment, is undeniable. However, IFT places formal medical responsibilities on the pregnant woman. Failure of a woman to take recommended steps to ensure the health of her fetus or any action she takes that would harm the fetus can now be called prenatal abuse and can lead to criminal prosecution.

As of 1993, eleven states had approved of judicial precedents or enacted statutes that for the first time seek to prosecute individuals (essentially women) for fetal negligence. These measures appear to reflect an effort on the part of public authorities to avoid complex and embarrassing court cases linked to wrongful life, as well as protective and preventive measures advocated by the medical community in their desire to minimize accusations of professional error. These measures also reflect lobbying on the part of pro-life groups who are anxious for the establishment of a legal status for the embryo/fetus.

No state or local jurisdiction has yet explicitly defined prenatal abuse. Instead, prosecutors seeking to indict women for fetal negligence refer to existing statutes relative to child abuse. The analogy they attempt to establish is that the fetus is a prisoner within the mother's womb, a victim of her behavior. Thus, pregnant drug abusers have been convicted, for example, of transmitting drugs to a minor. The Center for Reproductive Law and Policy has reported that one hundred sixty women in twenty-four states were convicted of such abuse in 1992.[15]

Five states have recently enacted laws requiring all medical agents to inform public authorities of their pregnant patients who are alcohol or drug abusers. In addition, eight states have enacted laws that require all medical agents to inform public authorities of newborn drug intoxication. Obviously, these measures facilitate the indictment procedure.

The case of Pamela Rae Stewart illustrates this judicial climate. In 1985, Stewart was arrested for refusing to follow her doctor's order to refrain from vigorous sexual intercourse with her husband. Charges against her also stated that she had not arrived on time at the delivery unit of the hospital. Consequently she was held solely responsible for damage to her fetus and was convicted of child abuse under California penal code statues. These statutes, recently amended, refer to: "Consciously omitting, without any legal pretext, to furnish a roof, food, clothing, as well as necessary medical care . . . for his/her child . . . *be he/she conceived and as of yet unborn* . . . considered as an existing person insofar as this section is concerned" (California Penal Code, Paragraph 270, cited in *People of the State of California v. Pamela Rae Stewart*).

Despite Supreme Court decisions guaranteeing fundamental rights to privacy and reproductive liberty, numerous state and legislative jurisdictions have chosen to embark on a path to bypass them. Their decisions and statutes are inspired by the notion that the embryo/fetus is, at the least, a potential person subject to the dangers of a hostile dwelling (the mother's womb).

THE RELATIONSHIP BETWEEN FETAL NEGLIGENCE AND WRONGFUL LIFE

At first glance fetal negligence convictions do not seem related to wrongful birth/life suits; nevertheless, a common denominator can be found: that is, an unprecedented status of the embryo/fetus. Indeed, the embryo/fetus takes on a new meaning relative to its previous judicial status and to the woman who carries it. The judicial and legislative void at the federal level with respect to artificial procreation, maternal/fetal medicine, and biogenetics in general (progressively pushing back the moment of fetal viability) has thus given rise to ad hoc, incoherent, and contradictory decisions in various states. This situation resembles the atmosphere prior to Supreme Court decisions relative to contraception and abortion.[16] Before these decisions, decentralized policies throughout the states contributed in maintaining a discriminatory environment of unequal access, wherein contraception and abortion were available only to those women or couples who lived in states with reformed laws, were rich enough to travel, or were lucky enough to know cooperative doctors.

The analogy exists today as one sees a lack of a comprehensive national public health program and national policy guaranteeing equal access to new medical technologies in maternal-fetal medicine, artificial reproduction, and genetic analysis. At this time, however, public authorities (especially those in the judiciary) are making decisions that, for lack of direction, are favoring the notion of fetal rights.

UNITED STATES POLICY: MAP AND BIOGENETIC RESEARCH

The only firm policy response of the federal government linked to biogenetic technology and MAP has been to limit public funding for research in these fields. Meanwhile, the private sector is given a free reign to carry out its practices as desired. In 1974, the Congress, responding to demands from the pro-life lobby trying to overturn *Roe*, imposed a moratorium on public funds for research on fetal remains as well as *in vitro* embryos. Immediately following this ban, the National Commission for the Protection of Human Subjects of Biomedical and Behavioral Research was created. This committee, similar to the French *Comité consultatif d'éthique* (see below) became the federal Ethics Advisory Board (EAB).

Laboratories involved in research covered by the ban vehemently protested the moratorium. On the front lines of protest were research laboratories seeking to determine the genetic origins of serious hereditary diseases, such as sickle-cell anemia, cystic fibrosis, and Tay-Sachs, among others. The birth of the first "test-tube" baby in England in 1978 (Louise Brown) prompted the EAB to issue a public statement severely criticizing the moratorium. The EAB called for a restoration of federal funding toward research on embryos until the fourteenth day of gestation. In 1979, the EAB recommended that federal funds should be allocated to research on fetal cells *in utero*, also coming under the moratorium. Despite these proposals Congress issued another three-year moratorium in 1984.

Once again, the scientific community (especially laboratories involved in research on embryos and genetic analysis) vigorously protested. In partial response, the National Institutes of Health (NIH) created the Human Fetal Tissue Transplantation Research Panel in 1988. Following four months of debate, the panel strongly encouraged the NIH to denounce the moratorium imposed on federal financing for embryo/fetal research. On January 7, 1991, the American College of Obstetricians and Gynecologists announced the creation of its own national consultant committee, designed to supervise fetal tissue research and artificial procreation.

The moratorium remained in effect until President Clinton's 1993 executive order. This order abrogated the 1974 moratorium on public funds for embryo/fetal research along with suspending the "gag rule" that had prohibited public funds for services offering abortion counseling and ending the ban on RU 486 testing and permitting its eventual importation.

In September 1994, a panel of nineteen doctors, lawyers, scientists, and philosophers, established by the National Institutes of Health (NIH), issued specific recommendations for embryo/fetal research.[17] The panel accepted experimentation up to the fourteenth day of embryonic gestation (equivalent to the closing of the fetus's neural tube). These experiments may include: a) research on excess embryos resulting from *in vitro* fertilization procedures, and following authorization by the genetic and/or social parents; b) research that involves the extraction of a cell from an embryo before transfer to the uterus in order to diagnose the existence of inherited diseases; c) the creation of a limited number of *in vitro* embryos (the number is not specified) solely designed for scientific experimentation (one approved method of obtaining the embryos is by extracting the ova from a female fetus either following an abortion or a miscarriage); and (d) gamete donors receiving financial compensation.

The NIH proposals call for the prohibition of public funding for any research involved in embryo cloning, the transfer of human embryos to animal uteruses, or embryo selection based on sex, even if the intention is avoiding transmission of diseases linked to sex. The main public policy issue is not what to allow or what to prohibit, but rather whether Congress will appropriate funds for research. Private laboratories and institutions throughout the country have already been involved in all the aforementioned types of research for the past thirty years. Indeed, the void in legislation has encouraged the proliferation of free-market forces as well as their consequences. If laboratories cannot obtain federal or state funding, then why not turn to private resources?

With no prospect of federal policy on the horizon, the most profitable scientific disciplines are now those that are developing at the fastest rate. According to George Anna, medical ethics expert at the University of Boston, the multiplication of biotechnology firms must be compared not to the development of science but to a "gold rush."[18]

In summary, it is not likely that the Congress will, in the near future, establish a comprehensive bioethics framework, one that avoids the extremes (total prohibition or the simple issue of public funding). It appears more likely that the courts will continue to be solicited to solve specific dilemmas. Meanwhile, the United States Supreme Court has already been called upon to serve as a final arbitrator with regard to some of the complex issues proposed by advances in fetal research (e.g., *UAW v Johnson Controls*, 499 U.S. 187, [1991]).

MAP POLICY IN FRANCE

In France, public policy responses to MAP have been affected by patterns of public debate that are different from those in the United States. The abortion issue, so central to many legal actions in the United States, is much less important in France. That, combined with the different constitutions and legal systems, has meant that the notion of wrongful life as a legal principle or serving as the basis for litigation, does not exist.[19]

Policymakers work in the context of debates that focus more directly on the ethical uses of science. Of great interest is the debate over eugenics carried out between historian Pierre-André Taguieff and biologist Jacques Testart. Testart is one of the "fathers" of the first test-tube baby in France, "Amandine." Subsequent to the publicity attending this birth, Testart took a firm stand against the "uncontrolled" proliferation of MAP practices. Taguieff, historian of political ideas and philosopher, is best known for his analytical critique of anti-racist discourse.[20]

Testart denounces techniques such as pre-uterine transfer of genetic material to diagnose inherited diseases. To him, such techniques valorize the trend toward "positive eugenics." While endorsing prenatal amniocentesis analysis, despite the fact that it can lead to the decision to abort a deformed fetus, Testart nevertheless prefers that pre-uterine transfer genetic analysis be prohibited since it can be performed much earlier in a pregnancy, creating an "artificial distance" between the parents and the desired child. With such methods the couple are selecting the most performant embryo and rejecting the others.

Taguieff maintains that opponents of the use of science for genetic purposes are motivated by outmoded ideologies, ignorant of history and essentially anti-modern. He sees three themes in the attack on the technologies of MAP. First is that it contradicts communist ideologies of egalitarianism. In Taguieff's view the egalitarian ideal shared by Testart and others cannot, if it wishes to remain coherent, accept the confirmation that, from the start, fundamental physiological and biological differences, whatever they be, do exist and contribute in distinguishing individuals from each other. Hence, eugenics, even in the strictest sense of the term, is rejected as being a scandalous and totally unacceptable confirmation that all human beings are *not* created equal. Applied biogenetics, as well as MAP, are thus immediately labeled as tools of racism, a first step toward the horrific Final Solution of Nazi Germany.

Taguieff goes on to describe the second category of anti-eugenic and anti-modern discourse as basing its argument on the sacredness or *sanctification of human life* that prohibits mankind to intervene or tamper with the *divine design*. Voluntary homicide, euthanasia, suicide, and abortion are defined as a satanic means of a presumptuous mankind eager to take God's place. In order to counter this evil force, God's will is for humans to refuse any human intervention whatsoever in the field of positive or negative eugenics.

Indeed, relative to MAP, Roman Catholicism specifically condemns mankind's "pretentious whim" to directly intervene in the process of procreation. As of yet, the Church remains relatively silent about applied biogenetics and gene therapy, preferring to focus on new reproductive technologies. Nevertheless, according to Church authority, mankind is presently over-whelmed and literally inebriated by the biotechnological power it possesses, refusing to remain a simple creature of God. Hence, the sacredness of life must be restored and urgent laws passed respecting the dignity of each and every human, and thus of the unity of mankind.[21]

Finally, another anti-eugenics discourse advocates "genetic fundamentalism," a form of belonging that is, according to Taguieff, based solely on the genetic makeup of *Homo sapiens*. Strictly speaking, this perspective can be defined as a biological variant of absolute conservatism; that is, prohibiting any modification of the human genome is a function of the unconditional requirement to conserve, preserve, and defend in the very name of conservation and preservation. According to Taguieff, "genetic fundamentalism" has provided modern humanists, deprived of religious institutions, with newfound spiritual aspirations. For "genetic fundamentalists," the *sacredness* of life takes precedence over the *quality* of life.

THE BIOETHICS LAW

In France, governmental response relative to applied biogenetics and MAP has been more forceful and centralized than in the United States. It began in 1983 when President François Mitterrand created the *Comité consultatif national d'éthique*. This commission's objective was to propose and construct a national scientific policy dealing with artificial procreation and applied biogenetics, among other fields. After eleven years of debate and numerous submissions filed by both social and natural scientists, the French Parliament adopted a bioethics law on July 29, 1994. The provisions of this law go into much greater detail than the NIH's recommendations. Some of the major provisions are still the object of controversy.

The law tries to strike a balance between the feared evils of experimentation on human beings and the expected benefits of fetal research:

a. Excess frozen embryos created before the July 29th law can be destroyed if they are not included in a family project. Those created following the law must be preserved.

b. As of July 1994, and each year thereafter, the genetic donors/parents of frozen embryos are asked to determine their outcome; that is, preserve them, donate them (to another couple or to scientific research), or destroy them.

c. Research on "orphan" embryos is accepted up to the fourteenth day of gestation, yet experimentation can only involve research related to the improvement of public health and/or scientific progress, and only if such research is incapable of being carried out otherwise.

Other recommendations addressed ethical questions about the use of MAP for family formation:

a. Artificial procreation techniques, under the national public health insurance, are solely reserved for married couples or couples able to prove that they have been living together for at least two years. IVF techniques are then fully reimbursed by Social Security up to four attempts.

b. Single women, homosexual couples, and/or menopausal women are prohibited from having recourse to these techniques, and private medical agents may not solicit their clientele.

c. Commercial surrogate motherhood is formally prohibited.

The law also sought the middle ground in the controversy reflected in the Testart and Taguieff debate about eugenics and reproductive technologies:

a. Pre-uterine transfer genetic diagnosis is authorized on a case-by-case basis and/or for couples with a family history of hereditary disease. In such cases, the law provides for all costs incurred by the national public health program (Jacques Testart and others would have liked to see this practice totally prohibited by the law).

b. All donations of human organs, cells, gametes, etc., are to remain anonymous, unless otherwise specified by the donor. Financial compensation for these donations is formally prohibited.

On July 27, 1994, two days before the French bioethics law was finally adopted, the *Conseil Constitutionnel*, which has powers of judicial review like the United States Supreme Court, confirmed that its contents were in conformity with the French Constitution. As previously mentioned, the law is more comprehensive and authoritative than the NIH recommendations. It goes so far as to regulate who can have access to the technologies for assisting procreation and places an outright prohibition on surrogacy. In the United States legal system, based on common law precedent within a decentralized federal structure, it would be very unlikely that such categorical provisions would be found in a Congressional statute. There are, however, some similarities. Both approve of research on excess embryos resulting from *in vitro* fertilization procedures, following authorization from the genetic and/or social parents. The United States panel went further in recommending the controversial extraction technique, while the French law limits its use to a case-by-case basis. The United States recommendations permit the creation of a limited number of *in vitro* embryos, solely designed for scientific experimentation. The French law fully prohibits this practice.

UNITED STATES AND FRANCE: THE STATE AND MAP

In his book, *L'Etat et la science,* Luc Rouban analyzes the relationships between the state and the scientific community in both France and the United
Sates.[22] According to Rouban, the capabilities of the United States federal system are weak when faced with universities, research foundations, and firms
acting as a strong lobbying force. In France, on the other hand, the state, with
a strong administrative apparatus and weak interest groups, seeks out and
sponsors researchers who then implement modernization projects elaborated
by the state. Thus in France, scientific research inserts itself within the state,
whereas in the United States a more distinct separation exists between state
authority and direction and scientific projects. As Rouban has concluded:

> *In France, corporatism coupled with state planning have served as
> major vectors permitting the integration of science and politics,
> and have likewise served as resources to those innovators
> who . . . have sought to associate a certain vision of science to a
> certain vision of the State in order to install a scientific policy. In
> the United States it is striking how these two reasonings remain
> foreign to the constitution of a similar (national) scientific policy
> since actors and agents have a more pronounced tendency to refer
> to a market evaluation, to the interaction of social actors, and to
> institutional fragmentation.[23]*

Rouban observes what he calls a "presidentialization" of national scien-
tific policy in both France and the United States, which we have illustrated by
Clinton's directive reversing the ban and Mitterrand's initiative in creating the
Comité national d'éthique.

Nevertheless, despite some guidance from above, the predominant role
of market forces in the United States is undeniable. In a 1990 interview, Leon
Rosenberg, Dean of the Yale Medical School, severely criticized the lack of
long-term planning in the field of scientific fundamental and applied research. Underlying the absence of direction, particularly in the field of health
and life sciences, Rosenberg went so far as to declare:

> *If, in the near future, it becomes impossible to significantly
> increase the federal budget for research in health and life sciences,
> then I would be in favor of diminishing public funds allocated to
> the Genome Project, and even to AIDS research.[24]*

Rosenberg's public declaration was meant to be provocative. His objective was
to underscore the face that it has become imperative that the executive branch

immediately create a commission whose aim is to develop a national policy for the sciences, especially for the biomedical sciences.

This commission was recently inaugurated by President Clinton. However, and despite advice from the Office of Science and Technology Policy (that a National Bioethics Advisory Commission replace the now-disbanded Biomedical Ethics Advisory Board), chances are that its impact will not carry as far as the French *Comité consultatif d'éthique*. If it did, it could perhaps lead to a similar version of the French bioethics law, itself highly controversial despite being the fruit of a long, extensive, and negotiated compromise. It appears that a future United States federal bioethics law would more likely involve (under pressure form the new conservative Congress) outright bans on research or a simple renewal of moratoriums on public funding. Naturally, both options would only serve to justify an intensification of the private sector's research and activity.

Meanwhile, United States state courts and legislatures will continue to be the sole decision makers in determining what policy to adopt when faced with the realities and formidable horizons offered by applied biogenetics and MAP. Such an incomplete, inconsistent, and contradictory policy must be avoided, yet this is not the case in the United States. In addition, and despite France's bioethics law (the first on the European continent), its application will likewise amount to little as long as other European nation-states do not enact a similar policy.

WHERE ARE THE FEMINISTS?

Public debate on issues discussed in this chapter seem to be framed, both in the United States and France, by politicians, scientists, and philosophers rather than by feminists, despite the fact that policy relating to MAP has profound implications for women's status and rights. One reason for the inability of feminists to control the debate in the United States is that positions on new reproductive technologies are fragmented, sometimes causing overt hostility within the American feminist community.[25]

One major issue serves as a pertinent illustration: the debate over surrogate motherhood raised by the case of "Baby M." The National Organization for Women (NOW), the largest U.S. feminist organization, is internally divided over the status of the surrogate mother. The New York NOW chapter lobbies in favor of prohibiting surrogate motherhood, stating that such practices allow for the economic exploitation of indigent women. On the West Coast, the California NOW chapter calls for full legal recognition of the surrogate mother in the name of the freedom of choice for all women regarding reproductive matters.

American feminists are in the midst of a third divide that extends beyond the question of equality versus difference. They have yet to position themselves with regard to other social issues that are bound to surface as a result of scientific research such as the status of frozen embryos, MAP commercialization, embryo cloning, etc. Nevertheless, as scientific and medical research continues to produce new discoveries, American feminists have taken some stands such as:

1. *Feminists who support the uterine mother or gestational mother.* Their position was developed during the "Baby M" case, as follows:

> Her gestational motherhood establishes her motherhood. We will not accept the idea that we can look at a woman heavy with child and say that the child is not hers."[26]

> At birth, the baby is literally her flesh and blood. Until moments before, it was part of her body and nourished like her own organs. To have provided a sperm or an egg is trivial by comparison. . . . At birth, the birthmother is in a special position to be the real parent.[27]

2. *Feminists who support the genetic parent.* They stipulate that if genetic parenthood is minimized (as they believe is the case today), the right to abortion will be even more severely curtailed. A woman's right to abortion was essentially based on her right to privacy and corporal integrity. This notion loses its meaning once a fetus is created outside of the woman's body, either through artificial means or in a surrogate mother.

> *To bear or beget a child is to bring into being another human life, to project further into the future a genetic community, and to create a physiological kinship bond regardless of by whom the child is raised. . . . The impact of knowing that one has a child continues long after even a successful adoption.*[28]

3. *Feminists who remain reluctant to pronounce themselves.* They do so primarily because of what they sometimes perceive of as an instrumentalization of women's bodies by the medical and scientific community. With the advent of new reproductive technologies, these spokeswomen point to the resurgence of the effort to "structure a woman's will to be a mother."[29]

> *The process of privileging birthmothers is likely to heighten the pressure on women to undergo* in vitro *fertilization and other technologically intensive routes to motherhood . . . the mystification of pregnancy may also have other detrimental effects . . . the "choice" to give birth may be weighted unduly by the fear of missing out on*

life's most meaningful relationship, one that cannot be matched by becoming an adoptive mother, let alone an aunt, godmother, or other honorary kin.[30]

Rayna Rapp, professor of anthropology at the New School for Social Research (New York), has researched a means to transcend these contradictory positions. Following extensive examination of women from various socioeconomic and ethnic categories of the American population, Rapp reveals that women's perceptions of childbirth, childbearing, and the medical community that takes charge of them during this period are as diverse as the women themselves. She concludes that no universal abstract language, be it that of feminists, anti-feminists, or political or medical spokespersons, can speak for each and every woman and her own needs. Rapp criticizes the submission of these needs to any type of collective negotiation. She writes:

Science speaks a universal language of progress. But women express their diverse consciousness and practices in polyglot multicultural languages. When women speak about the medicalization of reproduction, what they tell us must be placed in its historical, social context. Amniocentesis and other new reproductive technologies open a Pandora's box of powerful knowledge, constructed through scientific and medical practices. But messages given are not necessarily messages received. New technologies fall into older cultural terrains where women interpret their possibilities in light of older and contradictory meanings of pregnancy and childbearing. A feminist invocation of nurturing as a critique of technological rationality must first locate itself in relation to women's stratified diversity. Otherwise, it will reproduce the vexsome problem of false universalization it was initially developed to transcend.[31]

The struggle simply to maintain reproductive rights in the realm of contraception and abortion has become a full-time activity for United States feminist groups, leaving little opportunity to act upon, and not simply react to, the discriminatory decisions examined in this chapter. This does not prevent these groups, however, from being very preoccupied with this new challenge. As we have seen, the United States debate among feminists is complex and vigorous. In France, feminists appear to be much less interested or, rather, are much less heard regarding these issues. Perhaps the feminist perspective is absent in the political debate in France because feminism is less institutionalized and does not operate as an effective lobby.

During Mitterrand's presidential mandates, which included two periods of political "co-habitation" with a right-wing government and parliament, chief state advocates for women's rights, heading either the office of the *Secrétariat aux droits des femmes* or the *Délégué à la condition féminine* never came out with an official statement. They were rarely, if ever, heard as feminist spokespersons when these issues were addressed, even during the twelve-year-long Ethics Committee proceedings and ensuing parliamentary debate over the bioethics law.

Before Simone Veil left her responsibilities as Minister for Health and Social Affairs in 1995, her declarations on the twentieth anniversary of the *Loi Veil*, the decriminalization of abortion, were fully covered in the media. Yet, she never came out with a comprehensive analysis of the questions raised relative to women's status by the bioethics law, only expressing her satisfaction with passing of the law itself. Since the French presidential election of Jacques Chirac in 1995, more women than ever before in French history have been appointed to high-level governmental positions. At the same time, the high-power offices of the *Secrétariat aux droits des femmes* or the *Délégué à la condition féminine* have been abolished and replaced by a less influential *Service aux droits des Femmes* under the auspices of a new ministry headed by Colette Codaccioni, entitled the *Ministère de la Solidarité entre les Générations* (Solidarity Between Generations).[32] Neither Codaccioni nor Elisabeth Hubert (Minister of Health) took a stand when members of an anti-abortion commando action were acquitted of criminal activity. The basis for the acquittal was an article in the new French penal code absolving an individual from punishment when he or she is attempting to come to the rescue of a "person or thing in danger."

CONCLUSION

Biogenic engineering and medically assisted procreation have led policymakers in the United States and France to address the equation between science, procreation, and democracy in ways that will undoubtedly shape the future status of women and men. MAP has started a process of redefinition of the family far beyond the historical and traditional images known in industrialized nations since the end of the nineteenth century. These new perspectives of parenthood have created a decidedly bewildering situation for jurists, legislators, and especially for feminists.

Indeed, up to now, constructing a reproductive-rights framework in Western industrialized nations consisted of a quasi-Manichean exercise, i.e., the almost consistently antagonistic juxtaposition of individual rights (the private sphere) to the public interests and responsibilities. However, with applied biogenetics and medically assisted procreation, issues no longer derive from what medical technology can allow an individual to avoid, but rather from what this same individual can accomplish or realize. This transfer from a passive to a hypothetically active reproductive-rights framework has compounded what already is a highly polemical issue. Contrary to appearances, the present-day controversy opposing pro-choice to pro-life, in the United States and, albeit to a lesser extent, in France, is no longer the only conflict: feminists themselves are divided.

Throughout most Western nations, numerous ethics committees are advising legislatures on questions relative to scientific discoveries in the realm of biogenetic engineering and MAP. Undeniably, a new chapter in the history of women's rights is in the process of being written. One only has to look at the debate in the United States surrounding the notion of "fetal rights" in order to measure this sea change. While the technology continues its rapid advance, it is safe to predict that it will take a long time for policymakers to construct a consistent policy

NOTES

1. Among others see, John T. Noonan Jr., *Contraception: A History of Treatment by Catholic Theologians and Canonists* (Cambridge: Harvard University Press, 1965); Rosemary Radford Ruether, *Religion and Sexism: Images of Women in the Jewish and Christian Tradition* (New York: Simon & Schuster, 1974); James Mohr, *Abortion in America: The Origins and Evolution of a National Policy 1800–1900* (Oxford: Oxford University Press, 1978); Paul Carrick, *Medical Ethics in Antiquity: Perspectives on Abortion and Euthanasia* (Dordrecht: D. Reidel, 1985); Angus McLaren, *A History of Contraception: Antiquity to the Present Day* (Oxford: Basil Blackwell, 1990).

2. *Bonbrest v. Kotz*, 65 F. Supp. 138, p. (D.D.C. 1946), quoted in Patricia White, "The Concept of Person, the Law, and the Use of the Fetus in Biomedicine," in *Abortion and the Status of the Fetus*, ed. William B. Bondeson, H. Tristam Engelhardt Jr., Stuart F. Spicker, David H. Winship (Dordrect: D. Reiderl, 1984).

3. Key dates in MAP: 1791: first artificial insemination in Great Britain; 1804: first artificial insemination in France; 1884: first artificial insemination in Great Britain with donor sperm; 1940: successful cryogenic preservation of human sperm; 1970: first amniocentesis; 1979: birth of first *in vitro* fertilization (test-tube baby—Louise Brown) in England; 1982: birth of "Amandine," France's first test-tube baby; 1984: birth of "Zoe," first *in vitro* baby using frozen embryo transfer; 1994: birth of "anonymous" from micro-injected sperm insemination.

4. This figure, and many that follow, are taken from an extensive worldwide study entitled "La face cachée de la procréation médicalement assistée (The hidden side of medically assisted procreation)," *La Recherche* 213 (September 1989): 1112–28.

5. Office of Technology Assessment, *Artificial Insemination: Practice in the United States* (Washington, DC: Author, 1988), as cited in Robert Blank, *Regulating Reproduction* (New York: Columbia University Press, 1990), 25.

6.   In France, a recent debate opposed Dr. René Frydman and Jacques Testart, both members of the "Amandine" team. Frydman emphasizes the 25 percent success rate while Testart speaks of a 12 percent success rate; the difference is that Testart defines "success" as the birth of a healthy baby, not just the success in establishing pregnancy.

7.   B. Knoppers, *Conception artificielle et responsibiilité médicale* (Montreal: Editions Blais, 1986), quoted in *La Recherche*, op cit., 1116–19.

8.   H. Leridon, in "Recherches récentes sur l'epidéiologie de la fertilité," in J. Henry-Suchet et al. *Recherches Récentes sur l'Epidéiologie de la Fertilité* (Paris: Masson, 1986).

9.   D. Marchbank et al., "Annales du deuxième congrès mondial sur les maladies sexuellement transmissibles," *Abstract* 14.4, 1986, cited in *La Recherche*, op cit., 1119.

10. Frank Nouchi, "La qualité du sperme diminue progresivement depuis vingt ans," *Le Monde* (3 February 1995), 13.

11. For a fascinating discussion of this parameter, see Charles Rosenberg, "Culpable Failures of Volition: Disease and the Social Order in America, Perceptions and expectations," *Millbank Quarterly* 64, suppl. 1 (1986), especially pp. 44, 50.

12. Madeleine Rochon "Stérilité et problèmes de fertilité," *Etudes de santé*, Gouvernement de Quebec (Ministère de la Santé et des Services Sociaux, 1986).

13. *Curlender v. Bio-Science Laboratories*, 165 Cal. Rptr. 477 (1980), 488.

14. For example, in *Ellis v. Sherman* (No. J26052, Pa., 1994), the court emphasized the lack of scientific knowledge since the handicap involved (neurofibromatosis) is not yet detectable through prenatal genetic analysis. If it were, nothing prevents one from assuming that the court would have decided otherwise. In the case of *Alquijay v. St. Luke's-Roosevelt Hospital Center* (9 A.D. 2d. 704, N.Y.S. 2d. 1, A.D.1 Dept. 1984), the wrongful life concept was not rejected, rather the age of the plaintiff bringing suit (fourteen years). Finally, in the cases of *Di Natale v. Lieberman* (409 So.2d. 512. Fla., 1982), *Dorlin v. Providence Hospital* (118 Mich. App. 831, 325 N.W. 2d. 600, 1982), and *Nelson v. Krusen* (635 S.W. 2d. 582. Tex., 1982), the courts succeeded in avoiding judgment, declaring that " life had no price." In essence, this position was more or less a "wait and see" one pending legislation.

15. For implications of these convictions, see "Statutes that Unfairly Punish Pregnant Women for Behavior," *Reproductive Rights Update*, 2, no. 1 (January 5, 1990): 4; "Punishing Women for their Behavior During Pregnancy: A Public Health Disaster," *Reproductive Freedom* (1993). These are publications of the Center for Reproductive Law and Policy.

16. *Griswold v. Connecticut* (381 U.S. 479, 1965); *Eisenstadt v. Baird* (405 U.S. 438, 1972); and *Roe V. Wade* (410 U.S. 113, 1973).

17. *Science* (August 19, 1994).

18. "L'homme, propriété industrielle," *Der Spiegel*, reprinted in *Courrier International* (10 November 1993): 8.

19. The concept of wrongful life has rarely been analyzed by French social scientists or legal experts. An exception is David Le Breton, *Anthropologie du Corps et Modernité* (Paris: PUF, 1990). He translates the term "wrongful life" to that of *vie préjudiciable* (that which is deterimental, hurtful). Other possible translations are *vie injuste* (that which goes against justice, equity); *vie injustifiée* (that which is not or was not justified); or *vie injustifiable* (that which is unjustifiable, not defensible, unbearable). A multitude of connotations exists, each one capable of shaping, in a totally different manner, subsequent laws based on it.

20. The epistolary dialogue is in *Esprit* (February, March 1994). See also, for Testart, *le Magasin des Enfants* (Paris: Bourin, 1990); *La procréation médicalisé* (Paris: Flammarion coll. "Domino," 1993). For Taglieff, "Améliorer l'homme? L'eugénisme et ses ennemis," *Raison Présente* 105 (lst trimester, 1993): 59–104.

21. Taguieff, "Améliorer l'homme," op cit., 85. Also see Commission pontificale "Justitia e Pax" (president: Cardinal Etchegaray), *L'eglise Face au Racisme: Pour un société plus fraternelle,* Vatican (Paris: Editions du Cerf, 1989), 24.

22. Luc Rouban, *L'Etat et la science* (Paris: Editions du CNRS, 1988).

23. Ibid, p.12.

24. Dick Thompson, "The Growing Crisis in Medical Science: An Interview with Leon Rosenberg," *Time* (December 17, 1990): 20.

25. One major point deserves comment: the ongoing battle in the United States on the part of pro-choice forces to maintain abortion rights has no doubt prevented them from devoting the necessary time and energy to consolidate a common platform with regard to bioethical issues. This opinion was expressed by several activists in interviews: Terri Flan, California NOW (July 30, 1993) and Lynn Paltrow, Center for Reproductive Law and Policy (December 13, 1993).

26. Barbara Katz Rothman in *Gender in Transition*, ed. Joan Offerman-Zuckerberg (New York: Plenum, 1989). Rothman adopted this argument in testimony before the Joint Hearings of the New York State Senate and the New State Assembly Judiciary Committees on Surrogate Parenthood and New Reproductive Technology (October 16, 1986); reprinted in *France-USA: Comparaison des réactions de nos société devant le progrès des connaissances et des techniques en biogénétiques de la transmission de la vie,* AFFDU, International Colloquium Acts, March 3-4, 1988 (Paris: La Foundation Sterling-Currier/le Ministère de l'Enseignement Supérieur et de la Recherche), 108.

27. Ruth Hubbard, "A Birthmother is a Birthmother is a . . . ," *Sojourner: The Women's Forum* (September 1987): 71-72.

28. Nan Hunter, "Time Limits on Abortion," quoted by Nadine Taub in "Feminist Tensions: The Concept of Parenthood and Reproductive Choice," in *France-USA,* op cit., 112.

29. Gena Cora, "What the King Can Not See," in *Embryos, Ethics, and Women's Rights*, ed. E. Baruch, A. D'Adamo, J. Seager (New York: Harrington Park Press, 1988), 88.

30. Nadine Taub, "Feminist Tensions: Concepts of Motherhood and Reproductive Choice," in Offerman-Zuckerberg, op cit., 221.

31. Rayna Rapp, "Constructing Amniocentesis: Maternal and Medical Discourses," in *France-USA,* op cit., 160-61.

32. Before becoming Minister, Colette Codaccioni was an active participant in the bioethics law debate as she endeavored to have included in the text a definitive legal definition of the embryo/fetus as a "person." Codaccioni left her post in late 1995.

CHAPTER 10

FEMINIST PERSPECTIVES ON ABORTION AND REPRODUCTIVE TECHNOLOGIES

DOROTHY McBRIDE STETSON

INTRODUCTION

The abortion issue has been on the public agenda in North America, Europe, and Japan periodically during the past thirty years. In many countries, feminists have participated actively in the policy debate, but their part in defining the issues and influencing reform of restrictive laws has varied from country to country as well as over time (Lovenduski and Outshoorn, 1986; Dahlerup, 1986; Rolston and Eggert, 1994). At any one time the discursive strategy adopted by feminist advocates for abortion rights represents only a small portion of the complex issues at stake. Whatever the particular emphasis in a debate–choice, women's self-determination, equality, or sexual freedom–the feminist argument draws upon theoretical work which in turn is affected by changes in the political arenas. It is important to keep this interaction between theory and practice in mind when observing the public debate. Finding a feminist position on the abortion issue involves much more than devising a slogan like "right-to-choose"; questions of morality, personhood, family, democracy, the state, science, medical ethics, and gender relations are at stake.

The place of the abortion issue on the policy agenda varies cross-nationally as well. The compromises concocted in the 1970s and 1980s hold firm in most Western European states and Japan, making abortion a non-issue for feminist activists. Exceptions include Ireland and Germany where, thus far, acceptable compromises have eluded policymakers. Canada and the United States lack resolution as well; only in the United States, however, does abortion separate legislators, judges, and their constituents into two unyielding camps. In Eastern Europe, transition from communist regimes has forced newly elected parliaments to contend with efforts to restrict liberal abortion laws.

Throughout the period of abortion law reform, feminist theory has produced two well-established approaches for activists: liberal and radical. Each has provided rhetoric to assist women in gaining access to abortion services that is adaptable to a variety of political and legal environments. Today, a challenge looms that threatens to disrupt this established pattern of abortion politics: rapidly changing reproductive technologies. Developments in technologies have long affected abortion policy. For example, when improvements in surgical techniques made abortion available to more women, the American Medical Association campaigned to criminalize the procedure except to save the mother's life. Today, however, the technology is putting new powers in the hands of the medical profession so rapidly that it throws into question long-held beliefs and values about birth, life, death, and motherhood. Feminists have begun to sound the alarm, urging attention to the potential dangers, but these efforts reveal fundamental disagreements that may undermine the hard-won feminist cohesion over reproductive issues like abortion and contraception.

The goal of this chapter is to review contemporary writing of feminist commentators on abortion law and the new reproductive technologies.[1] The first section focuses on abortion and shows how slogans such as the "right to choose" may distort complexities pertaining to the place of abortion in the overall framework of gender relations. The second section will examine the division among feminists and the significance of the new reproductive technologies. Finally, the chapter will conclude with a consideration of the ways the debate over technologies has affected the abortion debate.

FEMINIST THEORIES OF ABORTION

The most widely known argument in the United States in favor of access to abortion is the liberal feminist demand for choice. The rhetoric of choice seems to be a powerful anchor in the face of efforts to restrict access to abortion services. Nevertheless, choice is a slogan that depends on a careful analogy between women's rights and classic liberal democratic theory.

The issue came to the public agenda in the 1960s and 1970s while many traditional laws and practices limited women's options in family, work, politics, and cultural life. Feminist arguments in support of gaining access to safe abortion services made ample use of liberal democratic ideals: freedom of choice, privacy, self-determination, control of one's body, and autonomy. Criminalization of abortion was fashioned as "compulsory pregnancy," forcing women to remain under the burden of pregnancy, childbearing, and family duties despite their own wishes and desires. The democratic idea of liberty to decide what to do with one's own life (life, liberty, and the pursuit of happiness) seemed just for women at a time when new options for work and education offered to expand their activities outside of the home.

The right of self-determination, the traditional claim of oppressed peoples for liberation, was appropriated to lend support to feminist claims for abortion rights. Advocates have argued that freedom for women as a group depended on having freedom to decide when and if they would bear children. This could be achieved by guaranteeing each woman the right to control her body, not to submit her body to the control of others. Women showed their determination to rebel against such control, even if it meant resorting to back-street abortionists and the risk of injury, even death. Framing the abortion question in terms of liberty, freedom, and self-determination versus submission, powerlessness, and compulsory pregnancy showed the way to a solution for many United States feminists: make abortion legal and limit government interference in women's lives through the guarantee of a right to privacy where women and their doctors could act freely. Choice came to be synonymous with removal of government regulations over abortion.

Two decades of experience with abortion debates have amended this early liberal feminist solution to the problem of abortion. Choice, if all it requires is that the government not limit abortion, has turned out to be a narrow foundation for policy. In Russia, for example, where the state allowed abortion more or less on demand, the law did not further choice because women did not have the means to prevent conception. Choice of abortion has meaning only if there is adequate contraception and information available to women. Similarly, privacy does little to advance the options of poor women who have neither the means to raise children nor the funds to pay for abortions. The decision to terminate a pregnancy takes place in a wider context of reproduction, including a culture that gives particular meaning to contraception, health care, economic conditions, and family life.

Women lack autonomy in the private sphere; putting limits on government power over the private sphere may leave structures of male dominance undisturbed. The earlier liberal feminist approach, focusing on choice, overlooked the issue of power between men and women in the family. More recent feminist writings about abortion law have tried to remedy this oversight by integrating another democratic ideal into their theory of abortion rights—equality: "If discrimination were at issue in the abortion debate, then treating women as 'different' from men in a way that limits women's opportunity would not be acceptable. Abortion would then be grounded in a woman's right not to be sexually discriminated against as a reproducer, as a pregnant body, or in terms of her 'difference'" (Eisenstein, 1988: 189).

Tying the abortion issue to powerful ideas of equality and anti-discrimination has policy potential. In the United States, such a linkage would place the matter of access to abortion services on a par with access to education, work, and health care; it would provide a way to apply constitutional doctrines of equal protection to abortion law. In many European countries, it would bring the issue under the umbrella of equality councils and commissions that are major state institutions enforcing the equality of the sexes (Stetson and Mazur, 1995).

In a sense, all arguments that tie women's reproductive rights to their civil rights are based on some notion of equality. Without the capability to make decisions about if and when to give birth to a child, women cannot have the education and work opportunities enjoyed by men. Abortion rights have come to be associated in some discussions with a less conventional idea of equality of sexual pleasure. This argument can be extended to sexuality. Being relieved of the fear of compulsory pregnancy by having access to abortion, along with contraception, allows women to participate and enjoy sex on an equal level with men.

Such appeals to equality will not make the problem presented by biological differences disappear. First of all, the fit between an argument for equality between men and women based on policies about these differences, like abortion, is uneasy at best. One can certainly make the case that where real differences exist between two groups of people that affect their opportunities, it is just to treat one group in a special way in order to achieve a more equitable outcome. However, where the difference is biological—reproductive biology at that—the claim for special treatment has the danger of emphasizing women's special reproductive capacities. For centuries, such an emphasis was the underpinning for the complex of religious, legal, and social structures that kept women from venturing outside their family roles. To establish a legal precedent based on women's special reproductive biology so recently after these systems have begun to erode may undermine hard-won advances in women's status. The feminist dilemma produced by aspirations for equality encountering sexual differences in reproduction detracts from the effectiveness of the equality argument.

The second problem arises over the claim that access to abortion gives women equal access to sexual pleasure. Appropriate abortion policies may relieve women of the fear of compulsory pregnancy, yet they are unlikely to make women and men equal with respect to sexuality. Sexuality is affected by a wide range of social and cultural factors, many of which make women submissive to men. Some feminist theorists argue that liberal abortion policies, far from liberating women, further strengthen men's sexual domination over women (MacKinnon, 1987; Dworkin, 1983).

With this realization, feminist writers have turned their attention toward the larger context in which abortion takes place. Sometimes called radical feminists, they work to integrate reproduction issues—abortion, contraception, sex education—with sexuality issues, such as the definition of female sexuality and male sexual aggression. They have found that rather than abortion law being a means to equality for women, it is the reverse, that equality between the sexes is necessary for abortion law to liberate women (Batiot, 1986). When a woman seeks an abortion, she is already pregnant; the important question is how she became pregnant. Did she have full freedom over her sexuality at that moment? When women and men meet in heterosexual encounters, they often-follow male-defined norms, with the result that women do not feel they have control: "Women feel compelled to preserve the appearance—which, acted upon, becomes the reality—of male direction of sexual expression, as if male initiative itself were what we want, as if it were that which turns us on" (MacKinnon, 1987: 95). The availability of contraception and abortion means more women available to more men for sex.

This argument has already been a major theme among Italian feminist groups when their abortion law reform was under consideration by parliament (Bono and Kemp, 1991; Caldwell, 1986). "We know very well that when a woman gets pregnant and has not wanted to, this has not happened because she expressed herself sexually, but rather because she has adapted herself to the sexual act and pattern which are certainly favoured by the patriarchal male, even if this could mean for her getting pregnant and having to face an abortion" (*Rivolta Femminile*, reprinted in Bono and Kemp, 1991: 214–18). For them, liberal abortion laws, while not opposed, would not in any way liberate women. They saw abortion in patriarchal societies as a sort of violence woman's body must undergo to satisfy the conception that sexual fulfillment is male orgasm in the vagina. Far from self-determination and choice, legalized abortion leaves women with the injury and the guilt. These feminists argued for a female-centered sexuality, free of procreative "vaginal finalization."

This trip to Italy brings us back to the feminist critique of framing the abortion issue in terms of choice and reproductive rights. While, as has been indicated, this rhetoric can be effective in gaining legitimacy for the reform claims by appealing to powerful democratic icons, its narrowness jeopardizes the contribution that access to abortion services could make toward under-mining gender-based social hierarchies. This difficulty is inherent in the con-cepts of choice, privacy, and reproductive rights. These ideas focus squarely on the individual woman; the right she has is to be left alone by the govern-ment to act. Individual rights mean little, however, if she is part of a social structure that limits her alternatives severely or lacks resources to break out of these constraints. Individual rights do little to challenge the institutions of class, racial oppression, and gender domination that limit choices for all women (to varying degrees) (Porter, 1994; Petchesky, 1985). And, since by definition rights mean that every individual has the same right, there is no mechanism for taking the disparate effects into account.

The individual-right-to-choose argument unwittingly reinforces the powerful rhetoric of anti-feminists through the idea of fetal rights. By defini-tion, rights pertain to every individual. The fetus, as a person or a potential human, has a right to life, to be protected by the government. This sets up a conflict of competing rights: of the woman to self-determination, freedom, and personality development; and of the fetus to be born. The debate is thus framed as a "clash of absolutes," as Tribe has labeled it (1990). Finding a compromise between absolute but contradictory rights has plagued the abortion debate, especially in the United States and Germany. In the early days of the abortion rights campaign, feminists came down emphatically on the rights of the woman over the fetus. But as long as they use the rights language they are thrust into uncomfortable position of finding justification for taking the life of the potential human.

Such difficulties have encouraged feminists to shift the debate from the idea of rights to the idea of reproductive freedom. The concept of freedom has advantages in the abortion policy debates. Whereas rights apply to individuals, not groups, the idea of freedom may apply to an individual woman as well as to women as a group. Rather than a woman being left alone in a zone of privacy, freedom implies the consideration of a set of their needs. It also connotes a wide range of needs, with access to abortion being only one of them. These include sex education based on exploration of female sexuality, attention to contraceptive methods and their availability, prenatal care, child care, economic status, housing—in short, all the social relations of reproduction. According to the concept of needs, activists should argue for liberal abortion policy as part of this larger set of needs to achieve reproductive freedom.

Liberal and radical feminist perspectives on the abortion issue have provided effective arguments for advocates for women in policy debates. One reason for this effectiveness is that by relying on the assumption that the capacity to give birth unites women, they found a way to form coalitions of different types of women's organizations in campaigns for abortion law reforms in many countries. However, similar to many feminist theories, they overlooked diversity among women, who do not see this assumed similarity among women in the same way. If one supports access to abortion on demand for all women, one must accept the fact that women will choose to abort fetuses for what may be perceived of as selfish and possibly unethical reasons. Disabled women, for example, have challenged the tendency of feminist activists to accept without examination the option for a pregnant woman to abort a fetus that may have a disability (Finger in Arditti, 1989: 281–97). Others are dismayed that access to abortion allows killing of fetuses of an unwanted sex.

The liberal and radical feminist analyses of abortion focus on gender relations, especially male domination over women. Arguments are portrayed as women against men and male-dominated institutions. Shrage (1994), however, points out that, in fact, the abortion debate over policy historically has been a debate between women. While abortion campaigns in the 1970s may have united women's movement activists for a time, the issue has polarized women, she argues, because they have different views of the centrality of motherhood. One group sees motherhood as one of a variety of life choices for women; other groups see motherhood as essential, although not necessarily singular, in women's lives. A belief in the centrality of motherhood to women is the foundation for some self-defined feminist views of abortion that contradict liberal and radical perspectives. Thus we find "feminists for life" as well as feminist arguments that emphasize responsibility of women for the well-being of their fetuses. "Women's capacity for reproduction gives them a special duty to consider their capacity for sustaining a pregnancy" (Porter, 1994: 80). These arguments bring the dilemma that the reproductive issue presents for feminists into focus. At the same time, it undermines the capacity of the abortion issue in the 1990s to unify women in the kind of sustained political campaign that took place in the 1970s. This potentially divisive effect is magnified by the puzzles arising from the rapid development of New Reproductive Technologies.

NEW REPRODUCTIVE TECHNOLOGY

As Merchant points out in chapter 9, scientific research since the 1930s has greatly increased the ability of doctors to intervene in reproductive functions of human beings as well as other animals. Called *New Reproductive Technology* (NRT), these tools include artificial insemination by husband and/or donor (AID); amniocentesis; fetal monitoring, diagnosis, and treatment; surrogacy; *in vitro* fertilization; ultrasound; and embryo transfer. The fundamental science underlying these practices is on an upward trajectory toward greater and greater capability of human control over conception, gestation, and birth.

In considering these changes, feminist theorists face a dilemma. For the most part, they are critical of the effects of these technologies on women. They fear that, in the hands of a male-dominated medical establishment, NRT is used to diminish women's status and power in reproduction. At the same time, a fundamental feminist tenet has been that women's lives have been narrowed due to their dependency on their biological functions and the way these functions have been interpreted. NRT promises to free women from the restrictions of biology, enhancing choice. In addition, women express their demands through their actions. Just as they act to end unwanted pregnancies, whether legal or not, many women seek help from such new techniques to overcome infertility or to be able to postpone childbearing until middle age without jeopardizing their own or their children's health.

The feminist argument in support of NRT recommends that women become fully informed about the uses of these various practices, but leaves it up to the individual to determine if and when a particular technique is appropriate for her. The technology permits more flexibility and choice for all people; along with that gain is the responsibility to exercise choice responsibly and with adequate information. Feminists should not presume that they or anyone should make such decisions for individual women.

In fact, supporters maintain that many of these choices offered by NRT are consistent with feminist goals. For example, women no longer need to choose between a career and a family. Before NRT, plans for education and launching a career in one's twenties had to be forsaken in order to ensure a healthy family. Today, advancements in reproductive knowledge, including amniocentesis and fetal monitoring and treatment, increase the likelihood that children born to women in their forties will be healthy. Motherhood is available to any woman with NRT. Lesbians conceive through AID without necessity of heterosexual contact. Older women can give birth, potentially after menopause. A woman can overcome problems of infertility, even to the extent of having a family member gestate her biological offspring. Surrogacy contracts, such as the celebrated case of Baby M, enhance the efficacy of both the birth mother, who controls her childbearing capabilities, and the adoptive mother, who satisfies her desire for a family.

A test of whether NRT in fact reinforces women's traditional status or gives them the choice of breaking traditional bonds would be to look at the politically active opponents of NRT. Leaders of male-dominated institutions apparently fear the effects of an open market in NRT. In the United States, Britain, and France, recommendations have been put in place limiting access by restricting use of NRT to heterosexuals, preferably married couples (see Merchant, this volume; Hanmer, 1987: 95). Surrogacy contracts are prohibited or severely circumscribed in many countries. And the Catholic Church is strongly opposed to the use of NRT to subvert the connection between procreation and sexuality, a connection which for centuries has been used to restrict women's lives to narrow roles of chastity and childbearing. Feminists who see NRT as potentially enhancing women's choice do warn that due to the excessive expense of these options, caution would have to be taken to ensure that poor women are not exploited by them but have access to them.

Janice Raymond calls these arguments that describe NRT as enhancing women's choice as *reproductive liberalism* (1993, chapter 3). These liberals claim that feminist arguments against the technologies are essentialist by clinging to a naturalistic idea of motherhood. Raymond disagrees: "Opposition to these technologies is based on the more political feminist perspective that women as a class have a stake in reclaiming the female body, not as female nature, but by refusing to yield control of it to men, to the fetus, to the state, and most recently to those liberals who advocate that women control our bodies by giving up control" (Raymond, 1993: 91).

Feminist critics of NRT tie the scientific theory and technological innovations directly to social gender hierarchies: they are tools that increase men's control over women. For the most part, these writers focus on the effects of NRT on women as a class. Sonograms and fetal monitoring during pregnancy have turned natural processes into the medicalized or "high-tech" pregnancy (Woliver, 1995). Knowledge about fetal development in the hands of the male-dominated medical research establishment has turned into prescriptions of what a "fit mother" or "fit reproducer" is. Failure to follow the prescribed course of "healthy" living can even be a basis for legal prosecution (see Merchant). This leads easily to the conclusion that science (read MEN) can do a better job than women in producing healthy babies (Hanmer, 1987).

It is not just scientists and physicians who can use this technology to enhance their control over women. Since science can now make previously infertile women fertile, there is no excuse not to have children. Women are compelled by husbands to have children at any cost, despite the heavy toll infertility treatments have on women's bodies and health. According to some feminist commentators, NRT promises to fulfill a centuries-old dream of men: full control of reproduction. Patriarchal society has developed an array of laws and customs whereby men could dominate reproduction by controlling women. But with NRT, men as a group along with their scientific brethren can finally appropriate women's bodies directly and exert continuous domination over the reproductive process (O'Brien, 1989).

Men exert this domination in part by dissection of women's bodies into its parts: eggs, uteri, blood, become the raw material for the technical reproduction of humans. This is the message of FINNRAGE (Feminist International Network of Resistance to Reproductive and Genetic Engineering, organized in the Netherlands in 1984) (Donchin, 1989: 137). Just as genetic technology has led to a market in body parts for the reproduction of animals, so NRT can become part of a market. Already women sell their wombs in surrogacy contracts. The analogy to prostitution is evident (Corea, 1989). In a social system where structures ensure men's access to women's sexuality through pornography, prostitution, and rape, NRT can easily be incorporated into enhanced control of women's reproductive capacities. Is it any wonder that feminist critics have sounded the alarm, alerting women to reclaim female bodies by fighting against these technologies?

EFFECT OF NRT DEBATE ON ABORTION

Feminist slogans from the 1970s for "abortion on demand" and against "biology as destiny" were effective in rallying women against restrictive abortion laws. Today, in light of the challenges presented by NRT, these slogans seem quaintly simplistic. The scientific advances in human control of reproduction have shifted feminist perspectives on a number of issues: in many cases, this shift has been from a position where they enjoyed a clarity of conviction to confrontation with a tangle of daunting questions that defy clear solutions.

Abortion rights seemed to place the decision of when to become a mother, a role that had potentially oppressive consequences, in women's hands. But complex NRT emphasizes that becoming a mother—reproductive freedoms—entails processes so complex that only scientists and specialists have the ability to understand and thus control them. Access to abortion gave women some control over their bodies; will NRT take this control away from them? "Is it possible to balance the medical benefits of these new technologies against their potential to shift control over reproduction into the hands of physicians, scientists, and technicians? How does one measure the individual woman's choice against the choices, or lack of choices, the institutionalization of these technologies will have for women in general?" (Franklin and McNeil 1988: 554). These questions reinforce the uneasy relationship between women's abortion rights and the wishes and behavior of the medical establishment (see chapters 5 and 7 in this volume).

Many of the technologies relating to fertility and reproduction, such as amniocentesis and genetic screening, depend on the availability of legal abortion (Woliver, 1995). Embryo transfer and *in vitro* fertilization allow for the destruction of excess embryos. This has led some feminist writers to ponder the greater implications of possible abortion practices in the context of gender and other social hierarchies. With amniocentesis a woman can not only abort a fetus, but also a particular fetus of a certain sex or with a particular disability. It is difficult for a feminist to defend choice in abortion when it is used, as it has been to a great extent in India and China, to kill female fetuses. Feminists concerned with disability also argue against defending the right of people to kill fetuses that are not considered perfect. Along with the fact that such actions perpetuate social hierarchies and prejudices, the close relation between such rights and eugenic threats is obvious.

Raymond argues that feminists must think about the pressures that might be put on women to conceive and abort embryos to provide fetal tissues, for family members, for example. Suspicions that scientists may use women's bodies for profit extend to the use of fetuses for research, especially genetic research. Others (especially FINNRAGE) warn about possible trafficking in fetuses "harvested" from abortions from the poor in Third World countries.

Awareness that medical experiments in reproduction raise important ethical issues has led to the consideration of bioethics laws in several countries (see Merchant in this volume). Considering limits on fetal research in

Denmark brought the debate over the relation of NRT to abortion rights into the meetings of the Women's Ethical Council (Rolston and Eggert, 1994: 80). A 1989 report sought to cushion potential criticism of unrestricted abortion in the first trimester by asserting that abortion was always a regrettable if sometimes necessary choice. Seeing a potential threat to abortion rights, feminist activists charged that such a statement was hypocritical, because the incidence of abortion was a reflection of the condition of women, not a moral question. The Council finally agreed to support the continuation of abortion on request in Denmark. The link between policy networks on bioethics laws and groups defending abortion rights found in Denmark is rare. Feminists are not usually heard in these deliberations.

Many of the new technologies, particularly those relating to pregnancy and fetal development, have provided a powerful means of representing the fetus as a distinct entity. Anti-abortion activists take full advantage of every opportunity to use language associated with personhood to describe the embryo and fetus. Many feminists who write about reproductive issues are concerned that the actualization of the fetus as a distinct entity in the public consciousness will further erode women's status.

We have seen how the idea of rights in the abortion debate, based on individual standing, has been applied to an idea of fetal rights, posing an opposition between the woman and fetus inside her. Visual references to the fetus have provided materials to be used to argue that the fetus's rights should take precedence over the women's rights. Champions of the fetus describe their constituents as weak, innocent, and vulnerable to the often selfish desires of the woman who would kill this little person for her own convenience. Feminists see that the medical establishment, in its mania for developing new ways to ensure healthy fetal development, often casts the woman's body as a receptacle, one that can be potentially harmful (through cigarettes, wine, and lack of vitamins) to their primary patient. Thus the innocent fetus's rights are set up against the selfish, even dangerous, body of the woman. In this debate, some feminists note, men are often the champions of the fetus, setting up the conflict in gender terms (Hanmer, 1987).

This focus on the fetus has even drawn in some self-styled feminists for life. There is, as we have seen, a radical feminist argument that abortion is a way for men to exercise control over women. However, even though these activists are not happy with the situation of abortion, whether legal or not, their focus is on its effects on women. But feminists for life are active on behalf of the fetus—as a weak and vulnerable social creature. If feminism stands for anything, they argue, it is the protection of the weak from oppression (Luker, 1984: 113; Finger, 1984). Thus, the growing emphasis on the fetus, brought about by new technologies, has the potential of dividing feminists on an issue, which, in the 1970s, was one of the most unified campaigns of second-wave feminism.

For feminists, the most horrifying prospect of this enhanced emphasis on the fetus is the disappearance of women altogether from the debate over abortion and reproduction. Markowitz notes that in the field of philosophy, the discussions of abortion have focused exclusively on the question of personhood of the fetus (Markowitz, 1990). Stabile (1994) points out that in all the visual representations of the fetus, the body of the woman disappears; in fact, the concept of fetal personhood may depend on that. When the fetus becomes the major focus of the discussion over abortion, a debate proceeds in gender-neutral terms, and the woman as an entity with needs and agency disappears. Gender-neutral abortion debates may jeopardize feminist goals.

Thus, reasserting gendered issues into the debates on abortion as well as on any other aspect of reproduction and the new technology is an important feminist priority. Advocates should avoid getting drawn into debates about the fetus (Petchesky, 1985: 341; Markowitz, 1990), except perhaps to make the point that fetal personhood means forced motherhood. Feminist arguments should draw on theories that elaborate the relation of abortion and women's decisions and attitudes about it in as wide a context as possible.

That is, the solution may be to consider the relation of women to all processes of reproduction, and to emphasize how the abortion decision is related to them. At the same time, it is important to see women in the social and cultural contexts of gender relationships. Evidence points to the need for a feminist theory of reproductive freedom, taking NRT into account, that is expressed in gender-specific terms.

NOTES

1. This essay is not intended to be an exhaustive review of feminist writings on abortion, but rather a sampling of the arguments and contemporary sources. Readers are urged to consult works cited here for suggestions of further reading.

REFERENCES

Arditti, Rita, Renate Duelli Klein, and Shelley Minden, eds. 1989. *Test-Tube Women: What Future for Motherhood?* London: Pandora Press.

Batiot, Anne. 1986. "Radical Democracy and Feminist Discourse: The Case of France." In *The New Women's Movement: Feminism and Political Power in Europe and the USA*, ed. Drude Dahlerup, 85–102. London: Sage.

Bono, Paola, and Sandra Kemp, eds. 1991. *Italian Feminist Thought: A Reader.* Oxford: Basil Blackwell.

Caldwell, Lesley. 1986. "Feminism and Abortion Politics in Italy." In *The New Politics of Abortion*, Joyce Outshoorn ed. and Joni Lovenduski, 105–23. London: Sage.

Corea, Genoveffa. 1989. "The Reproductive Brothel." In *Radical Voices: A Decade of Feminist Resistance from Women's Studies International Forum*, ed. Renate Klein and Deborah Lynn Steinberg, 121–32. Oxford: Pergamon Press.

Dahlerup, Drude, ed. 1986. *The New Women's Movement: Feminism and Political Power in Europe and the USA*. London: Sage.

Donchin, Anne. 1989. "The Growing Feminist Debate Over the New Reproductive Technologies." Review Essay. *Hypatia* 4 (Fall): 135–49.

Dworkin, Andrea. 1983. *Right-wing Women*. New York, Perigee Books.

Eisenstein, Zillah. 1988. *The Female Body and the Law*. Berkeley: University of California Press, 1988.

Franklin, Sarah, and Maureen McNeil. 1988. "Reproductive Futures: Recent Literature and Current Feminist Debates on Reproductive Technologies." Book Review. *Feminist Studies* 14 (Fall): 545–60.

Hanmer, Jalna. 1987. "Transforming Consciousness: Women and the New Reproductive Technologies." In *Man-Made Women: How New Reproductive Technologies Affect Women*, ed. Gena Corea, 88–109. Bloomington: Indiana University Press.

Lovenduski, Joni, and Joyce Outshoorn, eds. 1986. *The New Politics of Abortion*. London: Sage.

Luker, Kristin. 1984. *Abortion and the Politics of Motherhood*. Berkeley: University of California Press.

MacKinnon, Catharine. 1987. *Feminism Unmodified: Discourses on Life and Law*. Cambridge: Harvard University Press.

Markwitz, Sally. 1990. "Abortion and Feminism." *Social Theory and Practice*. 16, 1, (Spring): 1–17.

O'Brien, Mary. 1989. *Reproducing the World: Essays in Feminist Theory*. Boulder, CO: Westview Press.

Petchesky, Rosalind Pollack. 1985. *Abortion and Woman's Choice: The State, Sexuality, and Reproductive Freedom*. Boston: Northeastern University Press.

Porter, Elisabeth. 1994. "Abortion Ethics: Rights and Responsibilities." *Hypatia* 9 (Summer): 66–87.

Raymond, Janice G. 1993. *Women as Wombs: Reproductive Technologies and the Battle over Women's Freedom*. San Francisco: Harper San Francisco.

Rolston, Bill, and Anna Eggert, eds. 1994. *Abortion in the New Europe: A Comparative Handbook*. Westport, CT: Greenwood Press.

Shrage, Laurie. 1994. *Moral Dilemmas of Feminism: Prostitution, Adultery, and Abortion*. New York: Routledge.

Stabile, Carole A. 1994. *Feminism and the Technological Fix*. Manchester: Manchester University Press.

Stetson, Dorothy McBride, and Amy G. Mazur, eds. 1995. *Comparative State Feminism*. Thousand Oaks, CA: Sage.

Tribe, Laurence. 1990. *Abortion: The Clash of Absolutes*. New York: Norton.

Woliver, Laura. 1995. "Reproductive Technologies, Surrogacy Arrangements, and the Politics of Motherhood." In *Mothers in Law: Feminist Theory and the Legal Regulation of Motherhood*, ed. Martha Albertson Fineman and Isabelle Karpin, 346–59. New York: Columbia University Press.

CONTRIBUTORS

JOYCE GELB is Professor of Political Science and Director of the Program in Women's Studies at the Center for the Study of Women and Society at the Graduate Center of the City University of New York. Professor Gelb has frequently done research and lectured in Japan during the past decade. Her book *Women of Japan and Korea: Continuity or Change* (Temple University Press, 1994) brings together the ideas of Japanese and Korean scholars on a number of topics. Her book *Women and Public Policies*, co-authored with Marian Palley, is to be reprinted by the University Press of Virginia in the fall of 1996, with a new introduction and conclusion.

BRIAN GIRVIN is Senior Lecturer in the Department of Politics, University of Glasgow, Scotland. He has published journal articles on Irish, European, and American politics as well as European integration. Recent publications include "Between Two Worlds: Politics and Economy in Independent Ireland" (1989) and "The Right in the Twentieth Century: Conservatism and Democracy" (1994). He is completing a book, *The End of Traditional Ireland and the Threat of Modernity*, and working on a study of nationalism since 1945.

MARIANNE GITHENS, Professor of Politics and Director of Women's Studies at Goucher College, has written extensively on the topic of women in politics. Among her publications are *A Portrait of Marginality, Different Roles, Different Voices*, and a number of articles, the most recent of which is "Getting Appointed to the Court: The Gender Dimension." She has served as a major research consultant to the European Women project, sponsored by the European Union, and to the television series *Shoulder to Shoulder*, which dealt with the British suffrage movement. Professor Githens has received a number of grants and awards, including a NEH grant for research on American and European women's peace movements.

JENNIFER MERCHANT is a graduate of the University of California at Davis and the Institute of Political Science in Grenoble and Paris and is a lecturer in politics at the University of Evry Val d'Essonne in France. She is author of several articles and conference papers on public policy, women, and technology in France and the United States.

JOYCE OUTSHOORN is Professor and Chair of the Department of Women's Studies at Leiden University, the Netherlands, where she is also Director of the research program "Gender and Power." She has published extensively, most recently on the women's movement, women's public policy, women and poli tics, and feminist theory. Her book, *The New Politics of Abortion* (1986), co-authored with Joni Lovenduski, remains a definitive review of abortion policy reform in Europe. Recent publications include "Between Movement and State: 'Democrats' in the Netherlands" in the *Yearbook of Swiss Political Science* (1994) and "Administrative Accommodation in the Netherlands: The Department for the Coordination of Equality Policy" in *Comparative State Feminism* (1995).

KIM LANE SCHEPPELE is Professor of Law at the University of Pennsylvania and Co-Director of the Project on Gender and Culture at the Central European University, Budapest. Her current research focuses on comparative constitutionalism in general and on gender-related rights questions in particular. In addition to many articles on rape, domestic violence, abortion, and other gender issues in the law, she is the author of *Legal Secrets: Equality and Efficiency in the Common Law,* which won both the Corwin Prize from the American Political Science Association and the award for Special Recognition as a Distinguished Contribution to Scholarship from the American Sociological Association.

DOROTHY McBRIDE STETSON is Professor of Political Science at Florida Atlantic University, where she is an active participant in the Women's Studies program. A specialist in the comparative study of women and public policy, she is the author of three books: *A Woman's Issue: the Politics of Family Law Reform in England* (1982); *Women's Rights in France* (1987); and *Women's Rights in the U.S.A.* (1991, second edition 1997); and numerous articles and conference papers. Along with Amy Mazur she edited *Comparative State Feminism* (1995) and is convener of the Research Network on Gender, Politics, and the State.

DONLEY T. STUDLAR was selected as the first Eberly Family Distinguished Professor of Political Science by West Virginia University in 1993. He is Executive Director of the British Politics Association and has published widely in comparative politics of advanced industrial democracies. Recent publications include a book, *Great Britain: Decline or Renewal?* (Westview Press, 1996). Professor Studlar's many articles have appeared in such journals as *American Political Science Review, American Journal of Political Science, British Journal of Political Science, Canadian Journal of Political Science,* and *Journal of Politics.*

RAYMOND TATALOVICH is Professor of Political Science at Loyola University Chicago. His research focus is moral conflicts and public policy. Among his recent publications are *Nativism Reborn: The Official English Language*

Movement in the American States (University of Kentucky Press, 1995) and *The Politics of Abortion in Canada and the United States: A Comparative Study* (M.E. Sharpe, 1996).

LAURA R. WOLIVER is Associate Professor of Government and International Studies at the University of South Carolina, Columbia. She is author of *From Outrage to Action: The Politics of Grass-roots Dissent* (University of Illinois Press, 1993) and a number of articles on women's rights, civil rights, activism, and the politics of new reproductive technologies. She teaches classes on interest groups and social movements, American politics, political parties, and the politics of sex roles.

INDEX

LaVergne, TN USA
03 November 2009
162937LV00002B/139/P